A Happy Driver's Tales

Onward Towards the Golden Sun

By: Marshall J. Crawford

This book is dedicated to my parents for never giving up on me and to all those who are doing their best to find happiness in their lives.

Table of Contents

CHAPTER 1 - Introduction

Embracing Uniqueness: Into a Journey of Acceptance and Resilience

In the heart of Chicago's most dangerous neighborhood, I, a fearless ride-share driver, braved the treacherous streets at the stroke of 1 am on a pulsating Friday night. The city's underbelly simmered with electric energy as if holding its breath, waiting for the night to unfold. The air crackled with tension as I navigated my vehicle toward the designated location. Suddenly, a loud explosion shattered the silence, sending shockwaves through my body. My instincts kicked in, thinking that the sound was just construction work, but in an instant, a police vehicle drove by beside me, its flashing lights casting an eerie glow. As our windows rolled down, the officer's urgent voice cut through the night, "Did you hear that? That was a gunshot!"

My heart raced, realizing that the echoes of danger were much closer than I had ever imagined. "Of course, that couldn't be construction. It's 1 am on a Friday in front of a house!" as my thoughts recollected while waiting for the passenger. Just as I braced myself for the unknown, a shadowy figure emerged from the darkness—finally, after waiting more than 5 minutes, the passenger whose secrets were bound to transform this ride into an adrenaline-fueled journey of survival.

Meanwhile, as I headed south of Chicago on the highway towards the 100s, the passenger asked me, "Is this what you do full-time?"

I tightly grip the steering wheel, "Yes, it is, Sir. How about you? What do you do?"

Tyron smiled and said, "I'm a pharmaceutical. I work mostly on the streets. I am more of an illegitimate pharmaceutical."

First, I heard a gunshot outside the house while waiting for the passenger before the trip. I picked up the passenger and his friend. The next thing the passenger is telling me is that he is pretty much a drug dealer, and now this guy is in my car, and I am driving him to his next destination to do who knows what.

As I accelerated towards the destination, conversing with the passenger, my mind raced as I asked myself, "Should I have just canceled or not accepted the trip? I hope this guy doesn't try to rob me or kill me."

In the intricate streets of Chicago, where the city's heartbeat pulses through its bustling neighborhoods, I invite you to join me on a remarkable journey. As a native born and bred in the vibrant city, I have always felt a deep connection to the rich tapestry of cultures that make up the fabric of Chicago's identity. My story begins in the picturesque neighborhood of Lincoln Park, where I took my first breaths in and felt the city's energy envelop me in Grant Hospital. Growing up in the North Shore suburb of Skokie, just a stone's throw away from the heart of Chicago, I was fortunate to be immersed in a melting pot of diverse cultures and ethnicities.

I was exposed to a kaleidoscope of traditions, languages, and flavors that shaped my worldview early on. Walking the streets of my neighborhood, I could hear the melodies of different languages intertwining, see vibrant colors adorning storefronts, and taste the tantalizing aromas wafting from the eclectic mix of eateries that lined the streets. These experiences ignited a curiosity within me, a burning desire to explore and embrace the world around me. With its vibrant tapestry of cultures, Chicago became my playground, my canvas upon which I would paint my unique story.

In the upcoming chapters of my journey, I will navigate the labyrinthine streets of this magnificent city, forging connections with people from all walks of life. Together, we will unravel the mysteries, celebrate the diversity, and discover the hidden gems within this metropolis's bounds. So, step into my world, where the pulse of the city resonates in every beat of my heart, and let's embark on an exhilarating adventure through the vibrant streets of Chicago.

My parents, originally immigrants from Southeast Asia, instilled in me a strict cultural heritage of discipline and hard work. Still, my path to acceptance and growing up in the new homeland faced many challenges.

In my past life, the story of my journey unfolded in the most enchanting, unimaginable setting. It was a time filled with wrong turns, lousy GPS directions, unexpected detours, and incredible transformations in pursuit of true happiness.

Being the eldest of three siblings, I was caught in familial dynamics. My two younger brothers, who were closer in age —one year apart—often joined forces against me, the perceived "evil" older sibling, which the hands of fate dealt to my story. Little did they realize that I only wanted to lend a hand to my 1st generation of hardworking parents.

It all started when I made a right turn to a life-altering decision to enroll in culinary school. With a burning passion and desire for culinary arts, I dedicated myself to becoming the best pastry and corporate chef I could be. While balancing the demands of full-time night school for my bachelor's degree and an extremely social nightlife in Chicago, I also embraced the unrealistic challenges of working in culinary full-time with an unwavering determination. Each day, I absorbed as much information as I could. I worked on the creation and execution of delicious and beautifully decorated delights while sharpening my skills and expanding my culinary expertise. It was a thrilling time in my early 20s, filled with the excitement of pursuing my dreams and witnessing the fruits of my hard work.

However, a pivotal moment came when I embarked on a new path. A path filled with much winter and construction. As a few passengers entered my vehicle, their curious eyes met mine, and while learning about my life, they asked, "Why would you quit being a chef to be a driver?" With excitement in my eyes, I unraveled the untold truths. "You see," I began, "culinary TV shows may dazzle with their glamour, but behind the scenes, stress runs rampant. While others relish their holidays and weekends, we chefs toil tirelessly, crafting gastronomic wonders. Our social lives, intertwined with our fellow food and beverage colleagues, become our lifeline. Yet, the constant sacrifice takes its toll, leaving us yearning for moments of joy. So, I embraced the wheel, hoping to rediscover the simple pleasures of time spent with our loved ones. Now, as we race through the city's vibrant streets, I weave tales of flavors and camaraderie, eager to explore a world beyond the confines of the kitchen. Together, we venture into the unknown, where new horizons await, and the intoxicating aroma of freedom fills the air."

As I drove further into the journey of becoming a ride-share driver, I found myself being offered incredible other job opportunities by my passengers out of being impressed by my own experiences in my life and how I conduct my professional customer service interaction with them. Job offers from 5 Star 5 Diamond famous hotels and even job offers from well-known financial firms like IMF graciously strolled down my path. I even attempted to work as an office manager in the Financial District in Chicago for a short period until I realized there was still more freedom and more money made as a ride-share driver.

Amidst the whirlwind of success, I also had the privilege of experiencing the vibrant and unique character of Chicago's diverse neighborhoods. From the windy energy of West Loop to the cultural richness of Pilsen, each area offered a unique flavor and sense of community. I roamed the captivating streets of South Loop, marveled at the breathtaking views of Streeterville, and explored the artistic enclave of Ravenswood. Each neighborhood left an indelible mark on my heart, contributing to the mosaic of experiences that shaped my journey.

As fate would have it, my path took an unexpected turn. In my quest for true happiness, I found solace and fulfillment in

6

the most unexpected profession: a ride-share driver. This
seemingly ordinary role catalyzed a more profound sense of
purpose and joy in my life. While connecting with passengers
from all walks of life, I discovered the immense satisfaction of
positively impacting our intertwined paths. I found true
happiness on this journey in these simple acts of kindness and
human connection.

Looking back, grand achievements or prestigious positions did not define my journey solely. True happiness was found in the profound fulfillment of positively influencing one's life, embracing the unexpected journey, and finding contentment in the simplest moments. And so, in the first-person narrative of my extraordinary past life, my story continues to unfold. Roaming the vibrant streets of Chicago, I seek to bring joy, warmth, and inspiration to all I encounter and myself. With each passing day, I am reminded that true happiness lies not in the pursuit of success but in the meaningful connections we forge and the positive impact we make on the lives of others.

Imagine maintaining five stars as a ride-share driver, the epitome of excellence in the field. Picture this: cruising through all types of streets, your passengers smiling and satisfied, all because you've mastered the art of providing exceptional service. By adhering to the rules of the road, honing your customer skills, and embracing the principles of being a good person, you can transcend the ordinary and become extraordinary. Drawing upon my training in Culinary at Le Cordon Bleu Chicago, Hospitality Management at Kendall College National Louis University, and my experience working for prestigious 5-star, 5-diamond hotels, I've acquired a repertoire of lifelong skills. These valuable tools extend far beyond the culinary realm or the confines of the road; they apply to every facet of life, assisting in propelling one toward one's goals and aspirations.

Imagine the impact you can make, not only by delivering passengers safely to their destinations but also by creating memorable experiences while simultaneously getting paid for it after the end of the trip. Even imagine getting tipped out $5, $20, $50, and even $150. That happened to me, and I'm so grateful and appreciative. It's within the individual's grasp to become one of the best ride-share drivers, or perhaps even the best of the best if they choose to be. With anything, embrace the amazingness and possibilities of life, harness your training, and embark on a journey where your dedication and passion will yield extraordinary results! The path to greatness awaits you! As a ride-share driver, I also had the incredible opportunity to connect with individuals from all walks of life, spanning continents and cultures. From Ireland to England, Finland to France, Italy to Turkey, and Zimbabwe to Nigeria, my passenger list is a tapestry of diverse backgrounds and experiences. The adventure doesn't stop there. Europe beckons with its rich heritage and captivating destinations. I've met passengers from countries like Germany, Spain, Greece, Netherlands, Sweden, Switzerland, Poland, and many more. Each encounter always offers a chance to delve into the unique traditions, languages, and perspectives that make Europe fascinating.

Venturing further, I've also encountered the captivating allure where passengers from countries like Dubai, Saudi Arabia, Israel, Turkey, and Egypt shared their stories and insights. The cultures of Middle Eastern cultures have also unfolded before me, offering a glimpse into their rich history, traditions, and customs. Remember the Scandinavian countries, where passengers from Sweden, Norway, Denmark, Finland, and Iceland graced my rides. I was enlightened by the beauty of their landscapes and the warmth of their hospitality as I engaged with individuals from these Nordic nations. As I journey through the countless streets, passengers from Asia will bring the captivating cultures of China, Japan, Korea, Hong Kong, the Philippines, Malaysia, Laos, and more to your doorstep. Asia's vibrant diversity unfolded before me, offering opportunities to connect with people from different walks of life.

Get ready to embrace the opportunity to engage with individuals from South America, such as Argentina, Venezuela,

Honduras, Brazil, Colombia, Peru, and Chile, as you absorb the rich tapestry of their cultures. Through these encounters, you'll develop a profound expertise in engaging with individuals from different ethnic backgrounds, religions, and moral perspectives. Your conversations will transcend mere small talk, evolving into meaningful exchanges that broaden your understanding of the human experience.

In this story, a native-born in Lincoln Park, Chicago, and raised in the North Shore of Chicago, specifically in the village of Skokie, a first-generation Filipino-American, serves as a powerful reminder of the beauty within our differences. It is a testament to the transformative power of acceptance, which starts from within ourselves and radiates outward, shaping the world around us. Through resilience and the strength of choice, we can turn our challenges into stepping stones toward a life brimming with love, understanding, and authentic connection. As we fasten our seatbelts and embark on this remarkable voyage, you are invited to witness a world where cultural boundaries dissolve and our ability to connect with others soars to new heights. Each ride becomes an opportunity to gather stories and insights that will enrich our lives and expand our understanding of the diverse tapestry of humanity. In becoming actual global citizens, we bridge continents and build bridges of awareness, fostering a sense of unity and compassion that transcends borders. Through the experiences shared in this book, you may come to terms with the idea that differences are not obstacles to be overcome but rather invitations to learn, grow, and celebrate the richness of human existence. It is in embracing diversity and cherishing the unique perspectives and traditions of others that we create a vibrant, inclusive, and harmonious world. As I sat in my car, waiting for my next passenger in the West Town neighborhood in Chicago, I reached for my rose gold Apple MacBook, feeling its smooth, sleek surface beneath my fingertips. Just as I was about to delve into my digital world, I saw an older woman, Wanda, approaching the car. It was the last day of November, and the air was filled with anticipation for the holiday season.

   With a warm smile, I greeted Wanda and asked if she was ready for the upcoming festivities. In response, I cranked up the volume of my car's Bluetooth system, filling the space with cheerful holiday and Christmas tunes streaming from Spotify. Wanda chuckled softly, admitting she wasn't prepared for the holiday season. At 85 years old, her focus had shifted towards prioritizing her health, and she expressed gratitude for every day she remained vibrant and independent. As the music played, I couldn't help but share my appreciation for being alive. I conveyed to Wanda how each breath felt like a precious blessing, a reminder to seize every opportunity life offered. In my mind, I reflected on the adventures I had embarked upon as a ride-share driver. This job allowed me to travel to many breathtaking destinations in the Dominican Republic, such as Boca Chica and Santo Domingo.

To my surprise, I discovered a thriving Italian community in Boca Chica, a testament to the diverse tapestry of humanity. I relished the experience of savoring delectable Italian cuisine at charming cafes and indulging in mouthwatering pizzas. The abundance of fresh fish from the sea added an exquisite touch to my culinary explorations. The prawns, as large as lobsters, were a delightful delicacy that didn't break the bank. The opportunity to travel instilled a profound sense of gratitude reminiscent of Wanda's appreciation for life. It reminded me to seize the moments while I still had the vigor and freedom to explore different corners of the world, just as Wanda had done in her youth.

As Wanda shared her life story, she revealed that her journey extended far beyond the confines of our car. She spoke of a time when the responsibilities of parenthood and the joys of watching her children grow had occupied her days. Her voice conveyed a hint of nostalgia as she mentioned that her children were growing and carving their paths in the world.

"But you know, dear driver," Wanda said, her eyes glimmering with fondness and wisdom, "it's not just my children who have grown. I, too, have ventured into a new

chapter of life. Bless their hearts; my grandchildren have now started families of their own. Time moves swiftly, and before I knew it, I found myself visiting my loved ones in the nursing home."

Curiosity sparked, and I was eager to learn more about this facet of Wanda's life. With genuine interest, I asked, "Visiting the nursing home must bring a mix of emotions. What's it like for you, Wanda?"

She smiled gently as she said, "Ah, the nursing home, my dear. It's a place where memories intertwine with the present, where the frailty of age meets the resilience of the human spirit. I visit my family there, engaging in conversations that span generations. We laugh, share stories, and find solace in each other's company." Her voice, tinged with melancholy and gratitude, continued, "In the nursing home, I find a unique camaraderie. We swap tales of youth, love and loss, dreams and regrets. We become a tapestry woven together by the threads of shared humanity. It reminds me that **no matter our age or circumstances, our need for connection remains steadfast.**"

The journey continued amidst Wanda's heartfelt narration. Her visits to the nursing home painted a vivid picture of compassion and resilience. She spoke of finding joy in the simplest moments, sharing cups of tea with wise souls who had weathered life's storms.

*"There's a **beautiful wisdom** that can only be gained from those who have lived long and loved deeply," Wanda mused. "Their stories, their laughter, and even their tears all become a part of my own story. It's a reminder that life is fleeting, and we must treasure the time we have with those we hold dear."*

"Wanda," I said, my voice filled with admiration, "your presence in the lives of your loved ones, even amid their twilight years, is a testament to the love and strength that resides within you. Your visits bring light and comfort to those who may feel forgotten."

"So, Wanda, tell me, what's your secret to being such an extraordinary woman?"

*"Well, dear, it's all about **embracing life's rollercoaster of experiences**. I've had my fair share of ups and downs, and those moments have shaped me into the woman you see today. Wisdom comes from weathering the storms and finding humor in the chaos, don't you think?"*

*I accelerate as I enter the highway and roll up all the windows. "Absolutely! **Life's a wild ride, and we've got to hold on tight while laughing at the twists and turns.** Speaking of which, do you have any particular stories that left you questioning people's motivations?"*

"Oh, you bet I do! Let me tell you about when I went to a fancy dinner party. Everyone was dressed to impress, but beneath the shiny exterior, there were some interesting characters. One woman claimed to be a vegetarian, yet she couldn't resist sneaking bites of the meaty appetizers when she thought no one was looking! It made me wonder, what's the point of pretending?" Wanda giggles as she shares her story.

"Ha! That's quite the contradiction. It's like saying, "I'm on a seafood diet. I see and eat food...but only when no one's

watching!" It's funny how people sometimes forget their principles when faced with temptation."

"Exactly! It's like they're playing hide-and-seek with their true selves. But you know, dear, we're all human, prone to flaws and moments of weakness. It's important to remember that we're all just figuring things out as we go along."

"Wanda. The imperfections make life interesting and provide us with stories to share. So, what's the most valuable lesson you've learned from all your experiences?"

"Ah, the most valuable lesson... Well, dear, I'd say it's this: never take yourself too seriously. **Life's too short to fret about the small stuff. Embrace the laughter, find joy in the absurd, and** remember that everyone's just trying to navigate this crazy world in their unique way."

"Wise words, Wanda. Life's a comedy; we're all just characters in this grand theatrical production. Let's enjoy the ride together, shall we?"

Wanda glanced towards the front, "Absolutely, dear. Let's laugh, question, and ponder the mysteries of the universe as we journey on. And remember, if we encounter any more contradictions or peculiar characters along the way, we'll be ready to find the humor in it all!"

I smiled at Wanda, "You've got it! Buckle up because this journey was much more entertaining with you by my side. Onward we go, in search of laughter and wisdom!"

Wanda was an extraordinary woman during our journey, brimming with wisdom and life experience. She shared stories of the hardships she had endured, prompting her to question the motivations of others. I empathized with her sentiments, acknowledging that some people may not truly understand their actions.

In response, I recounted the advice I had received from another wise passenger to Wanda: "Just because someone wants to act up a fool, doesn't mean you have to act up a fool on with 'em."

Those words resonated deeply within me, guiding my choices on the road. When faced with reckless drivers, I prioritized safety and let go of any desire to engage in a race or confrontation. A lesson in humility and maturity spared me from countless accidents. As I drove along, following the unspoken rule of avoiding politics and religion, I couldn't help but wonder what kind of conversation would unfold with Wanda. She seemed like a woman with a spark, someone who wouldn't shy away from diving into the depths of controversial topics.

When I thought our journey would remain lighthearted, Wanda leaned forward and said, "I've been pondering some political and religious matters lately. Do you mind if we have a little chat about it?"

These are the types of conversations that I usually steer clear from to stay unbiased and not disrespect the passenger in any way. Still, whenever a passenger takes it to the next step in religion or politics, I am always up for learning about it as long as I am respectful and non-confrontational. A mischievous grin spread as I realized the game was on. This was where all the excitement lay, in those daring conversations that pushed boundaries and challenged perspectives.

With a twinkle in my eye, I responded, "Wanda, you've just opened Pandora's box. I'm all ears and ready for this thrilling discussion."

As the miles rolled by, Wanda shared her thoughts on the current political landscape, questioning the motives of politicians and the impact of their decisions. We delved into the intricacies of different religious beliefs, exploring the profound questions that often arise in matters of faith.

With each passing moment, our conversation grew more intense, our words fueled by passion and curiosity. We debated, we laughed, and we challenged each other's viewpoints. It was a verbal joust, a battle of wits, and we were both eager participants in this intellectual duel.

As we delved into more profound spiritual conversations, Wanda and I explored our beliefs in a higher power. I shared my upbringing in a Catholic private school and my attendance at Notre Dame High School during my first and second years. However, regardless of religious affiliation, I emphasized respecting and honoring each individual's beliefs. The car became a battleground of ideas, where we dissected ideologies and dissected the flaws in each argument. We navigated the minefield of sensitive topics, always respecting one another's opinions but unafraid to push the boundaries of conventional thinking.

Time went fast as we explored the depths of political ideologies and the intricacies of religious practices. It was exhilarating, like riding a rollercoaster of intellect and discourse. We reveled in the thrill of intellectual sparring, knowing that growth and understanding emerged through these challenging conversations. As our journey neared, we sat back, breathless but invigorated. We had danced on the edge of controversy. Yet, we never lost sight of the respect and camaraderie that bound our conversation—the car filled with a sense of accomplishment, as if we had conquered an intellectual summit together.

With a satisfied smile, Wanda turned to me and said, "Thank you for rising to the challenge, my dear driver. It's rare to find someone willing to engage in such conversations. This journey has been an adventure of the mind."

I nodded, feeling a sense of kinship with Wanda. "Likewise, my extraordinary passenger. Life's true excitement lies beyond the mundane and predictable in these discussions. Our willingness to explore these topics has made this journey truly unforgettable."

She smiled warmly, her eyes shining with gratitude and contentment. "Thank you, dear driver. It's a privilege to be there for my family, share their joys, and provide support during their challenges. Life has many chapters, and I'm grateful for the ones that bring us together, even aging and changing."

As Wanda stepped out of the car, her spirit radiating with resilience and compassion, I couldn't help but carry a newfound appreciation for the unwavering bonds of family and the significance of embracing every stage of life's journey.

While we bid each other farewell, I couldn't help but feel a renewed appreciation for the power of conversation. The forbidden topics had become our playground, the source of exhilaration and connection. From that day forward, I knew I wouldn't shy away from the game, for it was in those daring conversations that the true magic happened. It reminded me that we are all interconnected, each person carrying unique experiences and perspectives. By embracing this diversity, we can truly appreciate the uniqueness of humanity, fostering understanding and harmony in a beautifully complex world.

As the miles passed underneath our wheels on the way to the North Lawndale neighborhood in Chicago, Wanda and I found solace in our shared journey of gratitude, wisdom, and respect. In the quiet moments between conversations, the Christmas music continued to play, a gentle reminder of the joy and beauty of the simplest moments. We witness the resilience that arises from navigating the complexities of cultural identity and the power of choice in shaping one's narrative. We are reminded that our struggles do not define us but serve as catalysts for growth and transformation. Each challenge becomes an opportunity to cultivate empathy, understanding, and a deeper connection with ourselves and those around us.

Through these connections, we can create a society that thrives on love, acceptance and shared values. By recognizing our common humanity, we can dissolve the boundaries that separate us and foster a sense of belonging that transcends geographical borders. In this collective spirit, we can overcome challenges and build a better world for ourselves and future generations.

However, let us not forget that perfection eludes us all. As long as the world turns, problems will arise, and not everyone will share our views or like us. This is the ebb and flow of life, the intricate dance of human nature. But within these imperfections lies an opportunity for growth and understanding. With this book and its wealth of ideas and examples, I aim to provide my experiences to guide your journey toward happiness. I can not promise to solve all your problems, for that is the nature of our existence. Instead, I offer insights and inspiration, empowering you to navigate the complexities of life with grace and resilience. It encourages you to embrace your unique experiences and find ways to relate them to the broader human experience, fostering a deep sense of empathy and connection.

In a world that constantly seeks conformity, embracing uniqueness becomes a radical act of liberation. We embarked on a transformative journey, exploring the depths of acceptance and resilience, and what we discovered was nothing short of extraordinary. Through the lens of diversity, we shattered societal norms and stereotypes, uncovering the beauty within each individual's differences. As we delve into the stories of those marginalized and overlooked, we will witness the power of embracing one's true self unfold. These narratives will reveal the struggles and triumphs of individuals who dared to defy societal expectations and norms. The journey toward self-acceptance is often filled with obstacles and challenges.

These stories show us that embracing one's true self requires immense courage. It means standing tall in the face of opposition and refusing to conform to societal pressures that seek to define and limit us. On the path to self-acceptance, we will experience remarkable resilience. It may involve confronting internal struggles, unlearning societal biases, and finding the strength to live authentically. Yet, despite the challenges, these stories illuminate the undeniable rewards of embracing one's true self.

These resilient spirits find liberation, fulfillment, and a sense of belonging by embracing their identity and refusing to be defined by their circumstances. Their stories inspire us to question the status quo, challenge our own biases, and create a more inclusive and accepting world. As we delve into these marginalized and overlooked stories, we discover the transformative power of embracing one's true self. These narratives will teach us valuable lessons about resilience, authenticity, and the profound impact of self-acceptance on individuals and society.

Along this journey of exploring self-acceptance, we unearth the remarkable strength that emerges from embracing our quirks, flaws, and vulnerabilities. We learn that these aspects of ourselves are not weaknesses to be hidden or ashamed of but relative sources of authenticity and connection. Embracing our quirks means embracing the idiosyncrasies that make us who we are. It's about embracing our unconventional interests, ways of thinking, and unique perspectives on life. Accepting and celebrating these aspects allows us to fully express our true selves without fear of judgment or rejection.

Similarly, accepting our flaws is an essential part of self-acceptance. We realize that perfection is an illusion, and it is in our imperfections that our humanity shines through. Acknowledging our weaknesses and areas for improvement allows us to grow and evolve as individuals. It also fosters empathy and understanding towards others navigating their imperfections.

Furthermore, embracing our vulnerabilities is a testament to our courage and authenticity. It means embracing our fears, insecurities, and emotional fragility. By embracing vulnerability, we open ourselves to genuine connection and create a space for others to do the same. We forge deep and meaningful relationships in our vulnerability, which requires trust and openness. By celebrating our differences rather than fearing them, we create a tapestry of authenticity that enriches our collective existence. Each person's unique qualities contribute to the diversity and richness of the human experience. When we embrace and appreciate these differences, we create a sense of belonging and inclusivity where everyone can thrive.

In summary, our journey will teach us that the strength that arises from embracing our quirks, flaws, and vulnerabilities is a transformative force. By celebrating our individuality and accepting ourselves fully, we create a tapestry of authenticity and connection that enriches our collective existence. Through the prism of acceptance, we shatter the barriers that hinder progress and inclusivity. We realize that uniqueness is not a threat but an invitation to expand our horizons, challenge our preconceived notions, and create a more compassionate and understanding world. In embracing our differences, we find the courage to dismantle the walls that divide us, fostering a society that thrives on unity and respect.

Throughout this transformative journey, we will understand that resilience extends beyond simply returning from adversity. Resilience is intricately tied to finding strength in our uniqueness and embracing our differences. In the face of hardship, our actual characters and inner strength shine through, allowing us to overcome challenges and thrive.

When we embrace our uniqueness, we tap into a wellspring of resilience that empowers us to confront and navigate difficult circumstances. Our differences become sources of inspiration, pushing us to think creatively, adapt, and find innovative solutions. Embracing our uniqueness means recognizing that our diverse perspectives and experiences offer valuable insights and perspectives that can help us overcome obstacles. In the face of adversity, our unique qualities often give us the resilience to persevere. Our strengths, talents, and perspectives become tools that can be harnessed to overcome challenges. By embracing our differences, we cultivate a sense of self-worth and confidence that fuels our resilience.

Moreover, embracing our differences allows us to build a supportive community and draw strength from one another. When we come together, valuing and celebrating our individuality, we create a network of support that bolsters our resilience. We find solace in knowing that we are not alone in our struggles and that our collective strength can propel us forward. One day, I picked up a passenger named Carol, who was visiting from Ann Arbor, Michigan. As I drove her to the Lalapalooza Festival in Chicago, we went through different neighborhoods of Chicago, each with its character and culture. As we stayed longer on the trip, our conversation increased more and more. Carol had the chance to witness the different styles of architecture and the diversity in each neighborhood we drove by.

"You know, Marshall, I've been reflecting on our journey together, and I've come to appreciate the importance of embracing and celebrating our differences."

" Carol! It's incredible how much we can learn and grow by recognizing and valuing the unique perspectives and experiences we each bring."

"Exactly! By embracing our differences, we cultivate a mindset that views challenges not as roadblocks but as opportunities for growth and transformation. It's through these challenges that we truly discover our potential."

"That's so true. We become more resilient and adaptable when approaching setbacks with a positive mindset. It's not just about weathering storms; it's about harnessing the power of our uniqueness to overcome any obstacle that comes our way."

"Yes, resilience is key. As we've journeyed together, we've learned firsthand that strength lies in adapting and learning from life's curveballs. We've grown stronger by embracing our differences and using them as tools for success."

"Carol. Our journey has taught us that we open ourselves to endless possibilities by embracing and celebrating our differences. We've discovered that unity can be found in diversity, making our journey remarkable."

"Indeed, Marshall. Let's continue this journey with determination and the belief that our differences are our greatest assets. Together, we can overcome anything and create an even brighter future."

"I couldn't agree more. Our unity in diversity will guide us towards new horizons and remarkable achievements. Here's to embracing our differences and forging on this incredible journey!"

Our journey will illuminate the profound connection between resilience and embracing our differences. By finding strength in our uniqueness, we tap into a wellspring of resilience that empowers us to navigate adversity, foster supportive communities, and embrace the limitless possibilities of our individual and collective potential. Indeed, let us embark on this transformative journey together, hand in hand, as we celebrate the vibrant tapestry of human diversity. United in our quest for self-acceptance and authenticity, we can challenge the status quo, reject conformity, and wholeheartedly embrace our individuality. We create a harmonious symphony of voices, perspectives, and experiences by joining forces and valuing each individual's unique qualities. Together, we challenge societal norms and expectations that seek to limit and confine us. We dare to question the established narratives and carve out our paths, guided by the strength of our convictions.

In embracing our individuality, we unlock the true essence of who we are. We discover our most authentic selves by embracing our quirks, flaws, vulnerabilities, and passions. By embracing our uniqueness, we tap into our inner reservoirs of creativity, resilience, and empathy. We unleash our untapped potential and cultivate a purpose that propels us forward.

Through acceptance and resilience, we lay the foundation for a brighter future. By embracing our individuality and celebrating the uniqueness of others, we inspire others to do the same. We become catalysts for change, igniting a ripple effect that spreads far and wide. Together, we pave the way for a society that celebrates authenticity, respects differences, and thrives on the strength of its collective humanity. So, let us embark on this remarkable journey together, celebrating the rich tapestry of human diversity. Let us challenge the status quo, reject conformity, and fearlessly embrace individuality. In doing so, we unlock our transformative power and create a world of acceptance, resilience, and unity. Together, we can shape a future that is bright, inclusive, and filled with boundless possibilities.

Embracing uniqueness goes beyond individual growth; it encompasses a broader vision of fostering a society that appreciates and respects each person's inherent value. By embracing diversity, we acknowledge that everyone brings their perspectives, experiences, and contributions. When we unite to celebrate our differences, we create an environment where people feel accepted, understood, and valued for who they are. Through this collective effort, we can break down barriers, challenge stereotypes, and promote inclusivity. This journey towards embracing uniqueness is remarkable, as it requires courage to step outside of societal norms and embrace our authentic selves. It demands that we confront biases, prejudices, and discrimination within ourselves and society. Doing so will pave the way for a more compassionate and harmonious world. The kaleidoscope of human existence symbolizes the vast range of identities, cultures, and experiences that make our world vibrant. By embracing this diversity, we foster a society where everyone can thrive, all voices are heard, and no one is left behind.

So, dear readers, let us embrace the wisdom within these pages and embark on our journeys of acceptance and connection. Let us celebrate the beauty of our differences and recognize the power we hold to shape our narratives. May we choose resilience in the face of adversity, and may we seek to understand and appreciate the cultures and experiences of others? As we embrace our roles as global citizens, let us embark on a noble mission to build bridges of understanding and compassion, transcending the barriers that divide us. Together, let us weave a vibrant tapestry of unity that celebrates our world's beautiful diversity. In this tapestry, every thread represents a unique culture, language, and perspective, coming together to form a harmonious whole.

Let us stand together, hand in hand, and embark on this journey towards embracing uniqueness. The world eagerly awaits our collective commitment to creating a society that values and celebrates every individual.

Here is my exhilarating day as a ride-share driver. It all starts in the wee hours of the morning when the world is still cloaked in darkness. I do not spring out of bed at the first alarm. Nope, I like to give myself some time to wake up gradually, so I strategically set four alarms before my wake-up time. Absolutely! Before embarking on my day as a ride-share driver, I prioritize my well-being by ensuring I get 10 hours of sleep. I must wake up feeling refreshed and rejuvenated, allowing my senses to be fully alert as I take on the responsibilities of the road. My role as a ride-share driver extends beyond just transporting passengers. I also drive for other drivers who may need to be more attentive. This realization pushes me to operate with an unwavering focus, utilizing my entire 200 percent attention span. With every journey I embark on, I make it my utmost priority to adhere to traffic regulations and ensure the safety of everyone on the road. This means making complete stops at red lights and stop signs and respecting traffic signals without exception. I always use my signal lights well before turning, allowing fellow drivers to anticipate my actions and promoting a smoother traffic flow.

Moreover, I am acutely aware of the importance of yielding to pedestrians, cyclists, and motorcyclists. Their vulnerability on the road necessitates my utmost caution and respect. I prioritize their safety, always being mindful of their presence and watching for potential hazards. Accidents can have serious consequences, so taking every precaution to avoid them is essential. Having 25,000 trips, my chances are higher. Safety is the biggest priority. As a responsible ride-share driver, my top priority is the safety and well-being of both my passengers and myself. Accidents pose a physical risk and can lead to time-consuming and stressful situations.

Just imagine being involved in an accident. The immediate aftermath requires exchanging license and car insurance information with the other party. This process alone can be time-consuming, as details need to be accurately recorded. Then, the waiting game begins as you wait for a police officer to arrive at the scene. This can often take significant time, leaving you feeling frustrated and anxious. Once the police officer comes, a thorough investigation occurs to determine fault and gather evidence. This process can further prolong the ordeal. And let's remember the aftermath - reporting the incident to the insurance companies. This involves providing detailed accounts of the accident, submitting claims, and potentially dealing with legal and financial implications. This can quickly add up to 2-3 hours or more, leaving you drained and overwhelmed.

Avoiding accidents protects yourself from physical harm, saves valuable time, and eliminates unnecessary stress. It all starts with being kind to yourself, ensuring you get enough sleep, and starting your day earlier. Allowing yourself more time creates a buffer that eliminates the need to rush carelessly through traffic. This extra time grants you the freedom to navigate the roads responsibly and calmly, reducing the likelihood of making hasty decisions that could lead to an accident.

By taking the necessary precautions, such as driving defensively and remaining hyper-aware of your surroundings, you significantly mitigate the risks associated with accidents. You become proactive in preventing such incidents, giving yourself and your passengers a sense of security and peace of mind. It's about embracing a mindset of caution, responsibility, and consideration for your well-being and the safety of others sharing the road with you.

Ultimately, prioritizing safety and avoiding accidents saves you from potential harm and creates a positive ripple effect.

As a responsible driver, you inspire others to adopt similar habits, promoting a safe driving culture and reducing the overall number of accidents on the road. Together, we can contribute to a safer and more harmonious environment for everyone. So, let's remember the importance of avoiding accidents, not only for the physical risks they pose but also for the time, stress, and inconvenience they bring. By being kind to ourselves, getting enough sleep, and starting earlier, we give ourselves the gift of time and freedom. Let's drive responsibly, remain vigilant, and make the roads a safer place for all.

In this ever-evolving world of transportation, everyone on the road must contribute to maintaining safety. As a ride-share driver, I embrace this responsibility wholeheartedly. I strive to be a steadfast guardian of the street, ensuring every journey is comfortable, enjoyable, safe, and secure. Rest assured that when you hop into my car, you'll be in the hands of a driver who takes safety seriously. Together, we'll navigate the bustling streets, overcome challenges, and ensure your ride is memorable and incident-free.

The first alarm rudely interrupts my dreams at 1 am. I groggily hit the snooze button and drifted back into a light slumber. Thirty minutes later, at 1:30 am, another alarm pierces through the silence, urging me closer to consciousness. When the third alarm blares at 2 am, my mind begins to stir, and I feel excited. Finally, at 2:30 am, the fourth and final alarm rings, signaling it's time to rise and shine. I stumble into the bathroom and let the warm water from the shower wash away the last remnants of sleep. With each droplet that cascades down my body, I feel a renewed sense of energy and purpose. Drying off and slipping into fresh clothes, I'm ready to take on the day. Before I hit the road, one essential task must be refueling my trusty vehicle. I quickly stopped at the nearest gas station to ensure I started the day with a full tank. It's like giving my car a little boost of motivation, ready to conquer the miles ahead.

Now, here's where the real adventure begins. I navigate the quiet streets, my headlights cutting through the darkness like beacons of possibility. The city is still asleep, and tranquility is in the air. But I know that will soon change. With a growling stomach and a craving for that liquid gold, I make a detour to the 24-hour Dunkin' Donuts. The aroma of freshly brewed coffee hits me as I step inside, and the friendly faces of the early morning crew greet me. I order an excellent regular coffee, the perfect companion to kick-start my day. Savoring each sip, I feel the warmth spreading through my body, awakening every cell and energizing my spirit.

As a rideshare driver, I find that the early morning hours hold a special allure. As the sun timidly begins to rise, casting a soft glow on the horizon, it sets the stage for a unique experience.

My heart fills with anticipation in these moments, knowing I am about to embark on a journey beyond mere transportation. While the sun rises higher, illuminating the world around me, the passengers I encounter grow even more diverse. Among them are the unsung heroes of society, the first responders who tirelessly dedicate themselves to the well-being of others. I am privileged to drive doctors, nurses, and other medical staff on their way to work, ready to nurse people back to health and save lives.

These dedicated individuals, dressed in scrubs or white coats, carry an air of purpose and determination. Their mornings begin earlier than most, and they are driven by a deep sense of duty to alleviate suffering and heal those in need. As they step into my vehicle, I am filled with admiration and respect for their unwavering commitment.

In their presence, I am reminded of the selflessness that permeates their profession. They share stories of long shifts, sleepless nights, and the emotional toll of witnessing both triumph and tragedy. Their compassion and resilience shine through, even amid immense challenges. Beyond the medical field, I also encountered countless labor workers, each with unique stories. From construction workers to delivery drivers, their early mornings are filled with physical exertion and the pursuit of providing for their families. Their perseverance and dedication to their craft inspire me.

As I listened to their tales, my heart went out to my family members who were out there in the field. Thoughts of my mother, who works tirelessly as a nurse, and my two younger brothers, who are following in her footsteps, fill me with pride and concern. I understand their sacrifices, the long hours they put in, and the emotional toll it can take.

In those moments, I am humbled by the immense contributions of these individuals, who often go unnoticed or underappreciated. They are the backbone of our society, the ones who keep our communities running smoothly, and I am honored to have a small part in supporting them through my role as a driver. As the morning unfolds and the city awakens to the rhythm of bustling activity, I am reminded of the interconnectedness of our lives. Each passenger I encounter, whether a first responder or a labor worker, becomes a part of my narrative. Their stories, struggles, and triumphs become woven into the fabric of my experiences, shaping my understanding of the world and fostering a deeper appreciation for the resilience and strength of the human spirit.

In addition to the first responders, medical staff, and labor workers, my encounters as a rideshare driver extend to other remarkable individuals who contribute to our society. Among them are teachers, the unsung heroes who nurture young minds and shape the future. As I picked up teachers on their way to schools and educational institutions, I was struck by their passion and dedication. They carry the weight of responsibility, knowing they can ignite curiosity and inspire lifelong learning in their students. Their conversations are filled with anecdotes of breakthroughs, challenges, and the profound joy of witnessing a student's growth.

The city workers, too, form an integral part of the tapestry of passengers I encounter. From municipal employees to sanitation workers, they work tirelessly behind the scenes to ensure the smooth functioning of our urban environment. Whether it's maintaining infrastructure, keeping the streets clean, or providing essential services, their contributions often go unnoticed. Their stories remind them of the collective effort to create and sustain a thriving city. Teachers and city workers' presence gave me a deeper appreciation for individuals' diverse roles in building and nurturing our communities. Their dedication, often going beyond the call of duty, leaves a lasting impact on the lives they touch.

As I drive through the city, every passenger I encounter—a first responder, medical staff member, labor worker, teacher, or city worker—adds a new layer to my ever-growing book of stories. They broaden my understanding of the world, challenge my perspectives, and remind me of the intricate web of connections that make up our shared human experience.

Each interaction reminds us that while our journeys may differ, we are all interconnected, bound by our collective aspirations, struggles, and triumphs. It is an honor to witness the stories of these remarkable individuals who, through their chosen paths, contribute to the tapestry of humanity in their unique ways. In these fleeting moments, I become a temporary confidant in their journeys. Sometimes, conversations flow effortlessly, and we exchange tales of triumphs, struggles, and aspirations. Other times, silence prevails, and I find solace in the quiet companionship we share. Each passenger leaves an indelible mark, a subtle imprint on my perspective of the world.

As I navigate the city streets, I chauffeur them to their destinations and become a silent observer of the tapestry of life unfolding before me. The city awakens, and I witness its pulse, the ebb and flow of its inhabitants. The early morning light paints a backdrop of possibility, and I find myself immersed in the rich tapestry of human experience. For a brief moment, our paths intertwine, and I play a small role in their story. As they step out of my vehicle, their stories continue, and I continue on my journey, enriched by the encounters and narratives that have graced my humble car.

I find solace and fulfillment in these quiet moments before the bustling day fully awakens. The real magic happens, not in the destination reached but in the connections made, the stories shared, and the profound sense of humanity that permeates the early morning air. The city unfolds before me, revealing its many faces and secrets. I navigate through bustling downtown streets, where the pulse of urban life reverberates through every corner. Then, I venture into the serene suburbs, where white picket fences and neatly manicured lawns whisper tales of domestic bliss.

Every turn, every intersection promises an encounter that could change any perspective, challenge my assumptions, or make me smile. It's a constant dance of human connection as I listen to the stories, dreams, and fears of those who share my car for a fleeting moment. So, my day as a ride-share driver unfolds, a tapestry woven with countless threads of life's intricacies. From the predawn hours to the sun-kissed afternoon, I traverse the city, weaving through its veins and leaving a trail of memories in my wake. As the day draws to a close, I reflect on the privilege of witnessing the diverse tapestry of humanity. Every ride reminds us of the interconnectedness of our lives, the shared experiences that shape us all. As I park my car and bid farewell to the day, I can't help but feel grateful for the chance to be a part of something bigger, something that transcends the solitary act of driving.

So, if you ever find yourself in the backseat of a ride-share car, remember that behind the wheel is more than just a driver. There's a storyteller, an observer, and a companion on the road of life. And who knows, maybe one day, our paths will cross, and I'll have the honor of adding a chapter to your story, too. Fasten your seatbelts, dear readers, for the transformative voyage awaits. Let the pages of this book become a compass to navigate the vast ocean of life, guiding you toward moments of joy, fulfillment, and self-discovery.

As you turn each page, may you uncover the keys to unlocking your happiness and, in doing so, become a beacon of light that illuminates the path for others.

CHAPTER 2 - Always Do Your Best
Lessons from the Ride-Share Journey

Let us take a moment to return to when Uber and Lyft first started in Chicago. I was like the second or third batch of the first drivers to enter the ride-share market. I remember traveling close to Ogden Ave. to the office for a long time after being approved to be a driver. I recall going to one of the first Uber offices in Chicago. Waiting in line, I thought, what kind of new adventure awaits me? There's no way this could ever be a real job or make any money. This seems to be such a scam. I saw a separate line for Taxi drivers who wanted to join Uber Taxi. The other lane was the line for drivers to become UberX drivers.

Finally, after waiting in line for about twenty to thirty minutes, I reached the front!

There was a bearded man who looked at me reluctantly to hire me and give me a chance, but his colleague glanced at me, and she said, "Yes, you're approved!"

As she smiled, she handed me a bag of Uber stuff. Inside was an iPhone strictly for drivers' use, a car charger, water, snacks, and further information for Uber drivers. I was accepted, and so the real adventure finally began.

During the early days of ride-share apps, there was a significant amount of skepticism and misunderstanding among both passengers and drivers. As a driver at that time, I encountered challenging situations where passengers expressed their frustrations and treated us as inexperienced taxi drivers, sometimes worse than animals.

We were expected to encounter unpleasant encounters, such as being yelled at, cursed at, or receiving disrespectful comments. Passengers often assumed that we lacked common sense, didn't know where we were navigating or lacked driving skills.

Phrases like, "You don't know where the hell you are going."

"Is Uber even a legitimate company? It's a scam, and you are a scammer!"

"You don't know how to drive."

"You don't know where you are going."

All these words were, unfortunately, all too familiar. The negative experiences and skepticism between passengers and drivers in the early days of ride-share apps were primarily due to a lack of familiarity with how these apps worked. Many customers were still adjusting to the concept and were in the process of understanding how to use the apps effectively. Ride-share apps introduced a significant shift in the transportation industry, disrupting the traditional taxi model. This shift meant that passengers had to adapt to a new way of requesting rides, navigating the app interface, and understanding the pricing structure. This learning curve sometimes led to confusion and frustration.

For passengers accustomed to hailing taxis on the street or calling for a cab, the transition to using a mobile app could be challenging. They might have encountered difficulties inputting pickup and drop-off locations, understanding surge pricing during peak hours, or experiencing technical glitches with the app.

These uncertainties and frustrations often manifest as impatience or criticism towards drivers. In their confusion or annoyance, passengers might have expressed dissatisfaction by questioning the driver's knowledge of directions or their driving skills. This behavior was not indicative of the drivers' competence but rather a result of passengers grappling with the new system. As drivers, we needed to recognize that these negative experiences were not personal attacks but a byproduct of this learning process. We had to develop a thick skin and remain professional in such encounters. Patiently explaining the app's features, addressing concerns, and ensuring a smooth ride experience became essential in building trust and changing passengers' perceptions.

Over time, as ride-share apps became more prevalent and user-friendly, passengers became more comfortable with the technology. They started understanding ride-sharing's convenience and benefits, such as real-time tracking, cashless payments, and reliable service. As familiarity grew, passengers became more confident in using the apps, and the negative experiences stemming from confusion and uncertainty gradually diminished.

Ultimately, the ride-share industry's early challenges with passenger-driver interactions resulted from a transitional phase as people acclimated to the new technology and service model. Through patience, effective communication, and a commitment to providing excellent service, ride-share drivers played a vital role in helping bridge the gap and transforming skepticism into trust and acceptance. One of the passengers, Gabby, whom I picked up, couldn't point out enough how technology has greatly assisted us with GPS and finding our destinations.

I told the passenger, "Hey Gabby, do you remember when we had to rely on those big sheets of paper that needed to be unfolded maps to find our way to a destination?"

"Oh! It feels like a lifetime ago. We used to spend so much time figuring out the right route and navigating those complicated maps. It was quite an adventure!" as she sighed in relief.

"Indeed, technology has come a long way since then. Nowadays, our smartphones have become these incredible devices that revolutionize how we live our lives. We use them for so many things!"

"You're right! Our smartphones have become our lifelines. We can use them to communicate with friends and family worldwide, instantly connecting with loved ones wherever they may be."

"And it's not just communication, Marshall. With a screen tap, we can capture high-definition videos and photos, creating lasting memories. The quality and convenience are remarkable."

"Absolutely Gabby! It's incredible how we can document our lives and vividly share our experiences. We can now capture and relive precious moments with such ease."

"And let's remember the navigation aspect. GPS technology has made finding our way so much simpler. Our smartphones can pinpoint our exact locations and guide us to any destination we need to go to."

"Yes, it's like having a personal navigation assistant in our pockets. No more fumbling with paper maps or getting lost on unfamiliar roads. Technology has truly made our journeys smoother and more efficient."

"It's amazing how far we've come. From unfolding cumbersome maps to having the entire world at our fingertips, technology has transformed how we navigate, communicate, and capture memories."

"Marshall, our smartphones have become powerful tools that enhance our lives in countless ways. It's fascinating to think about how much more they'll evolve in the future."

"Indeed, the possibilities are endless. So, here's to embracing the wonders of technology and enjoying the convenience and connectivity it brings to our lives!"

"Cheers to that, driver! Let's embrace the advancements and make the most of this incredible technological journey."

Despite the initial difficulties, being part of the ride-share industry in its early stage allowed us to witness the transformation of public perception firsthand. It was rewarding to see how ride-sharing eventually gained acceptance and became a convenient and trusted mode of transportation for people worldwide.

Cashless transactions have proven innovative and have brought numerous benefits to customers and businesses. One significant advantage is eliminating the need for physical cash, which addresses several common concerns.

Firstly, it eliminates the hassle of dealing with taxi drivers who may need more change. With cashless transactions, customers can quickly pay the exact amount without worrying about carrying smaller denominations or being shortchanged.

Secondly, it minimizes the risk of losing or having cash stolen. Carrying a wallet full of cash can be risky, especially in crowded places or unfamiliar environments. By using digital payment methods, customers can securely complete transactions without needing physical money, reducing the chances of theft or loss.

Additionally, cashless transactions provide convenience. Customers no longer need to search for ATMs or worry about having enough money. With digital payment options, transactions can be completed quickly and seamlessly, whether it's through mobile wallets, credit cards, or online payment platforms.

Moreover, cashless transactions offer enhanced safety. Unlike carrying large amounts of cash, digital transactions leave a digital trail, making tracking and monitoring expenses easier. This can be particularly helpful for budgeting purposes and keeping financial records organized. The advent of cashless transactions has provided a safer and more convenient way for customers to make payments. It has streamlined the payment process, reduced the risk of theft or loss, and simplified financial transactions in various scenarios, including taxi rides.

Assuring confidently, "I know this has to be the right way."

Yet, amid that uncertainty, a glimmer of trust emerged as I conversed with my riders. Passengers would chime in, offering their insights. Looking confused inside the car while glancing through the windows, "No, Uber. I think this is the

right way. For sure, I know you need to take a left down
Belmont Ave", the intoxicated passenger replied.

Why was the passenger Erica intoxicated? Because she indicated earlier that she'd been drinking for a few hours at the bar. After a few hours, I examined the history and receipt of the trip. I saw that the company had taken several dollars off the original trip with Erica because she had reported that I had gone in the wrong direction. I disputed that the passenger was intoxicated and had directed me to go in the wrong direction, even though I knew exactly the area in the direction she had to go in the first place. Because why should I suffer loss and wages in gasoline from a situation that was not my fault? After review, the company refunded the money they had initially taken out. The company went through so much growth and so many transitions.

Other times, my instincts guided us correctly. As the miles ticked away, a symbiotic relationship formed, where my passengers and I would navigate the unknown together, weaving through the city's intricate web of streets, bound by a shared trust in the journey we embarked upon.

Certainly! Ride-share companies have revolutionized the transportation industry by offering increased convenience and safety, significantly impacting the traditional taxi market. One key advantage of ride-share services is the transparency and information available to customers. When booking a ride, customers can see essential details such as the vehicle's license plate number, make, and model. This information lets passengers quickly identify their designated ride and ensures they get into the correct vehicle, enhancing safety and minimizing the risk of getting into the wrong car.

Furthermore, ride-share platforms provide driver profiles with essential details such as ratings and when the driver has been with the service. These ratings are based on feedback from previous passengers, allowing customers to assess the driver's overall performance and professionalism. This rating system provides an extra layer of security and helps passengers feel more comfortable knowing they are riding with a driver whom other users have positively evaluated. Believe it or not, some still need to learn to check the license plate before entering the vehicle. As a responsible driver, I always greet and confirm the passenger's name for security. However, I had a passenger who had the same name, but the drop-off location was different, so the drop-off location also had to be confirmed. Two other Bobs came into my car at the same time this one time, but I could, of course, only drive home one of them.

The use of technology in ride-share services also contributes to safety. These platforms often have built-in GPS tracking, allowing passengers to share their trip details with friends or family in real time. This feature provides an added sense of security, as loved ones can monitor the journey and be aware of the passenger's location.

Additionally, ride-share companies typically have robust safety measures in place. They conduct rigorous background checks on drivers, verifying their driving records and criminal history. Some platforms offer features like two-way ratings and feedback systems, where drivers and passengers can rate and provide feedback on their experience. This accountability promotes professionalism and ensures that both parties adhere to specific standards of behavior. The combination of convenience, transparency, driver ratings, and safety measures provided by ride-share companies has attracted a large customer base. The ease of booking, the ability to track rides, and the overall sense of security have made ride-sharing a preferred choice for many passengers, leading to a decline in the traditional taxi market.

It's important to note that the impact on the taxi market can vary by region. Some areas may still have a significant presence of traditional taxis alongside ride-share services. However, ride-share companies' increased convenience and safety have undoubtedly disrupted the industry and reshaped people's commutes.

As I embarked on my first trip as a ride-share driver, a whirlwind of doubt and uncertainty swirled within me. Countless questions plagued my mind: Would the passengers warm up to me? Was I navigating the labyrinthine city streets correctly? Could I trust the GPS to lead me on the right path? In those early days, passengers sometimes provided their destinations upfront, leaving me to rely on my instincts and limited information. This means that at the beginning of Uber and Lyft, passengers were encouraged to input the drop-off location, but it was not required. Not until much later did the drop-off location become mandatory to request the ride successfully. There were moments when I would confidently choose a route, reassuring my passengers,

Mr. Johnson sighed heavily and explained that he was late for an important job interview. The position he was vying for could change his life, and the pressure weighed heavily on him. I assured him we would do our best to get him there on time, offering a comforting smile. Little did I know that this ride would teach me a valuable lesson about going above and beyond.

As we set off, I relied on my GPS for guidance, but it seemed determined to take us through bumper-to-bumper traffic. Mr. Johnson's anxiety levels skyrocketed with each passing minute, and I could feel his desperation. At that moment, I knew I had to take matters into my own hands.

Without a second thought, I made a daring decision. I veered off the main road and took a shortcut through a lesser-known side street. The move was a gamble, but I had a gut feeling that it would pay off. Mr. Johnson glanced at me, his eyes wide with surprise, but he trusted my judgment. As we raced through the narrow streets, dodging traffic and taking turns with precision, a sense of exhilaration washed over me. I was fully committed to delivering Mr. Johnson to his interview on time, no matter what it took. The mundane act of driving transformed into a thrilling adventure where time and space seemed to blur

To our amazement, the shortcut worked like magic. We emerged from the labyrinth of streets just a few blocks away from Mr. Johnson's destination. He let out a breathless laugh of relief, thanking me profusely. In that moment, I realized the power of taking risks and going beyond what is expected. As I dropped Mr. Johnson off at his interview, he turned to me with a newfound sense of confidence. He expressed his gratitude for my determination and willingness to explore uncharted paths. In his eyes, I saw a glimmer of hope that transcended the job interview's outcome.

That day, I learned that being a ride-share driver was more than just ferrying passengers from one point to another. It was about forging connections, building trust, and embracing the unknown. The ride with Mr. Johnson taught me that sometimes, to excel in life, you must take risks, trust your instincts, and always do your best. And so, as I continue my ride-share journey, I carry with me the lessons learned from that exhilarating chapter.

I approach each ride with unwavering dedication, knowing that every passenger holds a story and an opportunity for growth. Together, we venture into the unknown, weaving through the city's streets, bound by trust and always doing our best.

One particularly memorable evening, I received a ride request from friends heading to a popular downtown venue. Their laughter and excitement filled the air as they piled into my car, instantly brightening my spirits. Their destination seemed straightforward, and I confidently set off, determined to provide them with a smooth and enjoyable ride. However, what started as a routine trip quickly became a test of my problem-solving skills. We encountered unexpected road closures as we approached the downtown area due to a local festival. Gridlocked traffic surrounded us, and frustration began to replace the initial excitement.

Sensing his disappointment, I decided to take charge of the situation. I conversed with the passengers, discussing alternative routes and exploring different options. Together, we brainstormed and devised a plan to navigate the crowded streets. With their trust in my abilities, we embarked on a detour filled with twists and turns, hoping to reach their destination on time. As we maneuvered through unfamiliar streets, I relied on a combination of instinct and the occasional guidance from the passengers. It was a collective effort, with each of us contributing our knowledge and insights. The atmosphere inside the car shifted from frustration to determination as we embraced the challenge as a team.

After what felt like an eternity, we finally arrived at the venue. The passengers erupted into cheers and applause, grateful for our shared perseverance. They admired my dedication and resourcefulness as they stepped out of the car. At that moment, I realized the impact of always doing my best despite unexpected obstacles. In ride-share driving, some moments go beyond simply transporting passengers from one place to another. These moments become opportunities to connect with others and share stories that inspire and remind us of the power of doing our best.

One evening, I picked up a passenger who began sharing the misfortunes and struggles of life. I approached the designated location and saw a figure standing in the dimly lit street. The passenger got into the car, and as we drove deeper into the city, a sense of darkness and peril surrounded us. With a heavy sigh, the passenger began to open up, expressing the hardships and difficulties they had faced in life.

"You know, life can be so tough. There are homeless people scattered throughout the streets, individuals begging for a chance at survival. It feels like chaos out there. I even have family members who are homeless", his voice said with weariness and a disgruntled face.

"You're right. The world can be challenging, and it's easy to get caught up in the darkness surrounding us," I replied, my voice filled with empathy.

I nodded, acknowledging the harsh realities they described. As the passenger breathed a deep sigh, their weariness and contemplation were evident. Their gaze remained fixed on the bustling cityscape passing by, a vivid backdrop to their thoughts.

"I work tirelessly just to pay my bills," he expressed with a hint of resignation.

"Every day feels like a relentless grind, a never-ending cycle of obligations. But sometimes, amidst it all, I can't help but wonder if this is all there is to life. Is this the life we're meant to live?"

The city's vibrant lights and the rhythm of the passing streets echo his ponderings, reflecting the complexities of existence. The passenger's words conveyed a subtle longing for meaning and purpose beyond the mundane routines that consume much of our time. Amidst the busyness, a yearning for something deeper and more fulfilling emerged.

As I navigate the vibrant street of Milwaukee Ave. in Wicker Park, I often find myself accompanied by a lively presence: the cyclists who gracefully ride alongside me. Their agile movements and the rhythmic whir of their wheels create a symphony of motion, blending harmoniously with the urban landscape. While the traffic stops at a red light, I take the opportunity to observe and appreciate the cyclists' dedication to their chosen mode of transportation. Their commitment to sustainable and active commuting is evident as they effortlessly glide past, their bodies propelled by the power of their legs.

In these moments, I embrace the spirit of shared space and mutual respect. As a driver, I recognize the importance of yielding to these two-wheeled travelers. Their vulnerability on the road prompts me to exercise caution and prioritize their safety. I wait patiently at the red light, allowing them to pass by, acknowledging their presence, and granting them the right of way.

This act of yielding extends beyond mere traffic rules; it embodies a sense of understanding and solidarity. It reflects a recognition of the diverse ways people navigate the city, each mode of transportation contributing to the intricate tapestry of urban life. As the light turns green and we resume our journeys, I am reminded of the interconnectedness of our transportation choices. Whether on foot, on a bicycle, or in a vehicle, we are all travelers sharing the same streets, united by our collective desire to reach our destinations and engage with the world.

In yielding to the cyclists on Milwaukee Ave., I prioritize their safety and foster a culture of empathy and cooperation on the road. I am reminded that small gestures of consideration and respect can create a ripple effect, influencing the overall commuting experience for everyone involved.

As I continue driving along Milwaukee Ave., the presence of cyclists serves as a reminder of the importance of sustainable transportation, promoting healthier and greener alternatives for our communities. It encourages me to be mindful of the impact of my own choices as a driver and to seek opportunities to contribute positively to the coexistence of various modes of transportation. As I sat behind the wheel, my hands firmly gripping the steering wheel, I embarked on a journey that would take me through breathtaking landscapes and winding roads. The engine hummed with anticipation, ready to unleash its power on the asphalt. I accelerated, and my eyes scanned the surroundings, capturing the world's beauty as it whizzed by. And there, in the distance, I spotted a group of dedicated cyclists, each one a testament to their unwavering determination. Their synchronized pedaling and vibrant jerseys created a mesmerizing sight, a moving tapestry of passion and athleticism.

I maneuvered my car cautiously and respectfully, giving them ample space to continue their adventure. The bicyclists, focused and in their element, weaved gracefully through the twists and turns of the road. It was a dance, a symphony of motion, as they effortlessly conquered the terrain with every stroke of their pedals. As our paths aligned, a sense of mutual admiration filled the air. Their strength and resilience were palpable, their commitment to the ride undeniable. And then, one cyclist, catching sight of my vehicle, lifted their hand in gratitude. It was a sign of recognition, acknowledgment for the consideration I had shown, a small but significant act of kindness.

A surge of warmth enveloped me as their wave cut through the wind, their appreciation a testament to the harmony between drivers and cyclists. It was a shared understanding, a reminder that the road was big enough for us to coexist, embracing our passions while respecting one another's journey. With a smile and a renewed sense of unity, I continued, carrying that moment like a precious gem. The memory of the bicyclist's wave constantly reminded me of the importance of compassion and awareness, encouraging me to be a responsible driver and a supportive community member.

I pressed on, the engine's purr blending harmoniously with the rhythm of the cyclists' wheels. Together, we ventured forth, our separate paths intertwined in a symphony of motion, united by our shared love for the open road. In these shared moments on the road, I appreciate the diversity and interconnectedness of the individuals who make up the vibrant fabric of Wicker Park. From the cyclists who pedal alongside me to the pedestrians crossing the street, we are all part of a collective journey, navigating the city's streetscape together. The passenger's musings reflected a universal human experience, a quest to find significance and purpose during the daily grind. This introspection catalyzes personal growth and a search for a life that resonates more deeply with one's desires and aspirations.

As the cityscape continued to flow, the passenger's thoughts mingled with the possibilities beyond the routine. The passing moments offered a gentle reminder that life's true essence can be found in the pursuit of passion, connection with others, moments of joy, and the exploration of one's unique path. While the answers to the passenger's questions may not be immediately apparent, questioning can ignite a journey of self-discovery and open doors to new opportunities. The path to a more fulfilling life may require introspection, taking risks, and embracing change. In adopting these challenges, one can navigate the complexities of existence and uncover the potential for a life that transcends the confines of ordinary reality.

Ultimately, the passenger's contemplation invites us to reflect on our journeys and consider the possibilities beyond the daily grind. Through these moments of reflection, we can begin to shape a life that aligns with our deepest aspirations and brings us closer to a sense of purpose and fulfillment. In that moment, a surge of determination and compassion filled me. I felt compelled to respond to the passenger's contemplation, offering a perspective emphasizing each individual's transformative power.

With conviction in my voice, I affirmed, "Life is indeed what we make of it. While there are hardships and obstacles along the way, it's important to remember that we possess the power to shape our destinies."

The car smoothly traversed the vibrant city streets as I began sharing my personal experiences of perseverance and resilience.

A sense of camaraderie enveloped the conversation as I confided, "I, too, have faced my fair share of challenges. But through these trials, I've realized that it's not solely about the circumstances we find ourselves in; it's about how we choose to respond to them."

I elaborated on how our responses to adversity define us and shape our journeys. I spoke of the strength that can be found within, even in the face of seemingly insurmountable odds. I shared anecdotes of overcoming obstacles, recounting stories of resilience and the transformative power of maintaining a positive mindset. During our conversation, a subtle shift occurred. The passing cityscape echoed our shared belief in the potential for growth and personal agency. These Chicago streets, filled with diverse individuals pursuing their ambitions, symbolized the countless paths one could take in their quest for fulfillment. I emphasized that while life may present challenges, our choices and actions determine our trajectory. We can navigate life's twists and turns by embracing resilience, adaptability, and a courageous mindset. I spoke of the importance of seeking opportunities for growth, embracing change, and cultivating a sense of empathy and compassion toward ourselves and others. The conversation reaffirmed the human spirit's ability to rise above adversity as the car continued its journey. It was a reminder that external circumstances do not predetermine our individual stories but are shaped by our intentions, choices, and responses.

At that moment, we found solace in the shared understanding that life is a canvas waiting to be painted, and we hold the brush. With determination and compassion as our guides, we explored what it means to live a life of purpose, resilience, and fulfillment. Whenever I encountered passengers who seemed to have lost hope in the world, I found solace in sharing the inspiring stories of my Venezuelan friend, Manolo, and Greek friend, Clyde. Both had faced immense challenges when they first arrived in the United States, starting with very little and working tirelessly to create better lives for themselves. I began by recounting the story of my friends Clyde and Manolo, resilient individuals who had also faced challenges upon arriving in the United States. I described how both had left their homelands for better prospects, leaving behind the economic crisis gripping both countries. Starting with little more than a dream, they undertook various jobs, often working long hours to make ends meet. Despite the obstacles, they both remained steadfast in pursuing a better life. Through sheer determination and a willingness to learn and adapt, they eventually found stability and success, establishing their businesses and becoming an integral part of their communities. We formed a bond that transcended borders, cultures, and languages.

*We became a beacon of positivity, constantly uplifting one another in our group chat, aptly named "**Brothers Making It Happen**," as we journeyed through life.*

Throughout our close to 20-year friendship, these extraordinary individuals, my friends Clyde and Manolo, have

65

been the unwavering pillars of strength and inspiration in my life. The story of my friends exemplified the strength of the human spirit and the ability to rise above adversity. It showcased the power of resilience, hard work, and an unwavering belief in pursuing a brighter future. Despite the initial hardships and uncertainties, they persevered and carved out a path of success for themselves.

As I wove the stories of cyclists' determination and triumph, the passengers in the car leaned in, their eyes filled with curiosity and admiration. The passing cityscape mirrored the narratives I shared, its bustling streets as a vivid backdrop to the tales of resilience and triumph. The towering skyscrapers stood tall, like beacons of ambition, symbolizing the endless possibilities that arise from unwavering determination and perseverance. The streets, teeming with activity, echoed the vibrant energy that surged through the veins of the cyclists, propelling them forward against all odds.

I vividly depicted these cyclists' journeys with each passing landmark. Their uphill battles and relentless efforts resonated with the passengers, who began to visualize themselves in the shoes of those brave individuals. They marveled at the commitment and sacrifices made, finding inspiration in the tales of pushing boundaries and defying limits. A shared purpose filled the air as the car glided through the city streets. The passengers embraced the idea that within each of them lay the potential for greatness, just like the cyclists they heard about. The city's rhythm, the honking of horns, and the buzz of conversations harmonize with the stories, reflecting the symphony of determination and triumph that played out on both the road and in their lives.

With each turn of the wheel, the passengers became more engrossed in the stories, their dreams and aspirations intertwining with the narratives. The passing buildings and flickering streetlights witnessed the transformation within the car as the passengers absorbed the lessons of resilience, perseverance, and the pursuit of one's passions.

The passengers' faces glowed with a newfound purpose as the journey continued. They recognized that the city's bustling streets were not just a chaotic backdrop but a stage where their dreams could take center stage. The tales of the cyclists had ignited a fire within them, reminding them that amidst the noise and chaos, there were stories of triumph waiting to be written. As the car pressed on through the cityscape, the passengers' hearts were filled with inspiration, their minds buzzing with possibilities. They realized they, too, could embark on their journeys of resilience and triumph, weaving their own stories of adventure and growth. Together, we traveled through the city, united by the shared understanding that determination and perseverance can transform lives. The passing cityscape was a constant reminder that amidst the chaos, there lies a limitless opportunity waiting to be explored by those who dare to chase their dreams.

Despite the physical distance that separates us, we connect through social media platforms, communicating almost every day. We constantly share stories of triumphs, challenges, and life perspectives that enrich our understanding of the world. In the face of adversity, we encourage and motivate each other, reminding ourselves to never give up on our dreams. Here are some types of conversations that Clyde, Manolo, and I have in our chat room.

I said, "Hey, Manolo! How's everything going with your software engineering work and your family?

"Thanks for asking, Marshall. It's been quite a challenge juggling my software engineering projects while ensuring quality time with my family, but I'm making progress. On another note, I've been planning upgrades for my million-dollar home in West Palm Beach, Florida. It's exciting but also overwhelming," replied Manolo.

Clyde said, "Manolo, I can relate to balancing work and family. Managing hotels and caring for my family can be demanding, but it's all worth it. Have you made any progress on your home upgrades? You mentioned wanting to create a modern and stylish living space."

"Thanks, Clyde. I've been working with a talented architect and interior designer to bring my vision to life. We're incorporating smart home technology, redesigning the kitchen, and revamping the outdoor space for entertaining. It's a big project, but I'm excited about the result", replied Manolo.

Clyde said, "That sounds fantastic, Manolo! I've always admired your taste in design. By the way, managing my six properties has been quite a challenge lately. It can be difficult to handle between maintenance, bookings, and ensuring an excellent guest experience. However, I'm learning to delegate and streamline processes to make it more manageable."

I said, "Wow, Clyde, I can only imagine how much work it takes to manage multiple properties. It's impressive how you handle it all. Have you considered using any property management software or hiring a team to assist you?"

"I've been exploring different property management software options to streamline operations. Also, I recently hired a property manager who has been a great help in overseeing day-to-day tasks. It's significantly reduced my workload and allowed me to focus on other areas", replied Clyde.

Manolo said, "Clyde, that's a smart move. Delegating responsibilities and leveraging technology can be a game-changer in managing properties. Seeing how you're constantly finding new ways to improve and grow your business is inspiring."

I said, "Amazingly, both of you tackle such challenging endeavors while maintaining strong family connections. Your determination and dedication are truly admirable. Remember, we're here to support and encourage each other."

"Our friendship and shared experiences help us navigate through these challenges. Together, we can conquer anything that comes our way, whether it's managing properties, *upgrading homes, or sailing on the beautiful waters of Jupiter Beach", replied Clyde.*

Manolo said, "I couldn't agree more, Clyde. Let's keep pushing forward and supporting each other in our respective endeavors. With our collective motivation and determination, there's no limit to what we can achieve!"

I said, "Cheers to that, guys! Here's to overcoming challenges, pursuing our dreams, and enjoying the journey together."

During the darkest days, when the world's weight threatens to crush our spirits, Clyde, a faithful brother, would regale us with tales of resilience and unwavering determination. He shared his experiences of rising above seemingly insurmountable odds, inspiring us to overcome our obstacles and emerge more vital than ever. His words ignite a fire, reminding us that the human spirit can conquer any challenge. Manolo taught me the art of finding beauty and gratitude even in the simplest moments as he sent us pictures of him, his girlfriend, his daughters, and his dog, Milo. Through his stories of Greece's breathtaking landscapes and rich cultural heritage, he always reminds us to strive for the best through life's tiny treasures, appreciate every precious breath, and cherish the deep connections that make life meaningful. Together, we forged a brotherhood that grew stronger with each passing year. Through our group chat, we celebrate each other's victories, offering solace and encouragement during moments of disappointment and sharing countless motivational and inspirational quotes. In times of doubt, we remind each other that our dreams are within reach and that our potential knows no bounds.

As the years unfolded, we realized that happiness was not a solitary pursuit but a collaborative masterpiece, carefully crafted by friends who are as close as brothers who make it happen. By doing our best and surrounding ourselves with these extraordinary individuals, we find the strength to weather life's storms and the courage to chase our dreams.

Through the power of friendship and brotherhood, we discovered that the world might be filled with challenges, but it is also brimming with hope, resilience, and the unwavering support of those who share our journey. We are the architects of our happiness, and by nurturing relationships with good and positive people, we can navigate life's twists and turns with confidence and grace.

My Venezuelan friend, Manolo, began at the bottom, toiling away in various computer jobs, moving from one position to another. He climbed the ladder of success through sheer determination and unwavering commitment. He now resides in West Palm Beach, surrounded by movie stars and celebrities, enjoying the fruits of his labor.

Similarly, my Greek friend, Clyde, overcame immense obstacles. He had experienced homelessness, working as a pot washer to survive. However, he always retained his dreams and aspirations. With each step forward, he advanced from a banquet supervisor to a food and beverage manager, eventually becoming a hotel director. Currently, he holds a prestigious position overseeing 11 renowned hotel properties as a high-level executive over those general managers in a prominent hospitality firm.

"Never give up," Clyde said firmly, his eyes filled with determination as the Miami skyline glistened in the distance.

"Make it happen," Manolo added with a nod, their voice echoing with resilience as palm trees swayed in the warm breeze.

In that shared moment, our words intertwined while driving towards the Hard Rock Casino in Ft. Lauderdale in Manolo's Mercedes-Benz SUV, igniting a fire within us. United by our unwavering belief, we embrace the excitement of the city and the thrill of our destination, knowing that with a shared mindset, we could conquer any odds and create unforgettable memories in the vibrant heart of Miami. These stories of triumph in the face of adversity inspired me and reminded me of the boundless opportunities in the United States. Whenever I encountered passengers who felt disheartened or believed there were no opportunities for them, I would share the stories of my friends. I wanted them to understand that by always doing their best, they could achieve great things in life.

Amid our conversations, I emphasize the blessings of living in America, the land of opportunity. One can turn their dreams into reality with hard work, dedication, and a relentless pursuit of excellence. I remind them that the path to success might be challenging but not impossible. On top of that, we have the most billionaires living here in the United States and the entire world. We don't have any excuse not to be successful here. These stories served as a wellspring of motivation for my passengers and myself. Whenever I faced my struggles or encountered daunting challenges, I would draw upon the experiences of my friends. If they could rise above their circumstances and succeed, I could, too.

Once a year, Clyde, Manolo, and I would gather to celebrate our journeys and the rewards that came from always doing our best. We would indulge in the finer things in life, enjoying the company of one another and basking in the Florida sun while sailing on my Venezuelan friend's luxurious boat. In those moments, as the wind tousled our hair and the waters enveloped us, we would reflect on our experiences and the labor that had brought us here. We would be grateful for the opportunities we had seized, knowing that by doing our best, we had created lives filled with abundance and joy.

Reflecting on the present, I am amazed at the incredible heights my friends have reached. Manolo has ventured into information technology, working for the Pentagon in computer engineering. His expertise and dedication have propelled him to new heights, allowing him to reside in a magnificent million-dollar home that speaks to his achievements. Similarly, Clyde has expanded his horizons and become a successful entrepreneur in the real estate industry. He now owns several buildings, a testament to his unwavering work ethic and entrepreneurial spirit. His accomplishments remind us we can build a legacy that transcends our wildest dreams with determination and perseverance.

Their stories inspire me, reminding me that no matter where I am on my ride-share journey, there is always room for growth and the possibility of achieving greatness. They reinforce the notion that by always doing my best, I can carve my path to success, just like they did.

In moments of self-doubt or adversity, I draw strength from the incredible transformations my friends have undergone. Their accomplishments reaffirm my belief that I can overcome obstacles and reach new heights with dedication, hard work, and a commitment to always do my best. Their journeys have taught me the importance of resilience, adaptability, and continuous self-improvement. Through their example, I have understood that success is not merely about material possessions or societal recognition but about personal growth, fulfillment, and the positive impact we can make on others. The passenger seemed contemplative, their gaze shifting from the gloomy streets to their reflection in the rearview mirror.

"So, what can I do?" they asked, their voice filled with hope.

I smiled, knowing **a glimmer of light could be found even in darkness.**

"Start by acknowledging your strength and resilience," I suggested. "Remember why you work so hard and the goals you strive to achieve. Find ways to bring positivity into your life, even in the smallest ways. It's these small steps that can lead to significant change."

From one past protagonist to another, I couldn't help but feel a surge of hope as I shared my experiences with the passenger.

"You know," I began, my voice filled with conviction, "if my family could come from a third-world country like the Philippines and find success here in the USA, if my Venezuelan friend, Manolo could overcome the challenges of his homeland and work for the Pentagon, and if my Greek friend, Clyde could rise from being a pot washer and homeless to becoming a high-level executive overseeing multiple hotels, then I truly believe that anyone who gives their best in life can choose to fight for success in this land of opportunity."

The passenger's eyes widened, captivated by the stories of triumph against all odds. "But how?" they asked, their voice tinged with curiosity and a glimmer of hope.

I smiled, inspired by chance to share the power of determination and hard work. "It starts with a mindset," I explained. "You have to believe in yourself, your abilities, and the potential that lies within you. The path to success may not be easy, but with relentless effort, dedication, and a refusal to give up, you can shape your destiny."

The passenger leaned forward, their gaze fixed on me, eager to hear more. "But what about the challenges, the setbacks?" they asked, their voice tinged with concern.

I nodded, acknowledging the inevitable obstacles that life throws our way.

"Yes, there will be challenges," I replied, my voice steady. "But it's how we choose to respond to them that matters. Every setback can be seen as an opportunity for growth, a chance to learn and become stronger. **With resilience and a positive mindset, you can overcome any hurdle that comes your way.***"*

A sense of determination filled the air as we journeyed through the bustling streets.

"Remember," I said, my voice filled with conviction, "this land of opportunity is not limited to a select few. It is open to anyone willing to **work hard, dream big, and never give up***. Your background or current circumstances do not define your potential.* **It's up to you to seize the opportunities and create a successful future.***"*

As the passengers settled back into their seats, a radiant smile graced their faces, their eyes shining with a newfound sense of possibility. The stories of resilience and triumph had touched a deep chord within them, igniting a flicker of determination that had long been dormant.

They turned to me with heartfelt sincerity, their voices tinged with gratitude. "Thank you," they said, their words filled with genuine appreciation. I needed to hear this. It's time for me to choose the path of success and fight for a better life."

The car seemed to brim with electric energy at that moment as if the air around us cracked with anticipation. The passengers' declaration resonated not only within themselves but also with everyone else in the vehicle. It was a shared realization that the stories we had just witnessed held the power to inspire and ignite change.

Encouragement filled the car as the other passengers chimed in, their voices echoing a chorus of support. Each shared their dreams and aspirations, recognizing that this was a pivotal moment, a turning point where determination and action would pave the way to a brighter future.

The passenger's words reverberated in our hearts as the cityscape danced outside the window. We collectively embraced the truth that success was a mere possibility and a tangible goal within reach. The stories of resilience and triumph shattered doubts, leaving a tapestry of hope and determination.

With newfound purpose, the passengers committed silently to themselves, vowing to step onto the road less traveled, armed with courage and unwavering resolve. They understood that the path to success was not without its challenges, but the stories they had heard had infused them with the strength to overcome any obstacles.

As the car glided through the city streets, the passengers shared their stories of perseverance and growth. It became a collective journey, with each person supporting and encouraging one another, forming a tightly-knit web of inspiration and determination.

The passing cityscape, once just a backdrop, now had a new meaning. It became a symbol of endless opportunities, a testament to the transformative power of choice and the pursuit of a better life. The honking horns and bustling streets faded into the background, drowned out by the persistent voices of those ready to embark on their paths of success.

And so, as the car forged ahead, the passengers basked in the warmth of possibility and the unwavering belief that they held the key to their destinies. The stories of resilience and triumph had unlocked a door within their hearts, revealing a world where dreams were not merely wishes but tangible realities waiting to be claimed. Together, we embraced the journey ahead, knowing that the road to success might be bumpy. Still, with determination, perseverance, and a shared purpose, we were ready to defy the odds and create our stories of triumph.

I smiled, knowing that a spark had been ignited within them.
"You're welcome," I replied.

"Remember, you have the power to shape your destiny.
Believe in yourself, give your best, and never let go of that
fighting spirit. Success is within your reach."

As we reached their destination, the passengers stepped out of the car, their posture exuding determination. I watched them walk away, hopeful for the journey they were about to embark on. As I continued on my path, I couldn't help but feel inspired by our impact on others simply by sharing our stories of triumph and our unwavering belief in the power of hard work and determination. The passengers looked at me, gratitude shining in their eyes.

"Thank you," they said softly.

"Sometimes, we just need a reminder that we have the power
to create a better life for ourselves."

I nodded, feeling a sense of fulfillment.
"You're welcome," I replied.

"Remember, life may be challenging but also full of
opportunities. With hard work, resilience, and a
positive mindset, we can navigate through the darkness
and find our way towards a brighter future."

With that, we arrived at their destination. The passenger stepped out of the car, carrying a newfound sense of hope. As I drove away, I couldn't help but feel grateful for the chance to remind someone that even in the darkest times, there is always a glimmer of light waiting to be found.

As I navigate the winding roads of my ride-share journey, I am grateful for the lessons my Venezuelan and Greek friends imparted. They have shown me that by embracing challenges, maintaining a positive mindset, and consistently giving my best, I can shape a future filled with abundance, joy, and the freedom to enjoy the finer things in life.

So, armed with their stories as my guiding light, I press forward, ready to face whatever obstacles come my way. As long as I continue to do my best, the possibilities are limitless, and I can create a life that exceeds my expectations. As I continue my ride-share journey, I carry with me the stories of my friends, always ready to share them with passengers who may need a reminder of their potential. I am reminded that in this land of opportunity, where dreams can become reality, the power of always doing our best can lead us to places we never imagined possible. The stories of Clyde and Manolo brought forth a powerful and collective sense of hope and inspiration among my passengers. These narratives highlighted the resilience of the human spirit and served as a reminder that even in the face of immense challenges, there is always potential for growth and transformation.

As the tales unfolded, the passengers realized that their difficulties did not have to be permanent roadblocks. They saw that setbacks and hardships do not define us as individuals, but our response to these obstacles ultimately shapes our destinies. Clyde's story exemplified how one can rise above adversity. Despite facing numerous setbacks and obstacles, he never lost sight of his dreams and remained determined to achieve them. His unwavering resilience and persistence became a source of inspiration for those listening.

Similarly, Manolo's story demonstrated the power of personal transformation. He had experienced a period of self-doubt and uncertainty. Still, he found the strength to overcome his challenges and embark on a journey of growth and self-discovery. His story served as a testament to the inherent potential for change and the ability to rewrite one's narrative. With each passing moment, the passengers felt renewed optimism and belief in their capacities to overcome adversities. They understood that life's challenges were not insurmountable barriers but opportunities for personal growth and transformation. The stories of Clyde and Manolo served as a potent reminder that no matter how difficult life may seem, there is always a path forward, waiting to be discovered and embraced. As the car continued, the conversation became a celebration of the human spirit's ability to overcome obstacles and create a better future. The passengers, once disheartened, now embraced a renewed sense of possibility and determination. They started to reflect on their own lives, contemplating the steps they could take to overcome their challenges and forge their paths to success.

In sharing the stories of Clyde and Manolo, I intended to ignite a flame of hope within the passengers, reminding them that resilience, hard work, and the pursuit of a better life can lead to remarkable outcomes. It was a reminder that despite the difficulties we may face, we have the power to shape our destinies and find hope in the face of adversity.

In those moments when the weight of the world threatens to crush me, when the darkest clouds loom overhead, I find solace in the unwavering inspiration of my friends, Clyde and Manolo. They are beacons of resilience, their steadfast determination and unyielding spirit lighting the path before them.

Their shining example ignites a fire when I face the worst days of my life.

I always ask myself, "What would Clyde and Manolo do?"

And instantly, I am filled with a renewed sense of strength and purpose. I know, without a doubt, that they would never give up. Their unwavering resolve is like a force of nature, a reminder that they always find a way to make it happen, even in the face of the most compelling situations. They refuse to surrender to life's challenges, instead embracing them as opportunities for growth and transformation. Their words alone can lift my spirits and remind me that resilience is not just a trait but a choice. Their actions and unwavering pursuit of their goals in life serve as a constant reminder that success is not handed on a silver platter but earned through steadfast dedication and relentless effort. Their lives are a testament to the power of perseverance, to the unwavering belief that one can always strive to be at the top of their game. They embody the very essence of what it means to

85

push beyond limits, to rise above adversity, and to achieve greatness. In the face of their unwavering spirit, I find the motivation to always strive for the best. Their example fuels my ambition, propelling me to reach new heights and push the boundaries of what I thought was possible. When I feel the world crashing down on me, their presence, even in spirit, carries me through the storm.

And so, armed with their inspiration, I rise from the ashes of my worst days, ready to conquer the challenges that lie before me. I embrace compelling situations with unwavering determination, knowing I am not alone. For within me, I carry the indomitable spirit of Clyde and Manolo, a force that propels me forward, urging me never to settle for anything less than the best. Their unwavering belief in the power of resilience and the relentless pursuit of their goals remind me that greatness resides within me, waiting to be unleashed. As I take a deep breath, summoning the spirit of Clyde and Manolo, their words echo in my mind, fueling my determination.

"You've got this," Clyde's voice resonates, his unwavering confidence seeping into my being.

"No matter what the world throws at you, remember you can achieve greatness. Believe in yourself." Manolo's voice joins the chorus, his unwavering optimism shining through.

"Every challenge is an opportunity in disguise," he reminds me. *"Embrace them, learn from them, and use them as stepping stones towards your goals."*

With their words echoing in my mind, I feel a surge of courage and resilience. The world may conspire against me, but armed with the spirit of Clyde and Manolo, I know I can face any challenge head-on. As I step forward, ready to tackle the hurdles, I can almost hear them cheering me on.

"You've got this!" Clyde's voice booms with unwavering conviction.

"Push through the barriers, break through the limitations, and show the world what you're made of!"

Manolo's voice intertwines with Clyde's, his optimism infusing my every step.

"Remember, setbacks are just temporary," he encourages.

"They are opportunities for growth and learning. Keep moving forward, and success will be waiting for you." Their words become my mantra and guiding light in the darkest of moments. When doubt threatens to consume me, Clyde and Manolo's unwavering belief in my abilities pushes me to keep going and striving for greatness.

So, as I face the challenges that come my way, armed with the spirit of Clyde and Manolo, I hold their words close to my heart. I know that I can achieve greatness even in the face of adversity. Their inspiration fuels my determination, propelling me forward with unwavering resilience.

With each step I take, I almost hear them whispering,

"Believe in yourself. Embrace the challenges. You've got this."

And with their unwavering support, I forge ahead, ready to conquer whatever obstacles come my way. In those moments when the world conspires against me, I know that I am not alone. Clyde and Manolo's spirit reminds me I can overcome challenges and achieve greatness.

Remember that your journey is not meant to be walked alone. Seek out those who inspire you, believe in your potential, and radiate positivity. As friends who make it happen, you will create a symphony of encouragement, support, and unwavering camaraderie. And as you navigate life's path, always remember to do your best, for it is in the pursuit of excellence that you will find true happiness. This beautiful message emphasizes the importance of companionship and support on life's journey. When we surround ourselves with inspiring friends who believe in our potential and radiate positivity, we create a harmonious environment of encouragement, support, and strong friendships. We can accomplish great things and overcome challenges by uplifting and motivating each other. Along the path of life, it's crucial to always strive for excellence and give our best efforts, as this pursuit often leads to genuine happiness and fulfillment.

It encourages us to recognize that we are not meant to navigate life's journey alone. It reminds us of the significance of seeking like-minded friends who inspire us and believe in our potential. These friendships become a source of motivation and positive energy that uplifts us during good times and challenging moments.

When we surround ourselves with such friends, it creates a symphony of encouragement. Each person brings unique strengths, perspectives, and support, working together to help each other grow and achieve our goals. This symphony of encouragement fosters a

sense of camaraderie, where we cheer each other on,
celebrate successes, and provide solace during difficult
times.

Amidst life's twists and turns, it's important to remember the value of doing our best. Pursuing excellence is not just about achieving external success but also about personal growth and self-fulfillment. We cultivate a sense of purpose and satisfaction by striving to give our best effort in everything we do. Through this commitment to excellence, we can find true happiness as the journey becomes fulfilling and rewarding. This message encourages us to embrace the power of friendship, seek out those who inspire us, and nurture positive relationships. We create a harmonious symphony of encouragement and camaraderie by supporting and uplifting each other. As we navigate life's path, dedicating ourselves to doing our best allows us to find meaning and genuine happiness. Years before I took the wheel as a ride-share driver, I vividly remember the nerves and anticipation coursing through me as I embarked on my first ride.

Not every chapter of this ride-share journey is filled with
triumphs. There were countless moments of doubt and
frustration when I faced unjust accusations from passengers.

One particular incident stands out: a customer claimed I had intentionally taken a longer route to inflate the fare.

As accusations were thrown my way, I felt anger and sadness. However, I responded professionally and honestly instead of lashing out or succumbing to negative emotions. I calmly explained my navigation choices, providing evidence to support my claims. I maintained open lines of communication with the ride-share platform, ensuring that my side of the story was heard. It was challenging, but I refused to let it dampen my spirit. I continued to deliver exceptional service to my passengers, always striving to exceed their expectations. I embraced each ride as an opportunity to redeem myself and showcase the dedication and honesty that defined my character. The unjust accusations once directed towards me gradually became less significant as time passed. This was mainly due to the accumulation of positive experiences and glowing reviews that overshadowed those initial negative perceptions. The trust and appreciation expressed by passengers who recognized my unwavering efforts were a powerful affirmation, reminding me of the importance of always striving to do my best regardless of the circumstances.

Throughout my ride-share driver journey, I encountered moments of triumph and challenges. These experiences taught me the value of resilience and unwavering dedication. Each ride presented an opportunity to leave a lasting impression and positively impact someone's day. I discovered that the rewards of going the extra mile, both in terms of personal satisfaction and the connections formed with passengers, were immeasurable.

Starting as a ride-share driver can indeed be an anxiety-inducing experience, as various considerations may fill your mind. Let's explore some of the common questions and concerns I had:

1. What does the passenger think of me? As a driver, I naturally wonder about the impression I made on passengers. I asked if they found me friendly, professional, or accommodating. Remember that providing a safe and comfortable ride is crucial. Being polite, maintaining a clean vehicle, and driving responsibly can improve the passenger experience.

2. I hope they rate me five stars. Driver ratings play a significant role in ride-share platforms. High ratings can lead to increased demand and better opportunities. To improve your chances of receiving a good rating, focus on delivering excellent customer service, following traffic laws, and ensuring a smooth and efficient ride. Providing a positive experience can encourage passengers to rate you favorably.

3. Should I start a conversation? Should I stay quiet? Engaging in dialogue with passengers can depend on their

preferences. Some passengers may appreciate a friendly and chatty driver, while others prefer a calm and peaceful ride. Please pay attention to their cues and respect their desired level of interaction. Being attentive and responsive to their needs can contribute to a positive experience.

4. How is my appearance? The appearance of a driver can contribute to the overall impression we make on passengers. Dressing neatly and maintaining a professional appearance can create a positive first impression. However, balancing and ensuring you feel comfortable and confident while driving is also essential.

Remember that anxiety is normal when starting something new, and it often dissipates with experience. Over time, you may better understand passenger expectations and preferences, allowing you to navigate these concerns more confidently. Focusing on providing a safe and enjoyable ride while maintaining a professional demeanor is essential, as these factors greatly influence the likelihood of receiving positive ratings.

Additionally, take advantage of any resources and training materials the ride-share platform provides to enhance your skills and knowledge as a driver. Seeking passenger feedback or joining driver communities can provide valuable insights and support. With time and practice, you'll likely become more comfortable and adept at delivering an excellent ride-share experience, alleviating much of the initial anxiety you may have felt.

Being part of a company in its infancy as a ride-share driver was an incredibly fascinating experience. I witnessed firsthand how the company built and implemented new rules and policies to keep up with the industry's ongoing trends and comply with regulations.

As a driver, my input was highly valued during this crucial stage. I had the opportunity to contribute to discussions and actively provide feedback on various policies. Knowing that my experiences and insights as a driver significantly shaped the rules governing our work was empowering. The company's flexibility and adaptability were remarkable. They recognized the importance of staying up-to-date with market conditions, technological advancements, and legal requirements. It was a collective effort involving drivers like me to ensure that the policies we implemented were practical, effective, and beneficial for both drivers and passengers.

Being part of this collaborative process was both rewarding and fulfilling. I knew my contributions impacted the company and the more significant ride-sharing industry. It was exciting to witness the company's growth and its ability to establish itself as a trusted player in the market.

I am grateful for the opportunity to be part of a company's infancy stage, where I had the chance to shape the industry and be at the forefront of change. It was an exhilarating journey that allowed me to witness firsthand how a company evolves, adapts, and thrives in a dynamic and competitive landscape.

And so, as I reflect on the exciting chapter titled "Always Do Your Best: Lessons from the Ride-Share Journey," I share with you the knowledge that every challenge is an opportunity for growth.

No matter the obstacles we face, we shall continue to navigate through them with resilience and steadfast determination, knowing that the rewards of always striving to do our best will far outweigh any temporary setbacks.

Unfortunately, in ride-sharing, unjust accusations and exploitation of the system have become recurring issues. Some passengers have been accused of making false claims, displaying rudeness, engaging in flirtatious behavior, or even causing dangerous situations through reckless driving. These incidents have highlighted a troubling trend where sure passengers prioritize their gain over the well-being and safety of the drivers.

Facing unjust accusations and exploitation can indeed be disheartening and frustrating for ride-share drivers. These challenges can not only affect their emotional well-being but also impact their livelihoods. However, maintaining a positive mindset and resilience are vital qualities that drivers often cultivate to navigate these difficulties.

Firstly, a positive mindset allows drivers to approach each day with optimism and a focus on providing quality service. It helps them maintain their motivation and passion for their work despite the negative experiences they may encounter. By staying positive, drivers can better handle stressful situations and maintain a professional demeanor when faced with unjust accusations or difficult passengers.

Resilience is a crucial aspect of the ride-share driver's journey. It involves bouncing back from setbacks and maintaining composure in adversity. Resilient drivers develop coping strategies to handle challenging encounters through self-reflection, seeking support from fellow drivers or friends, or engaging in activities that help them recharge and rejuvenate. They understand that only some passengers will be pleasant, but they persevere and focus on providing most passengers with a safe and reliable service. Moreover, drivers often develop strategies to mitigate the impact of unjust accusations and exploitation. They may maintain meticulous records of their interactions, install dashcams to capture incidents or report any issues promptly to the ride-share platform. These proactive measures can help drivers defend themselves against false claims and provide evidence to support their side of the story.

Despite the difficulties, many drivers find fulfillment and satisfaction in their work. They take pride in providing a valuable service to the community and building positive relationships with passengers who appreciate their efforts. By focusing on the positive aspects and finding ways to overcome challenges, drivers can continue to offer a reliable and safe experience for their passengers despite the occasional negative encounters. In ride-sharing, I've encountered my fair share of challenges and obstacles. But in those moments, I find solace and inspiration from my amazing friends, Clyde and Penelope. These two individuals are indeed the best of the best, having honed their skills in the illustrious world of 5-star, 5-diamond hotels.

I vividly remember the days when Clyde and I worked side by side. Back then, I was a humble cook, and he held the esteemed position of banquet supervisor. We thrived in the vibrant energy of those luxurious establishments, where excellence was the only acceptable standard. Clyde's passion and dedication were palpable, and it was evident that he was destined for greatness. Then there's Penelope, a true embodiment of grace and sophistication. Like a shining star, she graced the halls of those prestigious hotels, leaving a trail of delighted guests in her wake. Her attention to detail, ability to anticipate needs, and unwavering commitment to providing an exceptional experience were unmatched.

When daunting challenges come my way, I often find myself silently asking, "What would Clyde and Manolo do?"

Their expertise and unwavering professionalism have become my guiding light. I imagine their confident smiles, calm demeanor, and steadfast resolve in the face of adversity. Their influence extends beyond their achievements. Alongside Clyde and Manolo, I am fortunate to have other mutual friends like Penelope and Haley, who are equally at the pinnacle of their professions. Their collective wisdom and expertise serve as a wellspring of inspiration, pushing me to reach new heights in my ride-share journey.

With their exceptional standards as my compass, I navigate the challenges, determined to provide the best service possible to my passengers. I channel their resilience, problem-solving skills, and unwavering commitment to excellence. Their spirits fuel my own, propelling me forward with a renewed sense of purpose and an unyielding dedication to creating unforgettable experiences. So, as I embark on each ride, I carry with me the spirits of Clyde, Penelope, Manolo, and Haley. I embrace the lessons they've taught me, drawing strength from their experiences. With their unwavering support, I am confident I can overcome any obstacle, deliver exceptional service, and leave a lasting impression on every passenger I encounter.

In this ride-share journey of mine, their influence is not just a mere thought but a beacon of inspiration, guiding me toward greatness and reminding me that I, too, can be the best of the best. It is crucial for ride-sharing platforms and the broader community to address these issues seriously. Implementing effective systems to handle complaints, conducting thorough investigations, and establishing clear guidelines can help prevent unjust accusations and exploitation of the platform. Drivers and passengers can contribute to a more positive and harmonious ride-sharing experience by fostering mutual respect and understanding of culture.

I found myself at a crossroads in the sprawling metropolis, where skyscrapers reached for the heavens, and the relentless buzz of city life filled the air. The dark cloud of a 4.8 rating, tarnished by unjust complaints, loomed overhead, threatening to shatter my dreams. Determined to find a lifeline, I embarked on a quest for a backup plan. As fate would have it, an unexpected encounter awaited me. In the depths of despair, a fortuitous meeting with a high-level manager from another ride-share company altered the trajectory of my journey. Though my initial driving try-out had failed, this encounter would be a turning point.

With unwavering conviction, the passenger, also a manager for the competing ride-share company, recognized my potential, looking beyond the flawed rating that had plagued me. In a remarkable display of advocacy, she championed my cause, highlighting my dedication and high-level customer service skills. Her unwavering belief in my abilities paved the way for a new opportunity, a door that swung open to reveal a fresh start with this alternative ride-share company.

Beth said, "You have truly remarkable customer service skills. I must say, I'm impressed. Have you ever considered working with our competition?"

"Thank you for the compliment! I did have a try-out with them, but unfortunately, I wasn't accepted. It was a disappointing experience."

"That's unfortunate to hear. However, I believe in your potential. Your dedication and commitment to providing excellent service have not gone unnoticed."

I drove on for a few weeks. I was surprised to have run into one of the Lyft Corporate Managers as a passenger by such a coincidence during an Uber trip. The world is small when we think about it. Sometimes, everyone does know each other. That's why treating everyone with kindness and respect is essential. What they say in life is so true. Sometimes, we don't know who we are talking to. In this case, that was very much true. Then, I finally received a text from Beth for my approval to drive with Lyft. I was so surprised and shocked this was happening. I felt as if I achieved the impossible in life. After going with Uber for a year, I wondered why Lyft wouldn't accept me to drive. I felt as if the clouds started to clear through the sky, allowing the sun's rays to glow through my life.

"Thank you for seeing that in me, Beth. It means a lot, especially after the challenges I am facing with my current company."

"I understand that it must be tough for you, but there's good news: our company values drivers like you. We prioritize creating a supportive environment where your skills can shine."

"That's a relief to hear. I want a fair chance to prove myself and continue doing what I love."

"And you'll get exactly that with us. We appreciate your dedication and passion for providing exceptional service to

passengers. We believe in giving our drivers the tools they need to succeed and grow."

"I'm grateful for this opportunity. It's a fresh start that I desperately needed. I'm ready to put my all into it."

"I do not doubt that you'll thrive here. Your commitment and skills make you an invaluable asset to our team. Welcome aboard!"

With Beth from Lyft's support and recognition, my ride-share journey took an unexpected turn. The passenger manager, unaware of the specific circumstances with the first company, believed in my potential and saw the value I could bring to their team. Their confidence in my abilities was a beacon of hope during a challenging time.

As I embarked on this fresh start, leaving behind the disappointment from the first company, I carried the passenger-manager's belief in my dedication and commitment. With determination and a renewed sense of purpose, I embraced the opportunity to provide exceptional service to passengers, knowing I was part of a supportive and empowering environment.

After years of dedicated service, I was removed from Uber due to what I believed were unjust charges. The reasons behind this decision remained unclear, but it highlighted the challenges older drivers face in an evolving industry. Despite this setback, I resolved to make the most of the opportunities presented by the competition company.

The false accusations and ban from the first company reminded me of my resilience. Rather than allowing them to dampen my spirit, I channeled the disappointment into a driving force to prove my worth and integrity. With the passenger manager's unwavering support and the new ride-share company's values, I was determined to create a positive impact and make a difference in the lives of the passengers I served.

This new chapter in my ride-share journey became a testament to my resilience and determination. It was a chance to rewrite my story, leaving behind the negativity of the past and embracing the opportunities ahead. With the passenger manager's support and my unwavering commitment, I embarked on this fresh start, ready to overcome challenges and provide exceptional service to passengers who believed in me.

This encounter was a revelation, a beacon of hope in adversity. It illuminated the power of perseverance and the profound impact that demonstrating exceptional customer service skills can have, even on those who hold influential positions. In the bustling urban landscape, where a mere number can shatter dreams, I learned that resilience, determination, and a commitment to excellence can forge a path to new and unforeseen possibilities.

As the days turned into months and years, I poured my tireless dedication and unwavering commitment into my ride-share journey. Every passenger's story, every conversation shared, and every mile traveled became a part of my experience. Countless early mornings and late nights were spent behind the wheel, building a reputation as a reliable and trustworthy driver. And then, on this particular day, my phone rang, interrupting the familiar hum of the city streets. My heart skipped a beat as I answered, not knowing what awaited me on the other end. To my surprise, it was the ride-share company I had been working with all along. With bated breath, I listened as they made an announcement that left me speechless. It was an unexpected turn of events, a testament to the journey I had embarked upon. The company recognized my exceptional service and chose me for an extraordinary opportunity.

Whether it was an invitation to join an exclusive program, a promotion to a higher tier of drivers, or an offer to become a brand ambassador, the details of the announcement remained a mystery, momentarily suspended in the air. But one thing was sure: I was overwhelmed with shock and joy, realizing that my dedication had not gone unnoticed. As I absorbed the news, a surge of motivation coursed through my veins. This unexpected turn marked a milestone in my ride-share journey that validated the countless hours I had invested and the passion I had poured into every ride. It was a reminder that hard work and commitment can yield extraordinary rewards. With a renewed sense of purpose, I eagerly awaited the next chapter of my ride-share adventure, ready to embrace new opportunities and challenges.

"Hi, is this Marshall?" the voice on the other end of the line asked.

"Yes, this is him," I responded, unable to conceal the curiosity in my voice.

And then came the words that would forever change the course of my story: "We are calling you because we would like to honor you as one of the winners of the Driver of the Year award. We invite you to the Driver of the Year Dinner Reception and a few upcoming concerts."

At that very moment, as my jaw dropped, I felt an overwhelming sense of awe and disbelief. The moment's weight crashed down, and I realized the magnitude of what had just happened. Being recognized as one of the Drivers of the Year, mainly for outstanding customer service, surpassed all my wildest dreams. It was a testament to the countless hours I had dedicated behind the wheel, tirelessly striving to provide an exceptional experience for every passenger. Each journey had become an opportunity for me to connect with people, to brighten their day, and to ensure their comfort and satisfaction. I had poured my heart and soul into my work, always going the extra mile to exceed expectations.

Receiving such an honor was not just a personal achievement but a validation of my impact on the lives of those I served. It recognized passengers' trust and confidence in me, knowing I would go above and beyond to ensure their safety and well-being. The journey to this moment had been filled with challenges and sacrifices. Long hours on the road, navigating through traffic, and dealing with various situations had tested my patience and resilience. But it was all worth it when I saw the smiles on my passengers' faces, heard their stories, and made a positive difference in their lives, even if only for a short ride.

Being named one of the Drivers of the Year for outstanding customer service was an affirmation of the impact I had made. It motivated me to continue pushing myself, striving for excellence, and delivering an exceptional experience to everyone who stepped into my vehicle. As the moment's weight sank in, I felt a surge of gratitude and humility. I was humbled by the recognition and grateful for the opportunity to serve others meaningfully. It was a reminder of the power of dedication, hard work, and genuine care for others. With this award, I realized that my efforts had not gone unnoticed. It was a powerful reminder that the impact of going the extra mile can be genuinely transformative in a world where exceptional service can sometimes feel rare. It inspired me to continue my journey as a driver, always striving to provide outstanding customer service and make a positive difference, one ride at a time.

Overwhelmed with gratitude, I couldn't help but express my disbelief. "But there must be others with better customer service skills than myself," I stammered, my mind grappling with the magnitude of this honor. The response from the company was resolute, assuring me that the award was based on tangible evidence - the five-star ratings, the heartfelt comments, and the generous tips I had received. It was a testament to my impact, as my passengers consistently expressed their satisfaction by bestowing me the highest tips through the app in Chicago. This recognition was more than just a shiny trophy or a night out for a celebration. It validated my unwavering commitment to providing the best experience possible for everyone who stepped into my car. It was a reminder that consistent effort and genuine dedication could bring about remarkable outcomes, even in a competitive industry like ride-sharing.

As I hung up the phone, a wave of pride washed over me. The road I had traveled was not always easy, but the satisfaction derived from knowing that my hard work had been acknowledged was immeasurable. With renewed purpose and a fire burning brighter than ever, I would continue to navigate the city streets, bringing joy, comfort, and exceptional service to every passenger crossing my path.

One particularly memorable day, I received a ride request from Mr. Johnson. As I arrived at the pickup location, I noticed Mr. Johnson standing by the curb, his face etched with worry. He quickly hopped into the backseat, his eyes darting anxiously from side to side. Sensing his unease, I greeted him warmly and asked if everything was alright.

This chapter delves deep into the profound lesson learned throughout the ride-share journey: the unwavering importance of giving your best effort. It is within the framework of embracing each day as an opportunity for growth, persisting in the face of challenges, and refusing to succumb to regrets that true fulfillment and happiness can be achieved. The rewards of striving to become the best version of oneself and maintaining a resilient mindset are explored in vivid detail.

The ride-share journey was a transformative experience that taught me the significance of doing my best in every endeavor. This chapter captures the power of persistence, resilience, and unwavering commitment, from the initial fears and uncertainties accompanying this new path to the triumphant moments of recognition and personal growth. It serves as a reminder that by always striving to do our best, we can navigate the roughest paths, find fulfillment even in the most challenging of situations, and leave no room for regrets.

Through the ups and downs of the ride-share journey, I discovered that giving my best effort wasn't simply about achieving external success or impressing others. It was about the internal satisfaction that comes from knowing I had poured my heart and soul into my work, no matter how big or small the task. It was about embracing the belief that each day is an opportunity for growth, a chance to push beyond my limits and uncover new capabilities.

As I persevered through the challenges that arose, I realized that the rewards of giving my best effort extended far beyond any external recognition. The sense of personal fulfillment came from knowing I had given my all, the growth and self-improvement that accompanied each step forward. It was the joy of seeing the impact of my efforts on those around me, whether it was a passenger who felt valued and cared for or a fellow driver who found inspiration in my dedication.

This chapter is a testament to the transformative power of striving to become the best version of oneself. It highlights the importance of maintaining a resilient mindset, refusing to give in to self-doubt or the temptation to settle for mediocrity. By embracing the philosophy of always giving our best effort, we open ourselves to a world of possibilities where personal growth and fulfillment drive our actions.

As my friend Manolo says, "It's not time that heals all wounds, but what we do with that time that matters."

Clyde replies, "That's it! Don't give up and make it happen."

I reply, "There is no better time than now."

So, dear readers, as we conclude this chapter, let us carry the profound wisdom gained from this journey. Let us embrace each day as an opportunity to give our best effort, persist in facing challenges, and refuse to live in regrets. Through these choices, we can unlock our true potential and live a life rich with purpose, fulfillment, and the joy of striving toward our personal best.

CHAPTER 3 - On the Way Up
The Power of Kindness and Good Choices

The theme of "On the Way Up-The Power of Kindness and Good Choices" resonates deeply within me, becoming the guiding principle behind every interaction I have. Stepping into the role of a driver, embracing a philosophy prioritizing exceptional service and passenger satisfaction is crucial. As I welcome each passenger into my vehicle, I strive to create a positive experience for them. A warm smile accompanies their entry, setting the tone for a comfortable and enjoyable ride. Recognizing that small gestures can make a significant difference, I ensure that my vehicle is equipped with phone chargers to cater to their charging needs. This simple amenity lets passengers stay connected and ensures their devices are powered throughout the journey.

Understanding that music preferences vary, I offer passengers the choice of music. By providing a selection of genres or even allowing them to connect their devices and play their music, I aim to create an atmosphere that aligns with their preferences and enhances their overall experience.

Temperature control is another aspect I consider attentively. I am mindful of maintaining a comfortable environment within the vehicle, adjusting the temperature according to their preference. Whether they prefer a cooler or warmer atmosphere, I strive to accommodate their needs to ensure their comfort throughout the ride.

By embracing this philosophy and incorporating these thoughtful touches into my role as a driver, I aim to leave a positive and lasting impression on each passenger. As a ride-share driver, I don't just see myself as someone who transports passengers from one place to another. I take pride in going beyond the basic requirements of my job by offering assistance with their luggage. I understand it's not just about the physical weight I help carry but also the emotional burdens I may alleviate.

I recognize that everyone has their struggles and challenges, and by lending a helping hand, I aim to make their journey more comfortable and reassuring. Whether helping someone with heavy bags or simply being there to listen and provide a kind word, I strive to create a supportive and caring environment during the ride. In addition to being a ride-share driver, I also take on the role of a DJ, setting the tone for the passengers' experience. I believe that music has the power to inspire and uplift, so I make it a point to play a wide range of genres, including classical, rock, rap, hip-hop, and R&B. By catering to the passengers' musical preferences and creating personalized playlists, I aim to make their journey more than just a ride—it becomes an immersive and enjoyable experience.

Combining my role as a ride-share driver and a DJ, I aspire to create a unique and memorable experience for each passenger. Whether through the power of music or by offering assistance and support, I am dedicated to making their journey comfortable, inspiring, and uplifting. In addition to my role as a ride-share driver and DJ, I aim to provide a personalized and enjoyable experience for each passenger. I go beyond the bare minimum by offering additional services that enhance their journey. I do this by allowing passengers to be the DJs themselves. I will enable them to connect their cell phones via Bluetooth and play their music playlists. By giving them control over the music selection, I aim to create a more interactive and enjoyable experience tailored to their unique tastes.

Furthermore, I understand the importance of comfort, especially during extreme weather conditions. That's why I go the extra mile to ensure the temperature inside the car is just right. Whether blasting the air conditioning during hot Chicago summers or turning up the heat during harsh winters, I strive to create a comfortable environment that suits the passengers' preferences. To further enhance the experience, I provide complimentary amenities such as bottled water and candy. These small gestures add a touch of hospitality and make the journey more enjoyable and refreshing.

Overall, my commitment to going beyond the basic requirements of my job is reflected in the personalized music experience, temperature control, and additional amenities I provide. I aim to create a comfortable, enjoyable, and memorable journey for each passenger, ensuring that their time with me is not just a ride but an exceptional experience. In addition to my other services, I have an Octopus tablet installed in the back of the car. This tablet offers a range of features to enhance the passengers' experience and provide entertainment throughout the journey. The Octopus tablet lets passengers stay informed with up-to-date weather updates and news articles. It keeps them connected to the world outside while they travel to their destination.

Moreover, the tablet also offers a variety of entertainment options, including videos and trivia games. The trivia games on the tablet are top-rated, especially during late-night rides when passengers are coming from the nightlife scene. The trivia games spark laughter, create a lively atmosphere, and make the journey a fun-filled experience. It's incredible how these trivia games can unite people, fostering camaraderie and joy among passengers. With the Octopus tablet, I strive to provide diverse entertainment options that cater to different interests and preferences. Whether staying informed, watching videos, or engaging in trivia games, passengers can pass the time and enjoy themselves during the ride.

By offering this additional source of entertainment, I aim to make the journey smooth, comfortable, enjoyable, and memorable. The Octopus tablet adds extra fun and engagement, ensuring that passengers have a great time from the moment they step into the car until they reach their destination.

In these small acts of service, I strive to demonstrate my commitment to making good choices. The choices we make, no matter how seemingly insignificant, have the power to shape our experiences and the experiences of those around us. By going the extra mile and extending kindness and compassion, I hope to create a positive ripple effect.

I want each passenger to feel valued and respected, knowing that their well-being and comfort are paramount to me. I aim to create a safe, efficient, uplifting, and inspiring atmosphere. I want them to leave my vehicle with a sense of warmth and gratitude, knowing they were in the presence of someone who genuinely cares.

Making good choices isn't always easy, but it's a commitment I hold dear. It reminds me that every action can contribute to the greater good, no matter how small. By infusing each interaction with kindness, empathy, and a genuine desire to make a positive impact, I hope to inspire others to do the same.

In the heart of a cold February 1, 2015, a relentless snowstorm transformed the city of Chicago into a winter wonderland. It was close to the beginning of my ride-share journey, and little did I know that this particular day would become an unforgettable test of my driving skills and a testament to the kindness of strangers.

As I continued driving, the winter sun illuminated the snowy landscape, creating a magical scene that seemed straight out of a fairytale. The sunlight danced upon the glistening snowflakes, illuminating the world around me with a warm and inviting glow. It was a picturesque day, where the sun's brilliance contrasted beautifully against the pristine snowy white backdrop.

I watched in awe as the snowfall intensified, transforming the surroundings into a winter wonderland. In just a short time, the snow began to accumulate astonishingly. What was once a few inches of snow had quickly transformed into a mesmerizing sight: a landscape buried under a thick layer of sparkling snow stretching as far as the eye could see.

As I momentarily paused to take in the breathtaking scene, my gaze shifted towards my trusty Toyota Corolla, parked nearby. The snow had piled up relentlessly, reaching almost surreal heights. The small vehicle was now enveloped in a cocoon of snow, its vibrant color hidden beneath the pristine white blanket.

The sight was both astonishing and slightly concerning. The snow had accumulated to the point where it reached the top of the car door, creating a formidable barrier that threatened to impede my journey. However, instead of feeling deterred, a surge of determination coursed through my veins.

With the sun's rays still shining brightly, infusing the air with warmth and possibility, I knew this snowy obstacle was another test along my ride-share journey. It reminded me that challenges may arise unexpectedly, but they can be overcome with perseverance and a positive mindset.

I took a deep breath, grabbed a sturdy snow shovel, and cleared a path around my vehicle. Each scoop of snow was a testament to my resilience and determination. The crisp winter air filled my lungs as I worked, the sun's rays providing a comforting embrace. As I cleared the snow away, revealing the vibrant color of the car beneath, a sense of accomplishment washed over me. The snow may have piled up, but it couldn't bury my spirit. It only reinforced my commitment to exceptional service to passengers, no matter the challenges ahead.

I marveled at the enchanting scenery as I drove through the snow-covered streets. The sun's rays reflected off the snowflakes, creating a dazzling display of shimmering light. It was a reminder that even in the face of adversity, there is beauty to be found and a sense of wonder that can uplift our spirits. With the sun shining and the snow-covered landscape as my backdrop, I ventured, ready to conquer the awaited challenges. Each passenger I picked up would be greeted with a warm smile and a determination to provide exceptional service, regardless of the weather conditions.

Bracing myself for what lay ahead, I started the engine on a Chicago Winter day to an unforeseen surprise blizzard. As I ventured out onto the streets, not only was it cold, but I noticed that the snowfall came fast to an astonishing four feet. Due to the continuous snow, mostly only the main busy streets of Chicago were lightly shoveled as a priority over the smaller neighborhood side streets, making navigation a daunting task. I had received pickup requests from nine different neighborhoods in Chicago: West Loop, South Loop, Lincoln Park, Lakeview, Roscoe Village, Logan Square, Wicker Park, Pilsen, and Hyde Park. Driving cautiously, I navigated the treacherous streets, each turn and curve requiring heightened attention and precision. Deep and unforgiving snow posed a constant threat, ready to engulf my car and make the journey even more dangerous. But with a steely resolve, I pressed on, determined to fulfill my duty as a ride-share driver, regardless of the adverse conditions.

With the engine humming and the sunlight glinting off the freshly cleared windows, I embarked on a journey through the snowy landscape. The sun's rays illuminated the road before me, casting a golden glow upon the winter wonderland. It was a reminder that amidst obstacles and adversity, there is always a glimmer of hope and beauty. As I continued my journey through the winter wonderland, I couldn't help but feel a deep sense of gratitude. The snowy roads and the radiant sun had come together to create a moment of beauty and resilience. It was a reminder that no matter the circumstances, as long as we hold onto hope and embrace the light within us, we can overcome any obstacle that comes our way.

I was in the East Side of Chicago, not too far from the Roseland neighborhood, at 4 am. I picked a passenger named Marcus. He had told me that the streets around this area were hazardous. He, too, was driving for Lyft a few blocks away from his home. He went to pick up, and before he knew it, he was carjacked by four teenagers who held a gun to his head. I felt nothing but empathy and compassion for Marcus. I explained to him it was miserable. As I drove Marcus toward the UIC medical district for his job, I also shared with him somewhat of a dangerous story. I'll never forget the day I picked up Juan, an ex-gang banger leader who had turned his life around and was now working at a community center to help at-risk youth. The car ride with Juan was filled with captivating stories and powerful insights that left a lasting impression. Certainly! Initially, when I picked up Juan, his demeanor and intense energy caught me off guard, feeling a sense of fear. Coming from a harsh environment and having been a former gang leader, Juan's presence exuded a raw intensity.

His loud voice and assertive mannerisms carried the weight of his past experiences. As he began speaking, his words resonated with a power that seemed to penetrate my very being. The passion and conviction in his voice were undeniable, reflecting the struggles he had faced and the determination he possessed to make a difference. In those moments, it was as if Juan's energy filled the car, creating an atmosphere charged with emotions. The intensity of his presence made me acutely aware of the harsh realities he had encountered and the transformation he had undergone. It was a stark reminder of his turbulent path and the strength it took to turn his life around.

Although initially intimidating, as the car ride continued, I gradually realized that Juan's energy wasn't meant to intimidate or threaten. Instead, it was a manifestation of his unwavering commitment to his cause. His loud voice and passionate demeanor were tools he used to capture attention and convey the urgency of his message to those he encountered. My initial fear gave way to a profound appreciation for Juan's journey. I was left with a deep sense of gratitude for the opportunity to witness his remarkable transformation. I was concerned for my safety to be driving an ex-convict in my car. I prayed and hoped not to say anything to anger this former ex-gangbanger leader. One wrong word, and it could have been game-over for dodging potholes like Mario Kart. It would have been game over because I can always fix or replace my car, but I can't regain my life if I lose it.

As I embarked on the journey, I could sense the weight of Juan's experiences and transformation. His determination to make a positive impact was evident as he shared personal anecdotes of his past involvement in the gang lifestyle. Juan's commitment to steering others away from similar paths was genuinely inspiring.

During the ride, I could feel the intensity of his passion as he recounted encounters with current gang members. Juan fearlessly engaged with them, emphasizing that they had a choice to break free from the cycle of crime and violence—his firsthand understanding of their struggles and redemption story compelling his message. Through the car's windows, I observed the diverse neighborhoods Juan had once navigated with a different purpose. The sights and sounds of the community served as a backdrop to the conversation, reinforcing the significance of his work. It was a reminder that change is possible and that individuals like Juan can make a profound impact on the lives of others.

"No worries, Marshall. The present is where we can truly make a difference. Every day, I wake up with the purpose of guiding these young ones away from the path of crime and violence", said Juan as he looked me in the eyes with such raw and piercing intensity.

"That dedication is admirable, Juan. It takes strength and determination to commit yourself to such a noble cause. Tell me more about the present work you're doing."

"Well, Marshall, it starts with building trust and establishing connections. I engage with these gang members, not as a judge or someone looking down on them, but as someone who has walked in their shoes."

"That approach is crucial, Juan. They need to see that you understand their struggles and challenges."

"Exactly. I share my story, my past mistakes, and the consequences I faced. I let them know there is a way out, a chance to create a better future for themselves."

Juan shared with me how he was in jail for 14 years, in which he was cut off from all communication. He didn't shoot or murder anyone, but he stated that he was in the meeting with the other people regarding the incident. His only contact was in the jail cell beside him, which was also in complete darkness.

"That's powerful, Juan. Being able to relate to them personally must make a significant impact."

"It does, Marshall. When they hear my story, they realize that change is possible. The community center I work for will provide them with resources, support, and opportunities they may not have had before."

Juan shared with me the story that he had been in jail for 14 years and that he had no light in 23 of those 24 hours in the day. In that one hour of the twenty-four hours, he had the choice to go for a shower or to go outside to the playpen. The playpen was supposedly the yard area where the inmates would go out. Juan said that he always opted in for the showers but would occasionally opt in for the playpen to communicate with the other prisoner, who was also a high-level leader of a ganger leader in the jail cell next to him, also in complete silence.

"It's incredible how you're breaking the cycle and helping them see alternatives to the life they've known."

"Seeing their transformation is the most rewarding part, Marshall. Witnessing those lightbulb moments when they realize they have the power to rewrite their narratives. I am doing this so these men don't need to lose their baby mamas to another guy while they are away. Yes, people visit for a year, but most forget about you after that. They also try to make it hard for visitors to see you, but I am here for the kids to show them that they don't need to go through this. We can help them find jobs and rearrange transportation for them for work, too, if we have to. We have the resources to help them turn their life around and show them the light."

"I can only imagine the fulfillment and joy that comes with knowing you've contributed to their journey towards a brighter future."

"It's indescribable, Marshall. Every day, I'm reminded of the importance of my work. I see the hope in their eyes, the determination to change their paths and make better choices."

"Juan, I am honored to witness your present journey and to be a part of these courageous conversations and life-changing moments."

"I'm grateful to have you by my side, Marshall. Your support and belief in the power of redemption mean the world to me."

"Here's to the present, Juan, and the incredible impact you continue to make. May your car rides be filled with hope, inspiration, and the unwavering belief that change is possible!"

"Cheers to that, Marshall! Let's keep driving forward, one life at a time, and creating a brighter future for everyone."

As I listened intently to Juan's stories and absorbed the energy he emanated, my fear slowly transformed into a deep respect and admiration for his resilience. I began to understand that beneath the loud exterior; there was a genuine desire to make a positive impact and guide others away from the path of crime and violence. By the end of the car ride, I recognized that Juan's intense energy reflected his unwavering dedication and the gravity of his mission. It was a transformative experience that allowed me to witness firsthand the power of conviction and the ability to channel one's past struggles into a force for change.

As the car ride ended, I was filled with emotions— admiration for Juan's courage, gratitude for the opportunity to witness his transformation, and a renewed hope for the future. This encounter with Juan left an indelible mark on my memory, reminding me of the power of compassion, redemption, and the ability to influence others positively. It was a genuinely exhilarating car ride, reinforcing the belief that everyone has the potential for change and that even the most difficult circumstances can be overcome.

"It is amazing, Juan, that you are working to make a profound impact in the lives of these young individuals."

So, as I continue on my journey as a driver, the theme of "On the Way Up-Making Good Choices" remains at the forefront of my mind. It propels me forward, reminding me of the profound impact we can have on each other's lives. Through this commitment, I aim to create a ripple effect of goodness that extends far beyond the confines of my vehicle, making the world a better place, one interaction at a time. Every step of the way, I understood the immense responsibility that lay on my shoulders. The safety and well-being of my passengers were paramount, and

I knew that I had to exercise utmost caution and skill. The slick roads demanded a delicate touch on the accelerator and a firm grip on the steering wheel. I adjusted my driving style accordingly, anticipating potential hazards and allowing longer braking distances.

The sound of the tires crunching through the snow echoed in my ears, a constant reminder of the unpredictable nature of the weather. I remained focused, eyes scanning the road ahead, searching for any signs of danger. I knew that even a momentary lapse in concentration could have serious consequences. As I continued my journey, I couldn't help but feel a sense of determination coursing through my veins. It was more than just fulfilling my duty—it was a testament to my commitment to providing a reliable and safe transportation service, even in the face of adversity. I knew that my passengers relied on me and trusted me to transport them to their destinations securely.

The challenges of the treacherous conditions only served to heighten my resolve. It was during these moments that my dedication as a driver was truly put to the test. I embraced the opportunity to demonstrate my professionalism and resilience, knowing that my actions had the power to make a difference. With each mile conquered, I felt a sense of accomplishment and satisfaction. I learned I was not just a driver but a guardian of safety, a beacon of reliability amidst the storm. As I continued to navigate the icy terrain, I did so with a sense of purpose, knowing that my determination to fulfill my duty was unwavering.

Driving through the snow-laden streets, I was reminded of the importance of perseverance, adaptability, and a commitment to service. It was a reminder that being a ride-share driver went beyond simply transporting passengers—it was about being a dependable companion during their journey, even in the face of adversity. As I pressed on through the unforgiving conditions, I was fueled by the knowledge that my dedication and unwavering commitment made a difference, one ride at a time.

However, as I turned into the intersections of each neighborhood, it seemed as if my wheels were destined to become trapped in the icy prison of the un-shoveled snow. More shovel trucks were needed to cover every small street and main busy street. Helplessly stuck in the snow, my wheels spun uselessly. While turning into a small street intersection in a neighborhood, I depended on the past tire grooves on the ice that had been driven before me to get me through the snow. Frustration threatened to rise within me, but I reminded myself to stay calm and composed.

Time and time again, as the trip requests poured in during this unexpected blizzard, I braved the elements and ventured into each neighborhood. However, what awaited me at every turn was a sight that tested my determination—a picture of my car engulfed in the clutches of the unforgiving snow and ice. With each new destination, I found myself facing a daunting challenge. The snowfall had blanketed the streets, transforming them into treacherous paths that threatened to immobilize my vehicle. The sheer force of the blizzard had created towering snowbanks that seemed impossible, as if nature conspired against my efforts to provide reliable transportation.

As I approached each location, my heart sank as I witnessed my car buried under the relentless snow. It felt like an icy, unforgiving grip had captured my trusty companion. The wheels were concealed, and the windows were frosted over as if mocking my attempts to navigate the storm. Yet, in the face of this formidable challenge, I refused to yield. With a steely resolve, I equipped myself with a shovel and ice scraper, preparing to battle the wintry forces that held my car captive. Each step I took through the knee-deep snow felt like a struggle, but I was undeterred. I knew my passengers relied on me, counting on my commitment to fulfill their transportation needs.

However, to my astonishment and gratitude, it seemed like a silent distress call had summoned residents from these Chicago neighborhoods. Like guardian angels emerging from a bright light, they rushed to my aid, time and time again. It was an awe-inspiring sight that amazed and humbled me as their breath became visible in the frigid air. They worked tirelessly, armed with shovels and garden hoes, to free me from my icy prison as if guided by divine intervention.

In the blizzard's fury, these extraordinary individuals selflessly came forward, driven by a shared sense of community and compassion. They braved the biting cold, their determination shining through as they rallied together, forming a united front against the formidable snow and ice. Their presence transformed the scene into a beacon of hope and solidarity. As they surrounded my car, their faces etched with determination, I felt overwhelming gratitude. These everyday heroes, who had their own lives and concerns to attend to, had chosen to extend a helping hand to a stranger in need. Their generosity of spirit and willingness to lend strength filled me with a renewed faith in humanity.

With synchronized movements, they attacked the snowdrifts, their efforts synchronized as if choreographed by an unseen conductor. The sound of shovels striking the frozen ground echoed through the neighborhood, intermingling with laughter and words of encouragement. It was a symphony of unity and resilience, a testament to the power of collective action. It felt that time stood still as they tirelessly worked to free my vehicle, their dedication unwavering. The frosty air was alive with a palpable energy, a shared determination to overcome the adversity that had befallen us. As their efforts bore fruit and my car slowly emerged from its icy confines, a collective cheer erupted, reverberating through the wintry landscape.

At that moment, I realized this was more than just a rescue mission. It was a bond forged in the crucible of adversity, a reminder that in times of hardship, communities come together to support and uplift one another. Their kindness went beyond the physical act of clearing the snow—it was a testament to the strength of human connection and the indomitable spirit of the human heart. I expressed my gratitude to these newfound friends, and I couldn't help but be moved by the moment's beauty. Their selflessness had turned a bleak, icy landscape into a tableau of warmth and compassion. They restored my faith in the inherent goodness within each of us.

From that day forward, I carried the memory of their kindness in my heart, a reminder of our incredible capacity to support and uplift one another. Their actions had transformed a seemingly ordinary blizzard into an extraordinary testament to humanity's resilience and unity. As I continued my journey, I vowed to pay forward their kindness, knowing that a single act of compassion can ignite a chain reaction of goodness in the world. With every heave of the shovel and every scrape of the ice, I slowly began to unearth my vehicle from its frozen prison. The bitter cold bit at my fingers, but I pressed on, fueled by the knowledge that providing a dependable service meant going above and beyond, even when faced with the most challenging circumstances.

As my car emerged from its snowy tomb, I couldn't help but feel a surge of triumph. It was a small victory amidst the chaos of the blizzard—a testament to my resilience and unwavering dedication. With my trusty steed freed from the clutches of winter, I was ready to conquer the next trip, undeterred by the formidable obstacles ahead. This experience served as a reminder of the unpredictable nature of life and the resilience required when faced with unexpected challenges. It highlighted my unwavering commitment to be there for my passengers, no matter the circumstances. As I embarked on each subsequent journey, I learned that I was not just a driver in a blizzard but a beacon of reliability, determined to overcome any obstacle that stood in my way.

I'll never forget the collective effort of one particular instance. I had just received a pick-up request from the Roscoe Village neighborhood of Chicago, heading towards the Lakeview neighborhood in Chicago. While arriving to pick up my passenger, my car got stuck in the thick snow again on one of the small side streets of the neighborhood. Without hesitation, the kind-hearted passenger joined the stranger named Adam, who had come to my aid. Together, we shoveled with determination, their laughter mingling with the falling snow as we worked side by side to dig my car out of the snow. It was a humbling sight, witnessing the unity and selflessness of strangers brought together by a common goal.

As Kaitlyn waited outside in the snow up to the calves of her snowboots, she saw the wheels of my car get stuck in the unforgiving snow.

"Oh no, not again! My car is in the snow on this small side street in Roscoe Village. This winter is relentless!"
"Don't worry, Marshall! I've got your back. We'll get you out of this snowy trap together!"

Suddenly, a stranger named Adam appears out of nowhere with two garden hoes.

"You're a true hero, my friend! I can't thank you enough for joining me in this snowy battle. Let's grab those shovels and show this snow who's boss!"

"Haha, you got it, Marshall!" said Adam with vigor as he started to shovel. "We'll shovel our way to victory. Nothing can stop us!"

"The snowflakes are falling all around us, but so is the laughter and determination. It's like we're in an epic movie scene, defying the forces of nature!"

Kaitlyn said, "Absolutely! The snow may be deep, but our spirits are even deeper. We're like a dynamic duo, united in our mission to free your car from this winter's icy grip!"

"With each shovel full of snow, our laughter mingles with the falling flakes, creating a symphony of determination and camaraderie. It's a humbling sight, isn't it?"

"It truly is, Marshall. Strangers are brought together by a common goal, working side by side to overcome obstacles. This is the power of unity and selflessness," said Kaitlyn as she automatically shoveled the snow, blocking the wheels onto the side of the road.

"And as we dig deeper, our bond grows stronger. We might have started as strangers, but now we're partners in this exhilarating snow battle!" I said as I gripped the garden hoe tighter with determination while scooping the hardened ice under the wheels.

"We're defying the odds, Marshall. The snow may be relentless, but so are we. We won't let it defeat us!" said Adam as he continued to break the hardened snow under the wheel with the garden hoe.

"Finally, after an eternity, we see the light at the end of the snowy tunnel. The wheels are free, and victory is within reach!" Kaitlyn smiles as she breaks the ice buried around the wheels' location.

Adam, Kaitlyn, and I were determined to free it when our car was stuck in the ice and snow in this wintry condition. Armed with garden hoes from Adam and a garden hoe from my trunk, we began our relentless digging. With each scoop, we gradually loosened up the ice and snow surrounding the front and back tires. As residents of Chicago, we were familiar with the technique of creating a rocking motion with the wheels, alternating between driving forward and backward. This method requires skill and finesse, almost like an art form, as it helps to gain traction and eventually break free from the grip of the icy terrain.

Kaitlyn gleams with happiness as she digs the car out of the snow and ice, saying, "We did it, Marshall! We conquered the snow, and your car is free once again. It's a testament to what we can achieve when we come together."

Adam pads the access snow off his gloves and says, "Indeed, my friend. This experience will forever be etched in my memory. The collective effort, the laughter, the sense of overcoming obstacles—it's a reminder of the incredible things we can accomplish when we lend a helping hand."

Kaitlyn, with a massive smile, said, "Absolutely, Marshall. Moments like these restore our faith in humanity. We're all connected, and together, we can conquer any challenge that comes our way."

"Thank you, my friend, for your kindness, laughter, and unwavering support. This snowy adventure wouldn't have been the same without you."

" There's no need for thanks, Marshall. Being part of this exhilarating and death-defying snow rescue mission was an *honor! Let's remember it as a testament to the power of*

teamwork and the indomitable human spirit!" Adam said.

Together: "Onward to more adventures and overcoming

obstacles together! We're unstoppable!"

\

I offered Adam some money as a thanks, but he refused because he said he was happy to help out for free. I saw him run as he disappeared into the snowy neighborhood of his home.

Each time I found myself stuck while turning into an intersection of a neighborhood street, a remarkable pattern emerged. It seemed as if there was an imaginary unwritten agreement between the residents of these nine to ten neighborhoods where I received ride requests, a shared understanding that they would come to each other's aid in times of need. Despite the relentless snowfall, which showed no signs of abating, these compassionate individuals emerged from their homes to dig my car out of the snow. Their selflessness was awe-inspiring, as they didn't expect anything in return. It was a testament to the power of human compassion and the willingness to extend a helping hand to a fellow human being, even in the most challenging circumstances. Mother Nature may have refused to cease her snowfall, but these kind-hearted individuals defied the elements with their acts of kindness.

An unexpected and exhilarating adventure unfolded across the diverse expanse of Chicago's nine to ten distinct neighborhoods. Fate, it seemed, had conspired against me as my car became trapped in the treacherous grip of the city's most formidable snowy season. The misfortune of finding myself stuck in multiple neighborhoods only heightened the thrill of the unfolding drama.

With each neighborhood I ventured into, the snow-laden streets transformed into an arduous battleground where nature's forces conspired against my mission. The howling winds, laden with frosty tendrils, seemed to dance mockingly, daring me to defy their icy grip. Yet, resolute and undaunted, I pushed forward, fueled by an unwavering determination to conquer the formidable obstacles in my path.

Navigating through the wintry landscape became a personal quest and a noble duty to safely transport Chicago's resilient people from point A to point B. Each journey took on a higher purpose as I became a guardian of warmth and comfort, shielding my passengers from the harsh elements threatening their well-being.

As I maneuvered through the snow-clogged streets, my senses were heightened, attuned to every subtle nuance of the treacherous terrain. My vehicle's wheels fought against the snow-packed roads' resistance, their grip tested with each turn. Yet, the collective determination of the city coursed through my veins, empowering me to push forward and overcome the challenges that lay before me.

The weight of responsibility rested on my shoulders as I recognized the trust placed in me by the people I transported. Their hopes, dreams, and daily routines intertwined with my journey, forming an unspoken bond of reliance. It was a testament to the unity and interconnectedness that defined the spirit of Chicagoans.

I felt a sense of accomplishment with each successful passage through a neighborhood. My passengers' smiles and gratitude, warm words of appreciation, fueled me forward. Through the relentless blizzard, we forged a path of resilience and determination, defying the odds and embracing the triumph of the human spirit over nature's fury.

In the face of adversity, I became a symbol of reliability and unwavering support, providing a refuge of warmth and safety amid the wintry chaos. The frigid winds and snowflakes might have conspired against the city, but they were no match for the tenacity that resided within the hearts of the Chicagoans.

As the blizzard gradually relinquished its grip, Chicago's neighborhoods emerged from their icy slumber, transformed by the collective efforts of brave souls who refused to be deterred. The triumph of reaching each destination safely resonated in the air, a testament to the power of resilience, community, and the unyielding spirit that defines the Windy City.

With every journey completed, I left a trace of hope and inspiration in the wake of my tire tracks. When the next snowfall blanketed their beloved city, Chicagoans could rest assured that a steadfast ally would navigate the wintry labyrinth and transport them through the storm, ensuring their safe arrival and keeping the flame of resilience alive.

As the blizzard raged on, the snowfall grew more relentless, transforming the urban landscape into a winter wonderland of epic proportions. The sheer magnitude of the storm was awe-inspiring, with four to five feet of snow accumulating around me, rendering the roads impassable and trapping my vehicle in its icy clutches.

Yet, amidst the frustration of being stranded, I felt awe and admiration for nature's power. The sparkling blankets of white, illuminated by the city lights, created a surreal and breathtaking scene. The serenity of the snow-covered streets starkly contrasted with the chaos and urgency of everyday life.

In those moments of isolation, I found solace in knowing I was not alone. The spirit of camaraderie and resilience permeated the air as fellow Chicagoans banded together, offering helping hands and a sense of community amidst the wintry tumult.

With determination as my guide, I navigated the labyrinth of snow-laden streets, embracing each neighborhood's challenge. The experience tested my resolve, pushing me to tap into hidden reserves of strength and ingenuity. Each community witnessed my unwavering spirit as I triumphed over the adversities that sought to confine me.

Ultimately, the blizzard sweeping through Chicago's neighborhoods was a testament to my indomitable spirit. It reminded me that even in the face of nature's fiercest storms, the human will can emerge more vital, more resilient, and ready to conquer any obstacles that come our way.

When the day finally ended, and I retreated to the warmth of my home, I couldn't help but reflect on the unfolding events. The snowstorm had tested my resolve but also reaffirmed the power of human connection. It taught me that even in the face of adversity, choosing kindness and making good choices will always be rewarded, sometimes in unexpected and heartwarming ways. I couldn't help but feel a profound sense of gratitude. I was grateful for the strangers who had come to my aid, gratitude for the passengers who had joined them in digging my car out of the snow, and for the opportunity to experience the power of human kindness firsthand.

This story became a constant reminder of the impact we can have on each other's lives through simple acts of kindness. As a ride-share driver, I vowed to continue spreading that kindness, knowing that it can create moments of unity, resilience, and hope even in the face of the harshest winters. These acts of kindness served as a powerful reminder of the impact we can have on one another. In a world that often feels disconnected, these moments of genuine care and support have illuminated the true spirit of community. It was a testament to the good choices I had made as a ride-share driver, fostering connections and leaving a positive mark on the lives of those I encountered.

It was a testament to the resilience and compassion of the people in Chicago. There's a saying in the city, "You know you're a true Chicagoan if you carry a garden hoe in the back of your trunk." When the snow turns into ice, the garden hoe becomes a mighty tool, capable of breaking through the frozen surface and freeing a trapped tire. This act of kindness and their preparedness showcased the deep sense of community and care ingrained in these neighborhoods' fabric. It was a reminder that even in the most challenging and unexpected circumstances, people are willing to lend a hand without hesitation or expecting anything in return.

The kindness and generosity of these strangers left an indelible mark on my heart. Their actions spoke volumes about the power of compassion and its impact on others. In those moments, I realized that being a ride-share driver wasn't just about getting passengers from point A to point B; it was about fostering connections and creating a sense of community. The simple act of showing kindness and compassion had a way of coming back to us, even in the most unexpected circumstances.

As the day wore on and the snow continued to fall, I encountered more and more people coming to my aid. Each time, I was reminded that the world is filled with individuals willing to extend a helping hand without ulterior motives. They embodied the good choices I had strived to make as a ride-share driver, and their acts of kindness became a beacon of hope and inspiration for me to become kinder to others eventually.

While embarking on each subsequent journey, I held onto the lessons learned from that snowy day. The memories of strangers and passengers coming together to dig my car out of the snow were a guiding light, constantly reminding me to be kind, lend a helping hand, and make good choices. These choices can transform not only your journey but also the lives of those around you.

From that day forward, I carried the memories of those strangers and their selfless acts of kindness. They were a constant reminder always to be kind and compassionate because you never know when your actions may touch someone's life in ways you could never imagine. As a ride-share driver, I vowed to continue spreading kindness and strive to make good choices, knowing that they can transform my journey and the lives of those I encounter.

In my commitment to fostering inclusivity and compassion, I consciously warmly welcome all animals, regardless of their role as service animals or beloved pets. As an ardent animal lover, I appreciate the profound connection between humans and animals, recognizing the invaluable comfort and companionship they bring into our lives.

Understanding the significance of the human-animal bond, I wholeheartedly embrace the presence of service dogs, acknowledging their vital role in assisting individuals with disabilities. These remarkable animals are companions and an extension of their handlers' independence and well-being. With utmost respect and consideration, I ensure these extraordinary creatures have a safe and comfortable space within my vehicle, allowing them to fulfill their invaluable duties.

Moreover, I extend my arms to passengers wishing to transport their beloved pets. These furry companions hold a special place in their owners' hearts, providing unwavering loyalty, unconditional love, and emotional support. Understanding the importance of their presence, I create an environment where the passenger and their cherished pet can feel at ease, fostering a sense of warmth and acceptance throughout the journey.

By welcoming animals of all kinds into my car, I aim to create a harmonious and inclusive atmosphere where the needs and well-being of humans and animals are respected. This approach not only enhances the overall experience for my passengers but also acknowledges the profound impact that animals have on our lives. Their presence adds an extra layer of joy, comfort, and connection that transcends the boundaries of language or culture.

Together, we embark on a shared journey where the laughter, wagging tails, and gentle purrs intertwine, creating a tapestry of warmth and companionship. It is my privilege to witness the joy that radiates from both passengers and their animal companions as the power of the human-animal bond becomes palpable within the confines of my car.

In embracing animals as part of my passengers' journeys, I want to contribute to a world where empathy, understanding, and inclusivity extend beyond our human realm. By fostering a safe and welcoming environment for all creatures, I strive to nurture a community that cherishes the profound connection between humans and animals, enriching the lives of both in immeasurable ways.

These choices reflect the values of kindness, compassion, and inclusivity. I create an atmosphere of care and consideration by assisting passengers with their luggage and accommodating their animals. It's about going beyond the transactional nature of the ride and fostering genuine human connections.

As I navigate the streets and weave through the tapestry of lives, I embrace the responsibility of being a ride-share driver. I remind myself that I am not just a driver but a catalyst for positive change. Each choice I make, whether offering assistance, showing empathy, or promoting inclusivity, can create a ripple effect that extends far beyond the confines of my car.

While the miles pass and the stories unfold, I find solace in the fact that I am contributing to a greater narrative of human connection and compassion. Each passenger becomes a chapter in my journey, and I, in turn, become a part of theirs. Together, we weave a tapestry of shared experiences, reminding ourselves of our power to uplift, inspire, and make a difference in the world.

With every mile, every choice, and every passenger, I am reminded that we are all on our way up, navigating the twists and turns of life. Our choices can shape the narrative, leaving a lasting impact on the lives we touch. So, I vow to continue making good choices, to be a source of kindness and positivity, and to embrace the power within myself to spread a positive influence, one ride at a time.

As I drive forward, I am filled with a sense of purpose. Each passenger I encounter becomes an opportunity to extend a helping hand, to brighten someone's day, and to reinforce the notion that even the most minor acts of kindness can shape our paths in remarkable ways. In this realm of possibility, where dreams intertwine with reality, I was in the driver's seat, my pulse racing with an undeniable sense of excitement.

The universe had conspired to reunite me with a long-lost companion, and the sheer joy of our reunion filled every fiber of my being. Memories of our shared high school wrestling triumphs flooded my mind, reminding me of my unwavering admiration for my older teammate. It was a profound moment, a reminder that life's tapestry is woven with threads of connection and purpose.

"Is that you?" I said to the passenger, my voice filled with excitement and disbelief. "Flex, what's up, man? Long time no see! I miss you."

Flex turned to me, his eyes widening with recognition. "Junior, my friend! I miss you too," he replied, a smile spreading across his face. "It's been such a long time!" I remember looking up to him as a role model on the wrestling team, especially when I was new and had just transferred to Evanston Township High School for my junior year."

I recalled those days on the wrestling mat; my heart swelled with nostalgia. "That's right," I said, my voice filled with warmth.

"You were an incredible teammate and mentor. Your guidance and support meant the world to me during that challenging time."

As we continued our conversation, the memories came flooding back. The grueling practices, the intense matches, and the camaraderie we shared with our teammates. We talked about our coaches, our strategies, and the lessons we learned on and off the mat.

I am deeply grateful to Flex for his warm and inclusive nature, which made my transition to a new school much smoother and more enjoyable. Having transferred from Notre Dame High School to Evanston Township High School during my junior year, I was apprehensive about starting anew and finding my place in a different environment.

However, I felt a sense of belonging and acceptance when I met Flex. His friendly demeanor and genuine interest in getting to know me instantly put me at ease. He recognized my uncertainty and went out of his way to make me feel welcome. He was also smooth with the ladies.

Flex became one of my first friends at the high school, and his support and companionship were invaluable during those initial weeks. He introduced me to his circle of friends, extending a sense of camaraderie and inclusivity to me. Through their kindness and openness, I quickly surrounded myself with a supportive group that eased my transition and helped me feel like I belonged.

Flex's presence and friendship provided stability amidst the new faces and unfamiliar hallways. He showed me around the school, sharing insider tips and tricks to navigate the campus and make the most of my time there. Whether it was finding the best study spots or introducing me to extracurricular activities, he played an instrumental role in helping me settle into my new school.

Beyond the practical aspects, Flex's friendship also brought joy and excitement to my high school experience. We shared laughs, inside jokes, and memorable moments that strengthened our bond. From attending school events together to exploring our shared interests, our friendship blossomed, and I cherished the memories we made.

Flex's kindness and inclusivity extended beyond our friendship. He was well-liked and respected by others in the school community, and his positive influence radiated wherever he went. He had a knack for making others feel seen and valued, effortlessly bridging gaps, and forging connections between different groups of students. His ability to unite people was remarkable, and I admired his genuine and inclusive nature.

"Hey Flex, I feel nervous about navigating the school hallways. They seem so big and confusing."

"Don't worry, Marshall. It's completely normal to feel that way in a new school. I remember feeling the same when I first started here. But trust me, you'll get the hang of it quickly."

"I appreciate your reassurance, Flex. It means a lot to have someone like you making me feel welcome. I'm glad I have you as a friend."

"You're welcome, Marshall. We're all here to help each other out. If you need guidance or have questions, just let me know.

Together, we'll make your transition into this new school smooth. We're in the same group on the wrestling team together. Let me know if you need anything. We always back each other up."

Looking back on my high school years, I am immensely grateful for Flex's friendship and his impact on my life. His welcoming spirit and unwavering support helped me navigate the challenges of a new school and taught me the power of kindness and inclusivity. Flex will always hold a special place in my heart as one of the first friends who made me feel at home in a new and unfamiliar place. I expressed how those experiences had shaped me, instilling a sense of discipline, resilience, and determination.

*"You were my role model," I admitted. **"Your work ethic and sportsmanship inspired me to push myself harder and never give up."***

*Flex smiled, humbled by my words. "I'm glad I could be there for you," he replied. "Don't forget, wrestling was a team effort. **We all supported and encouraged each other. That's what made our wrestling team so special."***

As we neared our destination, the conversation became our lives after high school. I shared how I had pursued a successful career as a chef while Flex had found his calling in law enforcement, dedicating himself to serving and protecting others.

Before parting ways, we exchanged contact information and promised to reconnect and reminisce about our wrestling days. It was a bittersweet farewell, filled with gratitude for the unexpected reunion and shared memories.

Driving away, I felt a renewed sense of appreciation and inspiration. Our chance encounter with Flex reminded me of our profound impact on others and how simple support and mentorship can shape someone's life. Life's tapestry had again brought us together, weaving our stories into a shared narrative of friendship and personal growth.

As I embarked on this journey, I couldn't help but wonder who the next passenger would be, knowing that each encounter would add depth and color to the mosaic of my existence. The road stretched before me, a boundless canvas waiting to be painted with the extraordinary stories of those I would meet. With a heart brimming with anticipation, I embraced the unknown, ready to uncover the poetic and philosophical wonders that awaited me on this exhilarating path.

I was on a routine ride-sharing trip on a Saturday afternoon when I picked up two passengers, Tim and Vicky. Once they were in the car, I confirmed their names and greeted them warmly. The passengers, who were quite stressed, told me things could be better. They recently moved to Chicago on short notice and were looking for a place to stay. Although it was a brief exchange, their stressed-out appearance and their story resonated with me.

"So, Tim and Vicky, what brings you both to Chicago? Moving can be quite stressful, huh?"

"Oh, you have no idea! We just got here on short notice, and we're still trying to find a place to stay. It's been a rollercoaster ride!" Tim said with a smile on his face.

Vicky makes eye contact and says, "Tell me about it. We've been scouring the internet, calling up realtors, and visiting potential apartments like crazy. It's overwhelming!"

"I can imagine. I have an idea that might make your apartment search a little easier. Have you guys heard about apartment search companies?"

Tim said, "Apartment search companies? No, I don't think so. What are those?"

"They're like matchmakers for finding apartments. You tell them your preferences, budget, and desired location, and they do all the legwork to find you the perfect place. It's like having a personal assistant for your apartment hunt!"

"That sounds amazing! Why didn't we think of that before?" Vicky expressed.

"Well, it's easy to get caught up in the craziness of moving. But lucky for you, I'm the Ride-Share Guru, and I've got all the tricks up my sleeve!"

"Ride-Share Guru, huh? I like the sound of that. Do you have any recommendations for these apartment search companies?" Tim asked.

"Absolutely! One is called 'Apartment Finders' and is known for its magical ability to find dream apartments. They wave their wands and poof! You've got a cozy new place to call home."

Vicky said, "Haha! That sounds too good to be true. Are you sure they're not actual wizards?"

"Well, I can't confirm or deny the presence of magical powers, but they're pretty darn good at what they do. They've got a nose for sniffing for bargains!"

Tim said, "I like the pun. We could use some help finding affordable places."

"Trust me, you're in good hands. Try these apartment search companies, and who knows? You might find your perfect Chicago nest sooner than you think!"

Vicky said, "Thanks for the tip, Marshall! You've truly come to our rescue."

"It's all part of the service, folks! Please sit back, relax, and keep searching for that dream apartment. Oh, and don't *forget to leave me a five-star rating for my apartment matchmaking skills!"*

We all simultaneously said, " Haha, will do!"

I could see how difficult it must be to be in their situation, away from home in a new city and trying to find a place to call their own. As we drove to their destination, I thought about how to help them. With genuine enthusiasm, I suggested they look into some apartment search companies and shared my belief that these companies are often helpful. They seemed grateful for the suggestion, and I felt a sense of accomplishment and joy knowing that their struggle might become a little easier now.

The next day, I was thrilled to see that I had been assigned a ride with one of the same passengers from yesterday, Vicky.

As Vicky entered the car, I recognized her immediately and said, "Hello again! You're not the person I picked up yesterday with the apartment search discussion, right?"

She replied with a huge smile, "Yes! Thanks to your recommendation, we found a place we liked!"

With a much more relaxed demeanor and sense of relief, she continued, "I'm so glad we met you and that you recommended those services! It helped turn our situation around."

I was filled with joy and excitement, knowing that my tiny act of kindness significantly impacted another person's life. Knowing how much stress they must have felt, it was enriching to see them find their place, relax, and not worry anymore. This shows how a small gesture of kindness can have a considerable positive impact.

Ultimately, they even tipped me $20 to thank me for my concern and suggestion. This shows that you can always go right by showing kindness to others. It is essential to help each other whenever possible, even in the minor ways.

In the heart-pounding pages of this captivating story, I found myself on another mission: transporting a husband and wife to the hospital. As I asked them if everything was okay, the husband's urgent reply revealed that his wife was in labor and about to give birth! Determined to navigate the treacherous path ahead, I assured them I would do everything possible to get them there swiftly and safely.

While we embarked on this high-stakes journey, beads of sweat formed on my forehead. Driving families with children was already a test of my skill, but to transport a pregnant woman in the throes of labor through the bustling streets of downtown Chicago on a Saturday night? It was a challenge, a true crucible of nerves and fortitude.

The pregnant passenger was breathing deeply and heavily as she spoke behind me and said, "I can't believe this is happening," the wife gasped, her voice strained with pain.

The husband, with a severe and stern look on his face, said, " Hold on, honey. We're almost there," reassuring her, gripping her hand tightly.

"Are you sure you can handle this?" the wife asked, her eyes searching mine for reassurance.

"I promise you, I'll do everything in my power to get you to the hospital swiftly and safely," I replied, determination etched into my voice.

As we weaved through the chaotic streets, the husband's voice broke through the tension, "How much longer? She can't wait much longer!"

With the husband anxiously questioning our ETA, I glanced at the GPS, my mind racing anxiously. The urgency in his voice was palpable, mirroring the adrenaline coursing through my veins. We were on a mission, racing against time to reach the hospital before his wife gave birth.

My thoughts spun like a whirlwind— Will we make it in time? What do we do if she gives birth inside the car? I wonder how much the cleaning fee would be? Visions of unexpected complications, the birth happening right there in my car, and the daunting aftermath of cleaning up the mess flashed before my eyes. The uncertainties swirled, threatening to engulf my every thought.

But amidst the chaos of my racing mind, a sense of determination surged within me. I couldn't let fear paralyze me. I had to focus on the task, channeling my energy into getting them to the hospital safely and swiftly. Every turn, every traffic light became a hurdle to overcome, a challenge to conquer.

The husband's grip on the seat tightened as we sped through the streets. His wife's pain grew more intense with each passing moment. I reassured them, my voice steady and calm, offering encouragement and support. Inside, however, my heart raced in sync with theirs, adrenaline fueling their urgency.

With each passing second, the anticipation grew thicker, the silence punctuated only by the wife's labored breaths. Minutes felt like hours, but we pressed on, determination propelling us forward. The hospital loomed in the distance, a beacon of hope amidst the uncertainty. The husband urged me to go faster, his desperation evident. I navigated the final stretch precisely, the car skimming through the streets as if guided by an invisible force.

As I fearlessly pushed the boundaries, adrenaline surged through my veins, propelling me forward at a breakneck speed. The city, determined to challenge our existence, unleashed a flurry of obstacles in our path. Taxis, their tires screeching in protest, executed daring U-turns from the opposite lanes while buses, like colossal beasts, lunged in front of me, daring me to outmaneuver them.

I refused to yield to the overwhelming situation! With lightning-fast reflexes and unwavering resolve, I deftly swerved and dodged, my car dancing with the rhythm of chaos. When I thought the ordeal couldn't become more treacherous, fate hurled a reckless vehicle into the opposite lane, its metal frame hurtling towards us in a deadly game of chance. In a split-second decision, I veered to the edge of reason, defying the laws of physics to avoid a catastrophic collision.

Yet, the trials were far from over. Into this cauldron of vehicular mayhem, a woman emerged from the shadows, tipsy and leaping into the middle of the street at the heart of danger.

The husband's eyes widened as he asked, "What was that lady thinking? She was intoxicated, jumping into the middle of the street like that, not on the walking lane!"

With the uneasy tension of dodging an intoxicated pedestrian and sweat streaming down my forehead, I said, "Yeah, that was out of control, nuts. She did not even look into her left side before leaping like that. Usually, pedestrians make eye contact with the driver while looking to their left and right before crossing, and usually on the pedestrian walking lane, and not so recklessly in the middle of the street."

The wife was breathing very heavy. It's as if I could feel her and the about-to-be newborn baby pushing to come out with each intense breath of the pregnant passenger, wishing everything to be alright with every second passing. Time seemed to slow as my instincts kicked into overdrive, my hands instinctively guiding the wheel, maneuvering with the precision of a maestro conducting a symphony of survival. The bustling Saturday night on Michigan Avenue became the backdrop for our battle against the odds.

Lurie Children's Hospital materialized like a beacon of hope right off Chicago Avenue amidst the tumultuous storm as the chaos around us reached its crescendo. With tear-filled eyes and hearts overflowing with gratitude, the husband and wife we had embarked on this challenging journey for expressed their profound thanks. It was as if the universe had conspired in our favor, weaving a tapestry of protection and guidance through the storm.

Our journey, a thrilling odyssey brimming with danger and uncertainty, became a testament to unyielding resilience and the indomitable power of positive energy. We emerged unscathed, our spirits emboldened by the triumph over adversity. In that moment, we became warriors of the road, forever bonded by the shared experience of defying the odds and embracing the unwavering spirit within us.

"Just a few more minutes, sir. Stay strong," I replied, my voice brimming with concern.

Finally, we arrived at the hospital's entrance; the husband let out a breath he hadn't realized he was holding. "Thank you, thank you so much," he said, his voice trembling with gratitude.

The doors swung open, and medical staff rushed to assist the expectant mother. At that moment, a wave of relief washed over me. We had made it in time. The husband's gratitude overflowed, his eyes glistening with tears as he thanked me for my swift and reliable driving.

"You're welcome. Take care and congratulations! I wish you the best; the new baby will be born!" I replied my words a mix of relief and joy.

In a heartwarming gesture, the husband pressed $40 into my hand, an expression of gratitude that went beyond mere monetary value. The husband looked me straight, saying, "Thanks for everything."

It was a token of appreciation for my pivotal role in their lives during those intense moments. They hurriedly made their way into the hospital, leaving behind an unforgettable journey that had tested us all but ultimately showcased the strength of the human spirit. Their decision to choose a ride-share driver over an ambulance saved them $500 at the time and forged a connection that would forever be etched in their memories. As I watched them disappear into the hospital, my mind finally settled. The whirlwind of thoughts and uncertainties that had consumed me during the journey began to dissipate. I breathed deeply, inhaling a sense of accomplishment and relief. Whatever challenges lay ahead, I played a crucial role in assisting this family during their need.

The uncertainties that once threatened to overwhelm me now became a testament to my resilience and ability to navigate through the storm. The visions of unexpected complications and cleaning fees faded into the background, replaced by a sense of pride and fulfillment. As I drove away from the hospital, the weight of the exhilarating experience settled upon me. I realized that in moments of uncertainty and chaos, our determination and focus guide us through. Life's unexpected twists and turns may leave us breathless, but they also present us with opportunities to rise above and make a difference in the lives of others.

This thrilling tale of trials and challenges of unwavering determination finally came to a close—a testament to the power of human determination, the world's unpredictability, and the extraordinary moments that can unfold when we find ourselves in life's most extraordinary chapters.

You never know who you might encounter or meet again on your journey. Therefore, it's crucial always to be kind and make positive choices. These encounters served as reminders of the importance of treating others with respect and the impact our actions can have on our lives. The joy of rekindling old friendships and reminiscing about shared memories created a sense of nostalgia and gratitude. It is of utmost importance to ensure that each trip as a ride-share driver is positive and enjoyable, as it not only reflects on personal ratings but also determines one's standing on the platform. Negative reviews can lead to removal, underscoring the significance of creating a welcoming and pleasant experience for passengers while safeguarding one's livelihood.

Through these encounters, I witnessed firsthand the importance of treating everyone with respect and kindness. The golden rule of treating others as we would want to be treated became a guiding principle in my interactions. It became clear that our actions, no matter how small, can shape our destiny and influence the experiences of others. By approaching life with kindness and consideration, we open ourselves to beautiful situations and endless possibilities for happiness.

"On the Way Up" is a poignant reminder of the power of making good choices and embracing kindness. As we travel, we may unexpectedly encounter familiar faces from our past, rediscover old friendships, and learn valuable lessons about respect and gratitude. These experiences become a testament to the idea that by treating others with kindness and embracing the opportunities that come our way, we can create a more fulfilling and enriching journey for ourselves and those around us.

With a renewed sense of purpose, I continued my journey as a ride-share driver, ready to face any challenges that may come my way. The whirlwind of emotions and uncertainties that initially accompanied this path had transformed into a driving force, propelling me toward new adventures and meaningful connections. The lessons learned and the relationships forged along the way became a constant source of inspiration, reminding me of the profound impact we can have on each other's lives.

As the final chapter of "On the Way Up" concludes, let us carry the transformative power of kindness and good choices. Dear readers, let us become the drivers of positivity and compassion in our own lives and the lives of others. In doing so, we shape our journey and contribute to a world filled with empathy, understanding, and the potential for extraordinary experiences.

As a ride-share driver and DJ, I have strived to provide more than an essential service. I have aimed to create a personalized and enjoyable experience for each passenger, going above and beyond to make their journey memorable. In these small acts of kindness, we can touch lives, make a difference, and create moments that truly matter.

In the vibrant city of Chicago, I have witnessed the resilience and compassion of its people.

The saying goes, "You know you're a true Chicagoan if you carry a garden hoe in the back of your trunk."

This seemingly unusual practice holds a deeper meaning. When the snow turns treacherous ice, that garden hoe becomes a mighty tool capable of breaking through the frozen surface and freeing a trapped tire. It symbolizes the readiness to lend a hand, the willingness to help without hesitation or expectation of anything in return. It showcases the deep sense of community and care ingrained in these neighborhoods' fabric.

Through my journey, I have encountered countless individuals who embody this spirit of kindness and preparedness. Their compassion and support have left an indelible mark on my heart. They remind me that even in the most challenging and unexpected circumstances, some people are willing to lend a helping hand. They are testaments to the power of community and the profound impact we can have on each other's lives.

As I continued driving, I couldn't help but wonder who the next passenger would be, knowing that each encounter held the potential to add depth and color to the mosaic of my existence. The road stretched before me, a boundless canvas waiting to be painted with the extraordinary stories of those I would meet. With a heart brimming with anticipation, I embraced the unknown, ready to uncover the poetic and philosophical wonders that awaited me on this exhilarating path.

Through these encounters, I witnessed firsthand the importance of treating everyone with respect and kindness. The golden rule of treating others as we would want to be treated became a guiding principle in my interactions. It became clear that our actions, no matter how small, can shape our destiny and influence the experiences of others. By approaching life with kindness and consideration, we open ourselves to beautiful situations and endless possibilities for happiness.

Among the many passengers I encountered, one stood out in particular. I had the privilege of driving a passenger whose wife was in labor—in that moment, time seemed to stand still as we raced against the clock to reach the hospital. The nervous excitement and anticipation filled the air, and I became an integral part of their journey, providing support and reassurance during a pivotal moment in their lives. Witnessing the power of human connection and the impact we can have on each other's most precious moments was a humbling experience.

And so, dear readers, as we conclude this chapter, let us carry the wisdom gained from "On the Way Up." Let us strive to be the drivers of positivity and kindness in our own lives and the lives of others. In doing so, we shape our journey and contribute to a world filled with empathy, understanding, and the potential for transformative experiences. May we embrace the challenges and opportunities that come our way, knowing that each mile we travel is an opportunity to create moments that truly matter.

Chapter 4 - Red Light again?!?!?

Mishaps, Roadblocks, and Challenges

In a time that took place much more recently in this chapter than in the other stories, it was Columbus Day Weekend, and I was excited to make that money and pay those bills. The sun had begun its descent, casting a warm golden glow across the city as I stepped out of my friend Mick's cozy Chiropractic office. It had been a long day, and I was looking forward to the familiar comfort of my trusty Red Toyota Corolla, parked just a stone's throw away.

I strolled toward the front parking spot in front of the Chiropractor's office. As I reached where my car should have been, my laughter vanished, replaced by a growing sense of unease. The parking space was empty, devoid of my beloved Corolla. Confusion swept over me like a sudden gust of wind, leaving me bewildered and searching for answers.

"Did I park here? I questioned my memory, desperately trying to recall the day's events. Yes, I did park here! I was sure of it. Panic began to bubble up inside me, threatening to consume my thoughts. Where could my car have gone?"

Just when despair threatened to take hold, a glimmer of hope emerged from the depths of my disarrayed mind. A flash of red caught my eye, and my heart skipped a beat. There it was—a red car performing a daring U-turn on Broadway Street in Chicago's Lakeview neighborhood, just across from the Jewish school.

Instinctively, I focused on the driver, hoping to glimpse the person behind the wheel. As the car drew closer, my eyes widened in disbelief. An African-American man with a crown of dreadlocks sat confidently at the helm, his hands gripping the stolen steering wheel.

Time seemed to stand still as my mind raced to process the impossible sight before me. Then, as if to confirm my worst fears, my eyes fell upon the license plate. It bore the same combination of letters and numbers imprinted in my memory—the unmistakable mark of my car.

A surge of realization coursed through me, jolting me out of shock. My car was being stolen right before my eyes. The gravity of the situation hit me like a ton of bricks, and a surge of adrenaline propelled me into action.

Without a second thought, I sprinted towards the scene, determined to reclaim what was rightfully mine. The thief's audacity fueled my resolve, igniting a fire that burned brighter with each step. I would not let my cherished Corolla slip away so easily.

As I approached the stolen car, fear and determination gripped my heart. I knew I had to act swiftly, seizing this fleeting opportunity to thwart the thief's escape.

With adrenaline coursing through my veins, I mustered every ounce of courage and called, "Stop! That's my car!"

The thief's eyes met mine in the rearview mirror, and for a split second, time hung in the balance. Our eyes locked, and I saw a flicker of recognition and defiance dance across his face in that brief, intense connection. But I refused to back down.

Determined, I chased after my stolen car, fully aware that this would be a battle against the thief and my doubts. The race against time had begun, and my journey to reclaim my Corolla had become an adrenaline-fueled odyssey through the city streets.

At that moment, I vowed to retrieve my car to reclaim the symbol of my freedom and independence. I would not rest until my Red Toyota Corolla was again parked in its rightful spot, a testament to resilience in the face of adversity. I was thinking of engaging with the thief driving my vehicle. As wisdom approached my senses, I thought caution was the best for survival. The thief may be desperate, carrying a knife and a gun. I then decided engaging with the thief driving my car at the stop light was not worth it as I watched my beloved money-making vehicle go away in the distance.

Little did I know that this unexpected twist of fate would lead me down a path of adventure, testing my limits and revealing the strength I never knew I possessed. With determination in my heart and the wind at my back, I embarked on a quest to reunite with my stolen car, ready to face whatever challenges lay ahead. With my heart pounding in my chest, I fumbled for my phone and dialed 911, desperately seeking help in this moment of crisis. The voice on the other end of the line belonged to an officer, his tone calm and reassuring.

Officer Jaxx said, "911, what's your emergency?"

"My car has been stolen! I need help!"

Officer Jaxx said, "Alright, sir, stay calm. I'll put your car on the hot list."

"Hotlist? What's that?"

Curiosity mingled with anxiety as I awaited the officer's response.

"The hot list is a database that automatically scans license plates when a police vehicle comes close. It helps us identify if a car has been reported stolen."

"Wow, I had no idea! That's impressive."

"Yes, Marshall, it's a useful tool. I need you to call 911 again to file a police report. Can you do that?"

"Wait, Officer Jaxx? I thought you could do it right now."

Doubt crept into my voice, hoping the police would swiftly apprehend the thief with the city's advanced camera technology.

Officer Jaxx said, "No, sir. I'm afraid you'll have to file the report separately. It's an essential step in our investigation."

"Okay, I understand. I'll call 911 again right away."

Resigned to the reality of the situation, I hung up the phone and dialed 911. This time, a different officer answered, ready to assist me in documenting the theft.

"Hi, I just spoke to another officer, and my car was stolen. I need to file a police report."

Officer Mike said, "I'm sorry to hear that, sir. Let's get started. Can you provide me with your name, address, and vehicle description?"

As the minutes ticked by, the officer diligently recorded the theft details. However, the process stretched, lasting far longer than I had anticipated.

"Alright, thank you for providing all the necessary information. I've filed the police report. Unfortunately, due to the city's shortage of police officers, it may take some time for further action to be taken," said Officer Mike.

"Forty-five minutes just to file a report? That seems quite long."

"I apologize for the delay, sir. The City of Chicago faces a shortage of around 3,000 police officers, and more are leaving the force daily. We're doing our best, but resources are stretched thin."

A mix of frustration and understanding washed over me. I realized that the city's challenges extended beyond my predicament, and the fight against crime was an uphill battle.

"I appreciate your help, officer, despite the circumstances. I hope you'll be able to catch the thief soon."

Officer Mike sighs contently, "Thank you, sir. We'll do our best. In the meantime, please watch for any additional information or updates. And remember, safety comes first."

As I ended the call, a sense of resignation settled upon me. The reality of the situation sank in—recovering my stolen car would require patience and cooperation as the police worked tirelessly to overcome the obstacles they faced.

In times of peril, when my world seemed to crumble, I sought advice from my friends Clyde and Manolo in the group chat. Manolo, residing in West Palm Beach, couldn't be there, but

Clyde, living in Chicago, arrived to offer much-needed moral support, offering to give me a ride home because, let's face it. I had no ride home since it was stolen. As Clyde, Mick, and I conversed in the Chiropractic office, a cloud of frustration and helplessness hung heavy as I navigated the daunting task of reporting the incident to my insurance.

I exhaled a breath of mixed emotions between frustration and depression that my work weekend was out of commission, "I can't believe this happened. It's so frustrating."

With a concerned look, Clyde said, "I know, buddy. It's tough, but we're here for you."

Dr. Mick asked, "How did it happen?"

As I recounted the conversation, my friend's words echoed: "Chop Shop, Chop Shop, Yep, It's in the Chop Shop!" sending shivers down my spine. The gravity of the situation began to sink in, and I turned to my friends for an explanation.

"Chop Shop? What's that?" I asked with a confused and disgruntled look on my face.

Clyde chuckles and says, "It's where thieves take stolen cars to dismantle and sell off the parts quickly."

On the phone, Manolo chimed in, adding his knowledge to the conversation.

Manolo sighed as mentioned, "Yeah, they're probably after your catalytic converter. It's been a hot item in the news lately."

The realization hit me like a sledgehammer. The possibility of my beloved Red Toyota Corolla being reduced to mere pieces in a Chop Shop seemed unimaginable.

With shock and anger on my face, I couldn't help but laugh at the situation I was in and the thought that my car stolen could be in a Chop Shop.

I wipe the panic sweat from my forehead, "I can't believe it. My car in a Chop Shop? It's most likely true! It's too nice of a vehicle not to end up in a Chop Shop."

Clyde said, "Unfortunately, that's how these thieves operate. They disassemble the stolen cars and sell off the components for profit."

Chucking with a grin, Mick said, "Yeah, it's quite likely that your car is already in a Chop Shop. I hate to say it, but chances are, you won't see it again. It's either that or on its way to a boat right now to get sold in another country for parts."

We all couldn't help but brainstorm where my car could be now. We all couldn't resist but laugh at all the cynical ideas we brainstormed. Mick, Clyde, and Manolo were on speaker phone, and I was trying to figure out the next steps for a possible solution, laughing hysterically about what had become of my vehicle. How unfortunate it was that I was expecting to make some decent money for this Columbus Day Weekend, but then poof! It's as if my car disappeared into thin air—my poor baby. My vehicle was my office, which assisted me greatly in making money as a ride-share driver. We have been on many adventures together. At that time, in all the chaos, I couldn't help but feel intense appreciation and gratefulness for the time I spent with my vehicle on all the long road trips going all over Illinois, Wisconsin, Indiana, and even Ohio! She made me a lot of money,

179

and I have gone on 11 vacations in five years because of her. I'll never forget all the memorable and heartfelt time we spent together. The weight of Mick's words settled upon me, adding to the overwhelming sense of loss and despair, and realizing that my cherished car, once a symbol of freedom and independence, might be forever lost in the underworld of illicit activities was a bitter pill to swallow.

As we sat there, the three of us in that chiropractic office, a sense of camaraderie and support enveloped me. While the situation's reality was disheartening, Clyde and Mick's presence reminded me that I was not alone in this ordeal.

Together, we navigated the uncertain road ahead, supporting one another through the highs and lows. Though my Red Toyota Corolla's fate remained hesitant, our friendship bonds endured, providing a glimmer of hope in the face of adversity.

As Columbus Day weekend arrived, my hope began to wane with each passing day. The initial shock of my stolen car had settled into a dull ache of frustration and helplessness. Determined to find solace amidst the chaos, I sought refuge at my Aunt Linda's place, where a warm embrace and the company of my cousin Tony and his children awaited. As I arrived at Auntie Linda's doorstep, my weary heart was met with open arms and a sense of familial comfort. With his infectious laughter and mischievous smile, my cousin Tony greeted me with a bear hug that momentarily lifted the weight of my worries.

Tony opened the door and said," Hey, man! Good to see you. Sorry about your car. That sounds like a rough situation to be in."
"Thanks, Tony. It's been a rough few days. But being here with family helps."

Entering the bustling household, children's laughter filled the air, a welcome distraction from my stolen car woes. Aunt Linda, a pillar of strength and love, welcomed me with open arms.

With relief, Aunt Linda said, "Marshall, I'm so glad you're here. We'll take your mind off things, even briefly."

Her words offered a glimmer of respite, a temporary respite from the relentless thoughts that had consumed me. As the days passed, I immersed myself in the joyous chaos of family life, finding solace in the simple joys of shared meals, laughter, and the sound of children's footsteps echoing through the house.

When they heard the news about my car, my parents expressed their surprise and concern. They had always been a source of unwavering support, and their presence brought a sense of grounding amidst the uncertainty.

With a concerned look, my Mom said, "Let's just pray everything will be alright."

My Dad said, "Make sure to follow up with the insurance company and the police."

Their words reassured me that I was not alone in this ordeal. The love and support of my family became a beacon of hope, guiding me through the stormy waters of despair.

A renewed sense of determination ignited as the Columbus Day weekend drew close. The stolen car may have plunged me into a temporary state of chaos, but the unwavering support of my loved ones reminded me of my resilience.

With my family's love and encouragement, I was ready to face the challenges ahead. Together, we would tirelessly pursue justice, hoping against hope for a glimmer of good news. The stolen car was merely a temporary setback in the grand journey of life—a journey that would be made all the more meaningful by the unwavering bonds of love and the strength found within the embrace of family.

My friends Haley and Penelope were utterly surprised when they heard the shocking news that my car had been stolen. Their disbelief was evident, and they struggled to accept the unexpected turn of events.

Questions flooded their minds as they attempted to grasp the reality of the situation. How could this happen? Who would do such a thing? Their disbelief transcended mere astonishment and morphed into a sense of vulnerability as they realized that unfortunate incidents could occur even in a seemingly secure environment.

I sighed as I sent my friends Haley and Penelope an updated group message, "You both won't believe what happened. My car got stolen!"

Haley said, "What? Are you serious? I can't believe it!"

Penelope said, "No way! How did this happen?"

"I know Penelope. It's so shocking. I never expected something like this to happen."

Haley said, "Who would do such a thing? This is insane!"

Penelope texted, "I can't wrap my head around it. It's like our sense of security has been shattered."

"I feel the same way. It's a wake-up call that unfortunate incidents can occur anywhere."

Haley messaged, "Did you report it to the police? Maybe they can find some leads."

"Yes, I already filed a report. Hopefully, they can help in recovering the car."

Penelope texted, "We're here for you. If there's anything we can do, please let us know."

"Thank you both. Your support means a lot to me. It's comforting to have friends like you during this tough time."

Haley said, "Absolutely. We'll be with you every step of the way, helping you rebuild and find resilience."

Penelope said, "Together, we'll overcome this setback. We're here for you, no matter what."

"Thank you to you both. I'm grateful to have you both as my best female friends."

After three days, Tuesday night finally came along. My phone rang, and my heart skipped a beat as it displayed the Chicago Police Department's caller ID. Excitement and anticipation coursed through me. Could it be? Did they find my stolen car? A million thoughts raced through my mind, wondering about the fate of my beloved vehicle. I answered the call with trembling hands, hoping for some good news.

To my surprise, it was indeed the 19th District Police Station on the other end of the line, located in the vibrant Lakeview neighborhood of Chicago. The officer's voice cut through the anticipation as they informed me that my car had been recovered just 30 minutes ago after a thrilling pursuit. My heart leaped with a mix of shock and relief.

As the officer continued, they said they were amazed to find my vehicle in such excellent working condition. A wave of gratitude and appreciation washed over me. The dedication and swift action of the police had not only brought my car back but

185

also preserved its integrity. It was indeed a remarkable turn of events.

Filled with excitement and gratitude, I hurriedly approached the police station, borrowing my cousin's car for the journey. Little did I expect the incredible scene that awaited me. As I stepped inside the station, I was greeted by a crowd of 20 to 30 police officers, all eager to congratulate me and extend their warmest wishes. They shook my hand with genuine joy, sharing the happiness of the car's recovery.

At that moment, I felt a profound sense of appreciation for the tireless efforts of law enforcement. Their dedication and commitment not only restored my faith in the police force but also reaffirmed the power of community and support. As I drove away in my recovered car, I couldn't help but reflect on the incredible journey, grateful for the extraordinary people who had played a part in bringing my car back to me.

"Officer Mike, I can't express how grateful I am to you and the law enforcement team for recovering my car. Thank you so much!"

"You're welcome! We must serve and protect the community. We're glad we could find your vehicle and return it to you."

With a sigh of relief, "I can't believe how fortunate I am. And to think, most of my belongings were still inside the car. My backpack had my gold bracelet, necklace, ring, and passports. I'm amazed they weren't taken."

Officer Mike smiled and was proud of being the one in charge of the officers in charge of retrieving my car. "That's a stroke of luck. We were able to catch two out of the four individuals who were in the vehicle. Surprisingly, two were teenagers, and one had a warrant for his arrest. The other was under house arrest."

I look frantically through my belongings and see most of them in my backpack, like my gold ring, bracelet, and necklace. "It's unsettling to know they were involved in such activities at a young age. I hope they receive the support and guidance they need to turn their lives around."

Officer Mike said, with a look of happiness and contentment," Absolutely. We'll do our best to ensure they are held accountable and provided with appropriate intervention."

"I am so grateful and appreciative. It feels like a true miracle has occurred, and I'm grateful to have my car back in good shape. I can't thank you and your fellow officers enough for your dedication and hard work. Thank you again for taking the time to congratulate me. It means a lot."

Officer Mike extended his hand for a handshake, "It's our pleasure. Seeing the positive outcome and the appreciation from the community is what keeps us going. If you ever need anything, don't hesitate to reach out. Stay safe and take care of yourself."

I go in to shake Officer Mike's hand, "I will. Thank you, Mr. Officer. I truly appreciate everything you and the police force do to protect and serve our community of Chicago. Thank you for all that you do."

Once I saw the inside of the car, my jaw dropped as far as it could. Oh, it was a huge mess! The inside of the car was dirty and had an overwhelming disgusting smell that could traumatize anyone beyond recovery. It was a combination of liquor, beer, cigar smoke, and possibly marijuana and other drugs. On top of that, there was a solid and nasty hygienic body odor and evidence of bodily fluids. It had been quite the undertaking of at least two weeks of cleaning, multiple car washes, and detailed work to eliminate this dreadful smell. The amulet my mom gave me, the two international phones I use when I travel, and my wallet were the only essential things missing, as well as the three entertainment tablets in the back, which were covered under their company's insurance. It's a shock to believe this car now operates as a 5-star ride for drivers on nearly 26,000 trips.

I found myself torn internally when deciding whether or not to press charges. The situation involved two teenagers, one of whom had a warrant for his arrest. However, he was released from this case due to a more severe crime and a potential sentence. This left me with the other teenager, who was under house arrest. I sought advice from my friends and family; they believed it wasn't worth pursuing charges, considering the potential consequences. They were concerned about my safety since the individuals involved knew where I lived and could retaliate.

On the other hand, I spoke with passengers from the South and West sides of Chicago who suggested that pressing charges would be beneficial. They believed it would create a paper trail that could help protect me if any further incidents occurred. Even some police officers I encountered as passengers agreed that holding someone accountable through pressing charges was important. They argued that nobody would be held responsible for their actions if nobody pressed charges.

It was worth pressing charges as they served as an example and contributed to the betterment of society. I received phone calls from the State Attorney, who assured me that I did not need to be present in court during the initial stages of the case. In a lighthearted moment, I joked about whether I could have or couldn't have Kim Foxx representing me, which elicited laughter between me and the State Attorney.

However, after a few months, I was disheartened to learn that all charges were acquitted. Tragically, the young man who was facing charges had been fatally shot and killed. This outcome was not what I had envisioned, as I had hoped he would see this experience as an opportunity to grow and secure a decent job in the future.

This was a red light for me, full of challenging situations, roadblocks, and mishaps. I am so grateful and appreciative that I got my car back, as this was my office and how I make money through ride-share. This lesson will be an excellent experience for those in a similar situation or looking for a good read.

As I continued my journey as a ride-share driver, I quickly realized that the road to success was only sometimes smooth and straightforward. This chapter is titled "Red Light Again? Mishaps, Roadblocks, and Challenges," I invite you to join me on a rollercoaster ride through the unexpected twists and turns that tested my resilience and pushed me to my limits.

This chapter stands as an exhilarating testament, a vibrant reminder that life's journey rarely unfolds according to our meticulously crafted plans. It vividly illustrates that trials and challenges are woven into the very fabric of our existence. In embracing the unexpected twists and turns, we find the essence of our humanity.

Amidst the pages of this chapter, we encounter stories of resilience and growth. These tales are tales of individuals who dared to face the unknown and embraced uncertainty with unyielding courage. These stories illuminate the beauty of vulnerability and the power of admitting when we don't have all the answers. In these moments of acknowledgment, we truly open ourselves to the lessons life yearns to teach us.

For it is in our imperfections that we find connection, empathy, and shared experiences. No one in this grand tapestry of life is impervious to missteps or untrodden paths. Each story within this chapter unveils the universal truth that perfection is an illusion, and the true beauty lies in embracing the unpredictable nature of existence. These narratives celebrate the human spirit, a testament to the strength forged through adversity. They reveal the triumphs from unexpected detours and the wisdom gained from unforeseen challenges. They showcase the resilience within us all, reminding us that the most extraordinary journeys often veer off course from our meticulously drawn maps.

In the stories within this chapter, we witness the power of resilience, adaptability, and the unwavering spirit that propels us forward. They serve as a poignant reminder that life's most incredible adventures often unfold when we relinquish control and surrender to the unpredictable dance of fate. So, let us embark on this exhilarating chapter, ready to embrace the imperfect, the unexpected, and the wondrous. Let us celebrate the beauty of our shared humanity and honor the stories that remind us that things don't always go according to plan in the grand tapestry of life. And that, dear reader, is where the true magic lies.

Life on the road is full of surprises, and I encountered my fair share of mishaps that left me in disbelief. From navigating treacherous weather conditions to inexplicable car malfunctions, fate prepared me with unexpected hurdles at every turn. Little did I know that these seemingly frustrating moments held valuable lessons and opportunities for growth.

Roadblocks, both literal and metaphorical, appeared when I least expected them. Traffic jams during rush hour became more than just a test of patience; they challenged me to find alternative routes and uncover hidden gems in the city's labyrinthine streets. Similarly, in the broader scope of life, my challenges taught me to think outside the box, adapt to unforeseen circumstances, and persist in the face of adversity.

I faced more than external obstacles. The internal battles, doubts, and insecurities that crept in when things didn't go as planned tested my resolve and forced me to confront my fears. During these moments of vulnerability, I discovered an inner strength I never knew existed—a resilience that propelled me forward despite the setbacks.

Throughout this chapter, you will witness the highs and lows of my journey as a ride-share driver. You will join me in navigating the intricate tapestry of human emotions as passengers come and go, leaving lasting impressions on my soul. And amidst the chaos and uncertainty, you will witness the power of perseverance and triumph from embracing challenges head-on. So, fasten your seatbelts and get ready for a wild ride. In "Red Light Again? Mishaps, Roadblocks, and Challenges," we will explore the unexpected detours, the valuable lessons, and the personal growth that can arise when we face adversity with courage and determination.

It all began during a pivotal time when I was 19 and had two adventurous friends, Penelope and Haley, who happened to be 16 years old. They convinced me to teach them how to drive, and although initially hesitant, I eventually agreed to embark on this journey with them. Little did I know that this decision would lead to an unexpected and unforgettable experience.

As I reminisce about the good old days, a particular memory makes me smile. It was a time when I was teaching my friends how to drive, and we were cruising around in a sliding van. The Toyota Sienna had large doors on the sides that could be opened with a swift slide. My friends, who are always enthusiastic, found a unique way to make their grand entrance. We embarked on our driving adventure one fateful day, armed with my parents' trusty 1998 Toyota Sienna. Excite and nervous anticipation filled the air as we gathered in the car. Teaching my younger 16-year-old girlfriends how to drive at a young age was not something I had imagined doing, but their determination and eagerness pushed me to embrace this newfound responsibility.

Penelope said with outstanding youth and vigor, " Come on, Marshall! Teach us how to drive! You promised us!"

"Absolutely, Penelope! Driving is an exciting skill to acquire. First, let's prioritize safety. Everyone, fasten your seatbelts!"

Haley, looking concerned, said, "Safety is crucial, Marshall. I'm all buckled up and ready to experience the thrill of driving through our beautiful town."

"Fantastic! Before we start our engines, let's familiarize ourselves with the basics of driving. It's not just about steering—it's also about understanding traffic rules, being aware of our surroundings, and practicing responsible driving."

With a happy look, Penelope said, "I'm eager to learn, Marshall. Teach us the fundamentals, and let's create unforgettable moments as we explore the roads of Skokie!"

Haley agrees with Penelope: "Yes, Marshall! We're ready to embrace this driving adventure and become skilled and responsible drivers. Marshall: Please slow down before making a complete stop at that red light! With your enthusiasm and determination, my friends, we'll confidently navigate the roads and embark on thrilling trips to new destinations."

Penelope, with dreams of the future, "Oh, the places we'll go, the sights we'll see! Let's embrace the freedom of the road and create unforgettable experiences together!"

Haley, in amazement, said, "I can already imagine the wind in my hair and the joy of discovering new corners of our town. What an incredible adventure awaits us!"

"Together, we'll unlock the joy of driving and embark on a journey filled with friendship, exploration, and endless possibilities. So, my dear buddies, buckle up, adjust your mirrors, and let's hit the road to create extraordinary moments!"

As we hit the road, I noticed their eagerness to embrace the thrill of driving. They were all buckled up, which made me happy, as safety should always be a priority. However, their excitement knew no bounds, and they wanted to add a touch of style to their driving lessons. So, they devised a plan to open the sliding van doors while we were on the move.

With their seat belts securely fastened, they coordinated their moves and simultaneously slid open their respective doors, creating a breathtaking spectacle. The rush of wind and a feeling of liberation filled the van as they reveled in the moment. Their laughter echoed through the air, adding to the sense of adventure.

Witnessing my friends enjoying the newfound freedom driving brought them was a sight to behold. Their carefree spirits and willingness to embrace life's joyful moments were contagious. Despite the unconventional door-opening technique, their commitment to safety by wearing seat belts reassured me that they were still mindful of their well-being.

Those moments of teaching my friends how to drive were about the technicalities of maneuvering a vehicle, creating memories, and embracing the sheer joy of life. Even though opening the sliding van doors while going may not have been the most conventional approach, it was a testament to our bond and the vitality we carried during those carefree days. As time progresses, I cherish these memories and the lessons they taught us about living life to the fullest, with a dash of spontaneity and a commitment to safety.

As we began our driving lesson, I took my place behind the wheel, ready to guide Penelope and Haley through the intricacies of the road. However, little did I anticipate the mischievous twist that was about to unfold. During one particularly eventful lesson, their mutual friend, Rebecca, joined us in the back seat. Rebeca, known for her playful nature, couldn't resist injecting excitement into our journey. Seizing an opportunity for mischief, Rebecca briefly attempted to cover my eyes with a mischievous prank.

"Are you sure you want me to teach you all how to drive?" I
asked Haley, trying to hide my nerves.

Haley looked determined, her eyes shining with excitement. "Absolutely! I can't wait to finally get behind the wheel. It's going to be so much fun!"

Penelope chimed in, her voice filled with anticipation. "Yeah, we've been waiting for this moment forever. Thanks for agreeing to teach us, Marshall. You're the best!"

I smiled, feeling a mixture of pride and responsibility. "Of course, guys. I'll do my best to guide you through this. Remember, driving is a big responsibility, and we must take it seriously."

Haley nodded earnestly. "Don't worry, Marshall. We'll listen to everything you say. We trust you!"

Penelope, always adventurous, added with a playful grin, "But maybe we can add a little adventure to our lessons, right? Spice things up a bit?"

I chuckled, knowing that Penelope's sense of adventure often led to unexpected twists. "We'll see about that, Penelope. Safety first, but I'm open to some fun along the way."

Excitement and nervousness filled the air as we settled into the car, ready to embark on our first driving lesson. I glanced at Penelope and Haley; their eyes showed their determination.

"Alright, let's do this," I said, gripping the steering wheel. "Remember, focus on the road, follow my instructions, and don't hesitate to ask questions. We're in this together."

Haley nodded, her hands gripping the edge of her seat. "I'm ready, Marshall. Let's make this a memorable experience!"

Penelope chimed in, her adventurous spirit shining through. "And who knows, maybe we'll add a little surprise along the way. Life is more exciting with a dash of unpredictability, right?"

I couldn't help but chuckle at Penelope's enthusiasm. "Well, as long as it doesn't compromise safety, I'm all for it. Let's see what this journey has in store for us!"

With those words, we set off on our driving adventure, ready to navigate the roads, learn valuable lessons, and create memories that would last a lifetime. Little did we know that

Rebecca's mischievous antics were just around the corner, ready to add an unexpected twist to our driving lessons.

"Rebecca, what are you doing?!" I exclaimed, my voice a mix of surprise and laughter.

The car filled with laughter and nervous excitement as Rebecca quickly removed her hands, realizing the potential danger her actions posed. With the brief moment of lightheartedness behind us, we focused on the task. It served as a reminder that driving requires responsibility and attentiveness, even amidst moments of playfulness.

As we continued our driving lesson, we navigated through the streets with renewed determination and a heightened sense of responsibility. The incident taught us the importance of trust, communication, and the need to prioritize safety while still enjoying learning to drive. That playful moment became a memorable part of our shared experience, adding a unique dimension to our journey. It solidified our bond as we learned to navigate the physical roads and the challenges that arise during life's journey.

From that day forward, our driving lessons took a more conventional approach, with a mutual understanding that safety and responsibility should always remain a top priority. The memory of that playful prank stayed with us, reminding us of the valuable lessons we learned together. As I reflect upon that formative time when I was 19 and my friends were 16, the memory of teaching Penelope and Haley how to drive, with Rebecca's mischievous attempt to cover my eyes, adding an unexpected twist, brings a smile to my face. It was a journey that taught us valuable lessons about friendship, trust, responsibility, and the importance of embracing the unexpected adventures that life presents us with.

After navigating through the ups and downs of life, I am thrilled to say that Penelope and Haley have become my lifelong best friends. They have become like sisters to me, and our bond has grown stronger. We have spent countless hours together, sharing laughter, tears, and all the adventures that life has to offer.

Our friendship has transcended time and distance. We have celebrated each other's successes, supported one another during challenging moments, and stood by each other's side through thick and thin. The trust and love we share are unbreakable. I had the honor of witnessing their love stories unfold as I stood by their side as an usher during their weddings. It was a testament to the deep connection we have and the role we play in each other's lives. Witnessing their joy and happiness on their special days was a true privilege.

As the years have passed, our friendship has expanded to include the next generation. I now enjoy playing and laughing with their children, creating new memories, and passing on the joy we have experienced together. Seeing the laughter and happiness in their children's eyes is a beautiful reminder of the enduring legacy of our friendship. Penelope, Haley, and I have become a support system for one another, a source of strength and encouragement. We have celebrated milestones, overcome challenges, and shared life's simple joys. The beginning of our friendship was full of twists and turns that became a pillar of stability and happiness, providing us with a sense of belonging and a reminder of the power of genuine connections.

As we continue on this journey called life, I am excited to see what the future holds for us. I know that no matter where our paths may lead, our friendship will remain steadfast and unwavering. Together, we will continue to explore the world, experience new adventures, and cherish the moments that make life truly magical. Penelope and Haley have become more than friends; they have become like little sisters to me. They have shaped my life in ways I could have never imagined, and I am forever grateful for their presence. Our bond is a testament to the beauty and power of true friendship, and I am excited to continue experiencing all of life's pleasures and happiness with them by my side.

I owe my thanks to Penelope. She was the one who planted the seed in my mind, convincing me to give ride-share driving a shot. At first, I brushed off her suggestion, skeptical that driving strangers around could be profitable. However, with her unwavering enthusiasm, Penelope insisted that I was missing out on a golden opportunity. Penelope, one of my extraordinary best friends, has embarked on an awe-inspiring journey of success. She began her career as a humble server, but her unwavering determination and relentless work ethic propelled her to new heights. She conquered obstacles and embraced challenges with each step, ascending to Food and Beverage Manager and Accounts Manager positions, but Penelope's ambitions didn't stop there.

Driven by her unwavering spirit, she set her sights on the real estate industry, where she found her true calling. Now, as a triumphant real estate agent, Penelope exudes confidence and expertise in every transaction. Her passion for finding dream homes and creating happy memories has transformed countless lives.

Beyond Penelope's remarkable professional journey, her essence resonates with warmth and generosity, creating a magnetic aura that draws people close. Her genuine spirit is reflected in her graciously extending invitations to the most enchanting gatherings, where joy and life intertwine perfectly.

When stepping into the realm of Penelope's gatherings, one is immediately enveloped in an atmosphere of pure magic. The air is filled with contagious laughter that echoes through the vibrant spaces adorned with twinkling lights and exquisite decorations. The tantalizing aromas of delectable cuisine waft through the atmosphere, enticing the senses and igniting anticipation. It is the company that genuinely brings these occasions to life. Penelope's family, an embodiment of love and beauty, radiates warmth and kindness to all who join them. Their genuine embrace and open-heartedness create an environment where friendships flourish and connections deepen. Every guest feels seen, heard, and valued in their presence, forming bonds that transcend the boundaries of time and space.

These gatherings are not mere social events but unforgettable celebrations of friendship and togetherness. Within shared memories, stories are woven, and laughter becomes the soundtrack to cherished moments. The vibrant energy of the attendees fuels the merriment, and the joy that permeates the air is infectious. Penelope's ability to curate such extraordinary gatherings is a testament to her innate talent for creating spaces where hearts are filled and spirits are uplifted. Her generosity of soul and genuine love for people shines through, transforming these occasions into unforgettable experiences that linger in the hearts of all who attend.

In the presence of Penelope and her beautiful family, time seems to stand still, and the world's worries fade away. These gatherings serve as a reminder of the power of connection, the joy of shared experiences, and the beauty of celebrating life's precious moments together. Penelope's journey is a testament to the indomitable human spirit and the boundless possibilities that await those who dare to dream. Her story inspires me to reach for the stars, embrace the challenges that come my way, and celebrate life's precious moments with unbridled enthusiasm. Haley, my remarkable therapist, and cherished friend has woven an extraordinary tapestry of support and connection in our lives. Beyond her exceptional therapeutic skills, she has become an anchor of solace and understanding. In our friendship's sacred space, we find comfort in the depths of our souls, pouring out our joys and sorrows without reservation or fear of judgment. Together, we navigate life's unpredictable currents, offering each other unwavering support, empathy, and a haven for vulnerability.

Haley's influence extends far beyond the boundaries of our therapeutic bond. She has a beautiful family, radiating love and warmth in every interaction. With open arms, she invites me to experience the magic of their wholesome gatherings, where laughter and cherished memories abound. In these moments, I am enveloped by a sense of belonging, embraced by the love and joy that permeate the air. Her presence in my life is a testament to the transformative power of friendship. She exemplifies the profound impact of genuine connection on our well-being, reminding me that we are not alone in our struggles or triumphs. With her by my side, I am fortified with the strength to face life's challenges and savor its most precious moments. Together, we navigate the tapestry of life, weaving threads of love, support, and celebration into the fabric of our extraordinary friendship.

In addition to her unwavering support and inviting gatherings, Haley brings a wealth of wisdom and invaluable advice to navigate the tumultuous seas of city traffic and challenging clients. She is a beacon of guidance when the chaos of the streets threatens to consume me, offering strategies to find calm amidst the relentless honking horns and gridlocked intersections. With her insights, I learned to breathe and embrace patience, transforming the stressful commute into a time of reflection and serenity.

Furthermore, Haley's expertise extends to client interactions, especially when faced with those who exude stress and tension. Her reservoir of knowledge equips me with the tools to navigate difficult conversations, giving me the confidence to maintain composure and empathetically address their concerns. Her guidance helps me uncover the underlying needs and find constructive solutions, transforming potentially challenging encounters into opportunities for growth and understanding.

Haley's ability to offer practical advice in the face of urban chaos and stressful client dynamics is a testament to her professional mastery. Her insights empower me to navigate these challenges with grace and resilience, ensuring that I can thrive amidst the ebb and flow of daily life. With her by my side, I am armed with a trusted friend and a wise counselor, ready to conquer the trials that come my way.

In the beginning, I reluctantly dipped my toes into the ride-share world. I started slowly, working a few hours daily while juggling my full-time jobs. The road ahead seemed daunting, filled with trials and challenges. However, as I witnessed the potential income that awaited me, I became determined to turn this side hustle into something extraordinary.

Day by day, mile by mile, I honed my skills as a ride-share driver. I navigated busy city streets, weaving through traffic with precision. I encountered all kinds of passengers, each with unique stories and destinations. Through it all, I hustled harder than ever, aiming to provide the best service possible.

However, my journey wasn't without its setbacks. I faced my fair share of obstacles along the way. Despite my best efforts, I was forever banned from my first ride-share driving position due to circumstances beyond my control. Nonetheless, I refused to let that setback define me.

Undeterred, I pressed on, striving to become the best ride-share driver I could be. I immersed myself in the intricacies of the job, constantly adapting to the industry's ever-changing landscape. With each passing year, my reputation grew, and so did my earnings. Then, after a decade of relentless dedication, my hard work paid off. I received the prestigious "Driver of the Year" award, recognizing my unwavering commitment to excellence. As I stood on that stage, clutching the ride-share key of the city in my hands, I couldn't help but feel a surge of pride and accomplishment.

Penelope, the catalyst behind my ride-share journey, stood beside me, her eyes brimming with joy. Because of her unwavering belief in me, I embarked on this remarkable ride, transforming my life in ways I never imagined possible.

So, as I reflect on the past ten years, I can't help but be grateful for the twists and turns that led me to this moment. From skeptical beginnings to becoming one of the biggest hustlers in the game, I owe it all to my friends Penelope and Haley for the ride-share driving adventure that changed my life forever. During my early years as a ride-share driver, a fateful and unfortunate mishap unfolded on a rainy Saturday night, leading to an inevitable collision that turned the course of the evening. It all began when I eagerly responded to a ride request at the bustling intersection of North Dearborn St. and made a seemingly innocent right turn onto West Illinois Street. Little did I know that this ride would take an unexpected and dangerous turn, leaving me with no choice but to face the impending impact. Oblivious to the imminent chaos ahead, I continued along the rain-soaked pavement, my windshield wipers struggling to keep up with the downpour.

While I navigated through the dimly lit streets, the rain poured relentlessly, creating hazardous conditions that tested my driving skills. I crank the defogger settings in my car to the highest setting I can go to. Despite my efforts to maintain control, the roads became increasingly treacherous, and visibility blurred. Fate intervened during this moment, and I was on a collision course with an unforeseen obstacle. As I made the turn, I saw a colossal party bus parked roughly 30 feet away, and time seemed to slow down as the scene unfolded before me. Suddenly, with a roar, the party bus driver slammed the accelerator, propelling the massive vehicle forward at full speed. My heart skipped a beat, and adrenaline coursed through my veins.

In that heart-stopping moment, my instincts kicked in, and I reacted on instinct. With a reflexive jolt, I slammed my hand frantically on the horn, its blaring sound piercing through the chaotic rain-soaked air. The cacophonous honk was my desperate plea, a primal cry to alert the reckless driver of the imminent danger

ahead.

My heart raced like a wild stallion, pounding against my chest as if attempting to break free. Despite the chaos, I held on to a glimmer of hope. The blaring horn, my final plea for safety, reverberated through the air, echoing in the face of impending disaster. The adrenaline coursing through my veins drowned out the city's clamor, leaving only the primal instinct to survive.

I could feel my breathing intensify, each inhale coming in sharp gasps as my lungs struggled to keep up with the adrenaline-fueled pace. Realizing the danger I faced sent a jolt of panic through my entire being. In that critical moment, I willed my car to respond, my hands gripping the steering wheel with a white-knuckled determination. Time seemed to slow down as I desperately tried to react, but the unavoidable collision was imminent.

The truth hung in the balance, the outcome uncertain. Would the reckless party bus driver heed the warning in time? Would fate intervene, granting me a narrow escape from this dangerous encounter? Only time would tell as the seconds ticked away, each feeling like an eternity. With lightning-fast reflexes, I veered my vehicle as far to the right as possible, desperately trying to create enough space between the oncoming party bus and my vulnerable car.

As the party bus lunged forward, time seemed to hang suspended in that harrowing moment. The collision felt inevitable, yet my heart refused to accept such a fate. I braced myself for impact, my body tensed, every muscle ready to withstand the force of the collision. Yet, despite my evasive maneuver, the party bus careened forward, its tires screeching against the wet asphalt as its massive frame bore down on me. The screeching sound of tires and plastic metal mixing as this careless gigantic party bus collided with me, sending shockwaves through both my car and my consciousness. The raindrops danced while the world around me blurred into a chaotic swirl of lights and sounds.

In that heart-pounding moment, I realized the fragility of life and the power of quick thinking. My heart, still racing from the adrenaline rush, reminded me of the inherent risks of being a ride-share driver. Despite that, it also fueled my determination to navigate these challenges and continue providing a safe and reliable service to my passengers. In a split second, I maneuvered my steering wheel to the right, trying to create as much space as possible. However, despite my best efforts, the party bus careened into the left side of my car, scraping off the entire fender. The sound of metal grinding against metal filled the air, sending shivers down my spine.

Thankfully, despite the violent impact that shook my car to its core, my car's engine miraculously emerged unscathed. The resounding crunch of metal against metal had threatened to shatter my sense of security. Yet, the sturdy machinery that powered my vehicle proved its resilience in adversity. As the chaos of the collision settled, a wave of relief washed over me, realizing that my physical well-being had been spared from harm.

With the adrenaline slowly subsiding, the rain continued to pour, accentuating the gravity of the situation. With a racing heart and a mix of fear and concern, I quickly assessed the damage and ensured my safety, that of the passenger, and that of the other party involved. It was a moment of realization that sometimes, despite our best efforts, circumstances can conspire against us, leading to unavoidable outcomes. Turning to my passenger, hoping to find solace and support in their account of the incident, I was disappointed as their response cut through the air like a frigid wind.

His face nodded a distinct no, and his voice, carrying an icy

detachment, coldly declined in an ignorant and jagged tone,

"No, I'm not getting involved in this. Sorry, man."

In response, I pleaded, "Please, you're the only witness to this

accident. Your account can help establish clarity and prove

that the party bus driver was at fault. You saw how they were

far behind us and then suddenly accelerated from behind to

cut us off at the turn!"

Despite my heartfelt appeal, the passenger remained steadfast in their refusal, leaving me puzzled. It seemed they were concealing something, although the reason behind their reluctance eluded me. A profound disillusionment washed over me, mingling with the ache of the impact's aftermath. I had expected camaraderie, a shared experience that would cement our bond in this unexpected ordeal. On the contrary, my passenger's indifference pierced through the tenuous thread of trust that had momentarily connected us.

Their callous refusal struck a dissonant chord, leaving me with frustration and disbelief. How could they pretend something significant didn't just occur with the truth unfolding before them? Did self-preservation so consume them that they were willing to abandon me in this moment of need? A torrent of questions flooded my mind as I tried to make sense of their apathy. Did they need to understand the importance of a witness to establish the truth? Did they genuinely believe that their silence would absolve them from the responsibility of their presence during the accident? The weight of their words hung heavily in the air, leaving a bitter taste of betrayal on my tongue.

Amidst the shattered expectations, I felt a renewed determination flicker within me. Though let down by my passenger's lack of support, I refused to let their indifference define my pursuit of justice. The scars on my car bore witness to the truth, and the sequence of events would speak for themselves. While disheartened by their refusal, I knew the path to resolution lay beyond their fleeting presence. I seek solace in the objective evidence, other witnesses' accounts, and the unwavering truth that would ultimately prevail. I straightened my posture resolutely, steeling myself for the battles yet to come. The disappointment of a lost ally would not deter me from fighting for what was right. I would navigate the complexities of insurance claims and legal processes, armed with the unwavering belief in my integrity as a responsible driver.

In the face of adversity, I vowed to chart a course toward justice, determined to prove that the truth would stand tall even without a witness. The road ahead might be rugged, fraught with challenges and setbacks, but I remained unyielding, ready to face whatever lay in wait as I pursued the vindication that both my profession and I deserved.

Feeling frustrated and skeptical, I couldn't help but protest,
"Are you serious? You were right there! You saw
everything!"

The passenger's face tightened with unease as they glanced away, avoiding eye contact.

"Look, I don't want any trouble. It's not my problem," they
muttered, unwilling to be caught up in the aftermath.

Just as our conversation reached an impasse, the bus driver, a towering figure, stepped out of the party bus.
He approached me with a mocking smirk, his voice dripping
with condescension. "Listen, man, you're young. Why don't
you go to school and find a real job? These Uber drivers are
always in a rush, driving like maniacs."

His words stung. His breath smelt of liquor and cigars, and insult and disbelief washed over me. I took a deep breath, determined to assert myself.

"Sir, you have yet to learn about my background. I have a college degree, and this is my full-time job. I take pride in providing a safe and reliable service to my passengers. Driving for ride-share is a legitimate profession, and I am committed to it."

The bus driver's smirk wavered momentarily, his arrogance momentarily faltering as my words sank in. He seemed taken aback, perhaps realizing that his assumptions were unfounded. The truth hung in the air, waiting to be acknowledged and accepted. Though my passenger's refusal to act as a witness left me disheartened, I hoped the undeniable evidence and sequence of events would ultimately prevail. In the face of adversity, I remained resolute, ready to fight for justice and vindicate my integrity as a responsible driver. In the chaos and disappointment, an unexpected glimmer of familiarity emerged from the periphery. As if by divine intervention, my friend Rick pulled up coincidentally in his sleek black Ford Explorer. Rick, a fellow ride-share driver, shared the same passion for navigating the city's streets and providing a safe journey for passengers. He was an accountant for some prominent firms in Chicago. With many years of accounting experience and taking big vacations around the world for eight months of the year, I was able to sign Rick up for Uber and Lyft. Rick found happiness in driving as a ride-share driver as a way of making short connections and sharing insights and experiences with passengers.

A surge of relief washed over me as I exclaimed, "Rick, it's so great to see you!" His concerned eyes scanned my face, searching for any signs of injury. "Is everything okay? Are you hurt?" he asked, his voice filled with genuine worry.

With a reassuring smile, I replied, "No, Rick, I'm fine. Just a bit shook up." Understanding the demands of his ride-share trip, I assured him I would be all right. "Don't worry, take care of your passenger. We'll catch up later."

As Rick reluctantly left to complete his ride, I watched his figure disappear into the distance, grateful for his presence, even if only for a fleeting moment. His promise to call later reminded me that I wasn't alone in this daunting ordeal. However, just as the dust settled, the unexpected arrival of the SWAT team added a surreal twist to the already dramatic situation. Like a scene from an action movie, their arrival injected adrenaline into my veins. The uniformed officers approached me cautiously, their eyes scanning the surroundings.

"Is everything okay here?" one of the Officers asked, their

voice laced with concern. I explained the accident and my

desire for a police report to document the incident.

However, their response shattered my hopes. "Since no one

was injured, you'll have to go to the police station to file a

report," they informed me, dashing my expectations of

immediate assistance.

Undeterred, I exchanged necessary information with the party bus driver, seizing the opportunity to establish a paper trail for the insurance claim. With a heavy heart, I bid farewell to the chaotic scene, my destination now the police station on Larrabee Avenue in Chicago. The following weeks became a blur of disconnection as my car underwent repairs, and I navigated the labyrinthine process of insurance claims. The roadblock this mishap presented tested my patience and resilience as a ride-share driver, but I refused to let this setback define my journey.

Finally, after an eternity, we resolved the insurance claims. As I anxiously awaited the ruling, hoping for justice to prevail, the verdict was delivered, and to my dismay, it shattered my expectations. Regrettably, the party bus driver was declared not at fault. I couldn't believe it. How could this be? The evidence seemed so clear, the circumstances so compelling. Nevertheless, the decision was made, and I was left with a bitter taste. It was a harsh reminder that justice doesn't always align with our hopes and desires.

At that moment, I felt an overwhelming mix of frustration, disappointment, and disbelief. I had put my faith in the legal system, believing it would right the wrongs and hold the responsible party accountable. Alas, now I faced the stark reality that justice can be elusive, slipping through our fingers when we need it the most. It was a bitter pill, a reminder that life doesn't always follow a neat and predictable script. Sometimes, things don't turn out how we want them to, and we're left grappling with the unfairness of it all. Despite the disappointment, I knew I had to find a way to move forward. I realized that dwelling on the injustice wouldn't change the outcome. Instead, I focused on the lessons learned and the strength gained from navigating this challenging journey. It was a reminder never to take justice for granted and to fight for what we believe in, even when the odds are stacked against us.

As I closed this situation, I carried with me the bitter taste of a verdict that didn't align with my expectations. However, I also had the resilience to rise above it, continue seeking justice, and hold onto hope. Ultimately, it's not just about the outcome but the resilience we find within ourselves when faced with adversity.

Though shaken by the collision, I resolved to handle the situation with utmost professionalism and empathy. I ensured that the passenger involved received the necessary support and assistance, doing everything I could to ease the distress. In the face of adversity, I remained steadfast, seeking solace in the knowledge that accidents happen, but our response and ability to learn from them genuinely matter.

Yet, this experience served as a powerful lesson, a reminder of the challenges of being a ride-share driver. It was a testament to the unpredictability of the road and the resilience required to navigate its twists and turns. Undeterred by this setback, I emerged from the ordeal with a newfound determination. I was ready to face the uncertainties ahead, armed with the knowledge that mishaps and roadblocks were temporary detours on the path to success. This mishap was a stark reminder that accidents can still occur even with the utmost caution and skill. It was a humbling experience that taught me the importance of being prepared for the unexpected and reinforced the need for diligence and responsibility as a ride-share driver.

As a ride-share driver, I would persevere, undeterred by the unexpected, and continue providing a safe and reliable service to my passengers, no matter the challenges that came my way. As time progressed, I emerged from the mishap with valuable lessons etched into my memory. It became a turning point in my ride-share driving career, fueling my commitment to safety and reinforcing the importance of defensive driving techniques. With a renewed sense of responsibility, I continued my journey as a ride-share driver, carrying the weight of that unavoidable collision as a constant reminder to prioritize the well-being of myself, my passengers, and everyone sharing the road.

During another phase of my life, I encountered Paulo, who left a small but significant imprint on my journey. Sometimes, these individuals may not exhibit the best character or influence us positively, but even from such encounters, valuable lessons can be learned. Let me tell you about a friend who seemingly had it all. He reveled in the nightlife, frequenting bars, indulging in substances, and keeping his wife waiting for him throughout the night. At one point, I considered Paulo one of my best friends, unaware of his hidden motives. Behind his friendly demeanor and countless favors, he harbored a secret competition with me. Despite already possessing immense wealth, including multiple luxurious cars, houses, boats, and properties, he was never content. It became evident that Paulo's pursuit of success and riches had become toxic.

Gradually, Paulo's true intentions emerged. He began using me as a means to an end, requesting that I drive him around all day without offering any compensation. He would invite me to parties, exploiting my skills as a chef, only to put me to work throughout the event. It became disheartening to realize that I was being taken advantage of and disregarded as someone who could provide free services.

As time passed, Paulo's lack of appreciation for the challenges of my profession as a professional driver became increasingly evident. The demanding nature of my job, the long hours spent on the road, and the commitment required to excel seemed to go unnoticed in his eyes. Instead, I felt reduced to nothing more than a chauffeur, a mere means of transportation, without any recognition of the effort and dedication I put into my work.

One aspect that particularly highlighted this lack of appreciation was Paulo's tendency to invite me to parties and events, only to have me end up in the kitchen, preparing food for the night. This pattern repeated itself numerous times, leaving me feeling overlooked and undervalued. While I understood the importance of lending a helping hand, it became clear that he needed to truly recognize the significance of my role and the expertise I brought to the table.

Furthermore, Paulo's invitations to lunch or dinner often involved him utilizing my services as a driver, expecting me to navigate the city and run errands without considering my time or effort. The absence of even a simple gesture like offering to cover the cost of gas in the car was disheartening. He took my services for granted, disregarding that I had my expenses and responsibilities to manage. The knowledge that Paulo possessed substantial wealth made matters even more frustrating. He had the means to request an Uber or Lyft for his transportation needs or even hire a professional driver, but he needed to recognize the value of my time and my services. It left me feeling unappreciated and taken advantage of, as if my profession and the challenges that came with it were inconsequential in his eyes.

In retrospect, this realization catalyzed me to reevaluate the dynamics of our friendship. It became clear that Paulo's disregard for my professional role and the lack of acknowledgment for the efforts I put into my work were indicative of a larger pattern of insensitivity and self-centeredness. It was evident that our values and priorities were not aligned, and it became necessary for me to assert my worth and seek relationships that recognized and respected the challenges and dedication that came with my chosen profession. As our friendship continued to deteriorate, I began to notice how others in his life questioned his choice of having me as a friend. Friends and family would ask him why he would associate with someone like me, implying that I was not worthy of his friendship. While hurtful, these remarks only solidified my belief in my self-worth.

One evening, as I sat across from my Paulo at a local pub in the South Loop of Chicago, the weight of our strained friendship hung in the air. I mustered the courage to address the issues that had been bothering me for far too long.

"You know, I've been feeling a bit used lately," I hesitantly began, searching for the right words. "It seems like our friendship has become one-sided, with me constantly catering to your needs without reciprocation."

Paulo's eyes darted around, a dismissive smirk playing on his lips. "Why are you making such a big deal out of it? You're just a driver, doing a job anyone can do."

I felt a pang of hurt and frustration, but I refused to let his words belittle me.

I took a deep breath, gathering my thoughts. "Being a driver is not just a job to me; it's my livelihood, my profession. It requires skill, dedication, and hard work. I had hoped you, of all people, would understand and acknowledge that."

He leaned back, his voice condescending. "Well, maybe you're taking it too seriously. It's not like your job is that important. All you do is drive around."

My heart sank, realizing he would never truly comprehend the value I placed on my work and the effort I put into it. It became clear that our friendship was built on unequal footing, with him only interested in what I could do for him. He then took it a step further, his tone even more demeaning.

"My friends and family often ask me why I even keep you as a friend. They think I shouldn't even be friends with you."

His words cut deep, but they also ignited a fire within me. I refused to let his belittling remarks define my worth. I straightened my back, looking him in the eye.

"I may not be important to you or your circle, but I have self-worth. Many real friends treat me like family and appreciate and support me for who I am. I deserve better than this."

He seemed taken aback by my response, faltering for a moment. Then he shrugged dismissively, refusing to acknowledge the truth in my words.

I told Paulo, "I have real friends who value my friendship more than you could ever imagine, and they would never consider not being there for me. Even after all the help I gave you and your family. I don't need this negativity in my life."

With a mix of conviction and determination, I realized that this friendship had run its course. I deserved to be surrounded by people who uplifted and respected me rather than belittling me based on my profession.

As I walked away from the café, I felt liberated. Ending that toxic friendship was a bittersweet but necessary step toward finding healthier connections in my life. I vowed to prioritize my well-being and surround myself with people who genuinely appreciate and value me.

Looking back, I don't regret my choice. Ending that friendship allowed me to reclaim my self-worth and seek relationships built on mutual respect and support. It was a challenging lesson learned, but one that ultimately led to personal growth and the realization that I deserve to be surrounded by friends who uplift and cherish me for who I am.

I realized that I should not measure my value based on the opinions of others, especially those who failed to see beyond superficial judgments. I had a strong sense of self-worth that stemmed from my accomplishments, my dedication to my profession, and the genuine connections I had built with others who treated me like family. Also, this past friendship has given me better standards for whom I want to surround myself with. I am now able to sense toxicity in a relationship and deal with it as swiftly and accordingly as possible. My friend Haley also had a similar issue with her friend Gina, and we were able to feed each other as much advice and realizations on how to deal with toxicity in our lives. For Haley, it was Gina. For me, it was Paulo. It was a pivotal moment of realization. I understood that I deserved better than being belittled, exploited, and questioned by someone who claimed to be a friend. I made the conscious decision to distance myself from this toxic friendship and focus on nurturing relationships with people who truly appreciated and respected me for who I was.

Severing my ties with this friend allowed me to grow and thrive. I surrounded myself with individuals who celebrated my successes, acknowledged my hard work, and treated me with the respect I deserved. These real friends became my chosen family, supporting me through life's highs and lows. Looking back, I am grateful for the lessons learned from this challenging friendship. It taught me the importance of recognizing toxic relationships, setting boundaries, and valuing myself beyond the opinions of others. It reinforced the significance of surrounding myself with genuine connections, where mutual respect and support form the foundation of lasting friendships. This experience empowered me to prioritize my well-being and seek relationships that uplifted and cherished me for who I truly am. As I continued to navigate life, the experiences with this friend shaped my perspective and understanding of human relationships. Despite the toxicity that seeped into our friendship, I reflected on the lessons learned and the personal growth that emerged from those challenging moments.

One of the most profound realizations was the importance of self-worth and not allowing others to define my value. Being referred to as "someone who just drives around" by someone I once considered a close friend stung, but it also sparked a deep self-reflection. I began to question why I allowed myself to be treated in such a dismissive manner and why I had tolerated the imbalance in our relationship for so long. Through self-reflection, I discovered that I had been seeking validation and acceptance from someone incapable of providing it. I had allowed my sense of worth to be dictated by external factors, such as the approval of others or the accumulation of material possessions. This friendship catalyzed me to redefine my priorities and focus on my sense of self-worth, independent of others' opinions or worldly success.

Furthermore, this experience highlighted the importance of setting boundaries and recognizing when a relationship harms one's well-being. It became clear that maintaining a healthy dynamic required me to assert my needs and establish boundaries to protect myself from being taken advantage of. It was a lesson in self-preservation and self-care, reminding me that I deserved to be treated with respect and reciprocity in all my relationships.

While this friendship may have left a bitter taste in my mouth, it also served as a powerful reminder of the importance of surrounding oneself with genuine and supportive individuals. It highlighted the significance of cultivating relationships built on mutual respect, trust, and appreciation. Through this experience, I learned to be discerning in choosing my friends, focusing on the quality and depth of the connections rather than the superficial trappings of success or material wealth.

This friendship that started with promise and potential ultimately taught me invaluable life lessons. It taught me to be resilient in the face of disappointment, value my self-worth, and prioritize healthy and balanced relationships. These lessons continue to guide me on my journey, reminding me of the importance of authenticity, self-care, and the pursuit of genuine connections that uplift and inspire. Reflecting on the past, I am grateful for the growth and insights from that challenging friendship. It may have been painful to let go, but it opened the door for new friendships that truly cherish and support me. I now find solace in the company of friends who recognize my worth beyond my profession, celebrate my achievements, and inspire me to be the best version of myself.

As I entered the highway entrance on Addison Street, heading eastbound, little did I know I was about to witness another dramatic event unfold. As I merged onto the highway, I was drawn to an SUV entering through the Kimball Avenue entrance. To my shock, I watched an SUV collide with an object on the merging entrance, propelling it into the air with incredible force high up to the sky! It soared upwards, reaching a height comparable to even higher to one of the light posts on the highway, before gravity took hold and it descended, landing upside down. At first, I thought I was dreaming. I had hoped this situation was not actual, but it was as natural as the wind blowing unto my hair and face with the windows down.

At that moment, a rush of concern and adrenaline surged through me. I knew I had to act quickly. Without hesitation, I consciously decided to drive up and see if the person in the overturned vehicle needed any assistance. My first thought was for their well-being, hoping everyone involved was safe and the SUV hadn't landed on any other cars. Grateful that luck had spared me from the vehicle landing on top of mine, I approached the scene with caution and a readiness to help. As I neared the upside-down vehicle, relief washed over me as I saw that it had come to rest on the curve of the highway rather than crashing into other cars. I noticed that five other vehicles had also stopped; their drivers were compelled to lend a helping hand in this time of crisis. They formed an impromptu team united by a shared desire to assist those in need.

With a sense of urgency, they approached the overturned vehicle. It was a sight that sent chills down my spine. As I drove closer, I could see a man trapped inside, struggling to free himself from the wreckage. Without hesitation, each person positioned themselves under one of the man's arms, working together to lift him out from under the car. With careful coordination, three people on his right side and another three on his left put themselves under his arm, supporting the man to walk away from the accident scene, ensuring that he was safe and away from any potential danger. Luckily, in this crazy accident, the man's limbs were still intact, and he was conscious. At that moment, I was reminded of the incredible power of human compassion and unity. Strangers from different walks of life had come together, setting aside their concerns to help someone in distress. It was a testament to the strength of the human spirit and the capacity for kindness that exists within us all.

As the man was guided to safety, sirens grew louder. Emergency responders were on their way, ready to provide further assistance. Knowing that help was on its way, I felt a sense of relief and gratitude. Though the incident had been shocking and filled with uncertainty, the collective effort to ensure the man's well-being brought a glimmer of hope and reassurance amidst the chaos.

Reflecting on this extraordinary chapter of life, I am humbled by the experiences and encounters that continue to shape my journey. It serves as a potent reminder that we all can make a difference, big or small. In those moments of crisis and adversity, our true character shines through, and the bonds of humanity unite us in ways we may never have anticipated.

Time is a precious commodity, and it is easy to become consumed by our busy lives. However, this unexpected detour reminded me of the importance of being present and willing to lend a helping hand when life presents us with an opportunity. It was a valuable lesson in prioritizing compassion and selflessness over personal convenience.

As I resumed my journey, I couldn't help but feel renewed gratitude for the moments that truly matter in life. The time spent in traffic while watching strangers assist at the accident scene may have caused a temporary disruption, but it reminded us of our incredible impact on others when we put their needs before our own. I carried a profound sense of fulfillment and a renewed commitment to being a force for good in the world. The memory of that day serves as a constant reminder that sometimes, the most rewarding experiences come from unexpected detours and selfless acts of kindness.

In the crisp autumn of 2019, as the world stood on the precipice of the tumultuous year that would soon follow, I found myself grappling with an inexplicable illness. It was a time of uncertainty when the whispers of an impending pandemic had yet to fill the air. Once a vessel of vitality, my body was weighed down by an unrelenting fatigue. I struggled to draw breath, my chest constricted by an invisible force that fought against my every inhale. Coughs wracked my body, echoing through the hollows of my weary bones. The simplest tasks became herculean feats as my energy reserves dwindled to mere flickers, lasting only three to four hours before fading to nothingness.

In October of 2019, amid my battle, I unknowingly stood on the precipice of a global struggle that would reshape the very fabric of our existence. With each negative test result, with each day I pressed forward, I became a testament to the strength and resilience that resides within us all. And in that, I found hope. Determined to reclaim my health, I turned to the healing powers of vitamins, doubling my intake in a desperate bid for strength and going to the gym regularly. Yet, the answers to my ailment remained elusive. Seeking solace and solutions upon the official announcement of COVID-19 in January 2020, I sought guidance at the health clinic, hoping for a glimmer of understanding amidst the darkness that enveloped me. The doctor's diagnosis brought relief and confusion. No infections ravaged my body, and my temperature remained steady, devoid of the telltale fever that had become synonymous with the looming pandemic. In those early days, a lack of fever was synonymous with an absence of COVID-19, a virus that would soon grip the world in its merciless clutches. If there was no fever, there was no COVID-19 as an automatic diagnosis.

As the months passed, I underwent numerous tests that served as a testament to my resilience. Swabs were taken regularly to ensure my safety and the safety of those around me. I diligently followed social distancing guidelines, maintaining a physical distance from others whenever possible. I anxiously awaited the results of each test, relieved when they repeatedly returned negative. The world was undergoing a profound transformation, and I stood on the frontline of an epic battle against an invisible enemy. It was a battle that defied comprehension, yet I faced it head-on, fulfilling my duties as a ride-share driver with unyielding determination and unwavering caution. Then everything changed. Suddenly, the aisles of every store were stripped bare, as if a hurricane had swept through, leaving nothing but an eerie emptiness in its wake. Hand sanitizer, that once ubiquitous shield against germs, had vanished into thin air. Anti-bacterial cleaners, the guardians of cleanliness, had become a rare treasure. Even the humble bar of soap, a symbol of basic hygiene, had become a scarce commodity. I vividly remember the day I ventured into the chaotic battleground of a Sam's Club, a fortress that promised supplies for my anxious parents. The line stretched like a serpent, its coils wrapping around the building. I joined the queue, determination etched on my face, and time crawled, each passing minute a testament to the desperate thirst for protection and prevention.

Finally, I stepped inside the store, my heart pounding with anticipation. But what I saw left me stunned. The aisles resembled ghost towns, devoid of the products we once took for granted. Signs limited purchases to one or two items per customer, a stark reminder of the scarcity that gripped our world. It was a scene straight out of a dystopian novel, a surreal sight that defied all logic.

Then, amidst the eerie silence, chaos erupted. Voices rose like thunder, arguing over something as ordinary as toilet paper. People jostled and shoved, desperation transforming into a primal need to secure even the necessities. I watched in disbelief, my eyes wide with shock and disbelief. It was a sight I never thought I would witness in my lifetime—a world turned upside down, where the simplest of things, once taken for granted, became coveted treasures. The battle against an invisible enemy had not only tested our resilience but also revealed the fragility of our everyday existence. As I left the store, carrying the limited supplies I managed to secure, I couldn't help but reflect on the profound transformation that had engulfed the world. The battle against this invisible adversary had thrust us into a new reality—where scarcity reigned, and the extraordinary replaced the familiar.

From that moment forward, I knew that every ride I embarked upon and every interaction I had carried the weight of this unprecedented battle. I would navigate these uncertain times with unwavering determination, knowing that even in the face of scarcity and chaos, I had a role to play—doing my part in restoring hope and resilience to a world forever transformed.

Among the many experiences I had during this time, there was one that left a lasting impression. A couple had traveled from London to celebrate St. Patrick's Day, only to find that much of the festivities were discouraged or canceled to prioritize everyone's safety. It disappointed the couple who had journeyed overseas with expectations of vibrant celebrations. I vividly recall driving the couple from downtown Chicago to O'Hare airport. It was a sad ride, filled with disappointment and missed opportunities. I empathized with their sadness, knowing that circumstances beyond their control had dampened their experience. The cancellation of St. Patrick's Day festivities due to the relentless grip of the pandemic left me in awe, and even now, a part of me struggles to comprehend the magnitude of the situation entirely. The mighty St. Patrick's Day, known for its vibrant parades, cheerful gatherings, and overflowing merriment, suddenly fell silent as caution took precedence over revelry. I couldn't help but feel a tinge of sadness as I witnessed this extraordinary holiday, steeped in history and cultural significance, lose its familiar luster. The streets that would typically be adorned with festive green decorations and filled with laughter and cheer remained eerily quiet. The familiar melodies of Irish music, usually drifting through the air, were replaced by a solemn stillness.

It was a sight that struck a chord deep within me. The collective decision to cancel the celebrations was undoubtedly necessary, driven by the paramount need to prioritize the safety and well-being of everyone involved. Yet, the absence of the St. Patrick's Day festivities was a poignant reminder of the pandemic's profound impact on our lives. St. Patrick's Day, a day that symbolized unity, joy, and cultural pride, had been subdued by the weight of a global crisis. The decision to forgo the celebrations was a testament to our collective responsibility, demonstrating our commitment to protecting one another in the face of adversity. It was a sacrifice made for the greater good, a temporary pause in the vibrant tapestry of life.

While it was disheartening to witness such a fantastic holiday go uncelebrated, I couldn't help but appreciate the gravity of the situation. The cancellation served as a reminder that our actions, no matter how small or grand, could have profound consequences on the well-being of those around us. It was a sad yet necessary choice, a testament to our resilience and the unwavering spirit that binds us together. As I reflect on those canceled St. Patrick's Day festivities, I'm reminded of the immense strength and determination within us all. Through these challenges and sacrifices, we forge an unbreakable bond, knowing that by staying apart, we protect what makes us human —our ability to come together, celebrate, and create cherished memories.

Though the cancellation of St. Patrick's Day was a poignant reminder of the times we live in, it also ignited a glimmer of hope within me. One day, we will reclaim the vibrancy and joy of this remarkable holiday, celebrating with a newfound appreciation for the unity and resilience that define us.

Such encounters served as a reminder of the pandemic's profound impact on individuals and their plans. I witnessed firsthand the disappointment and adjustments people had to make to safeguard public health. As a ride-share driver, I became an unwitting witness to the personal and collective stories shaped by the pandemic. These experiences deepened my understanding of the challenges faced by individuals from all walks of life, and they further fueled my determination to navigate the uncertain road ahead with resilience and empathy.

As a ride-share driver, I navigated a turbulent world during those challenging times. It was a time when the true extent of our trials became apparent. The enforced distance between loved ones left them yearning for the warmth of an embrace, which was now forbidden. The once-bustling streets of downtown Chicago transformed into eerie ghost towns on Friday and Saturday nights. Curfews were implemented, requiring people to stay home, except for essential workers like first responders and ride-share drivers. During the period of isolation, ride-share drivers faced increased difficulties in making a living and paying bills. Despite the necessity to avoid close contact with others, their job required them to be in close quarters with passengers. This created a challenging situation that needed to be addressed with the implementation of safety measures.

Ride-share companies and drivers took several precautions to mitigate the risks of proximity. One measure was to leave the window partially open to ensure a continuous fresh air flow. This helped improve ventilation within the vehicle and reduce the concentration of potentially infectious particles. Another step was to turn off the recirculated ventilation and rely solely on fresh air ventilation. Recirculated air could carry contaminants, so disabling this feature prioritized the safety of both drivers and passengers.

Moreover, wearing masks at all times became mandatory for ride-share drivers. Masks act as a barrier, reducing the risk of respiratory droplets spreading between the driver and passengers. These safety measures were crucial in minimizing the transmission of COVID-19 and ensuring the well-being of everyone involved. By implementing these protocols, ride-share companies aimed to create a safer environment for drivers and passengers. However, it undoubtedly presented additional challenges for the drivers to navigate their jobs while upholding these safety standards.

Amid the pandemic's chaos, my dear friends Penelope and Haley embarked on a journey to fill their lives with unimaginable joy and heart-wrenching anxiety. They both brought beautiful lives into this world, their newborn babies becoming beacons of hope in a time of uncertainty. Yet, alongside the overwhelming love that enveloped them, a cloud of worry loomed overhead. The anxiety gnawed at their souls, the fear of the unknown. Would everything be okay? Would their precious little ones remain untouched by the invisible threat that haunted their thoughts?

With each passing day, as the world grappled with the relentless spread of the virus, Penelope and Haley found themselves immersed in a delicate dance of caution and protection. They meticulously followed safety guidelines, every action fueled by an instinctive need to shield their newborns from harm. The fear persisted, relentless in its grip. The mere thought of their babies contracting COVID-19 sent shivers down their spines. They couldn't bear the idea of being separated from their little ones, isolated and unable to hold them close, to feel their tiny heartbeat against their chests.

Every cough, every sneeze, every sniffle from anyone in their vicinity became a source of heightened concern. Their minds raced with worry, analyzing every symptom, every potential risk. The weight of responsibility pressed upon them reminded them of the delicate balance they had to maintain for their children's well-being. Yet, amidst the anxiety, Penelope and Haley found strength in each other. They shared their fears, their doubts, and their hopes. They became support pillars, providing solace and reassurance when the world's weight threatened to crush their spirits. Together, they navigated the uncharted waters of motherhood during a global crisis, their bond unbreakable.

While the months passed, their little ones blossomed, their laughter filling the air with pure joy. Penelope and Haley marveled at the resilience of their babies, their innocence untouched by the chaos surrounding them. It was a testament to their unwavering dedication and tireless efforts to shield their children from harm. The anxiety never indeed vanished, a lingering presence in the depths of their hearts. But with each passing day, a glimmer of hope emerged as the world slowly regained its balance. They began to believe that their babies would be okay.

Penelope second baby and Haley's first baby's journey through motherhood during the pandemic was a testament to the strength of the human spirit. It was a reminder that even in the face of adversity, love and determination could conquer the darkest of fears. Their stories would forever be etched in their hearts, a testament to the extraordinary resilience of mothers who, even in the most uncertain times, could move mountains to protect their precious children. Lyft, one of the Ride-Share companies, also provided support by offering the option to order a free plexiglass partition. This partition served as a transparent, protective barrier between the driver and the passenger, ensuring an added layer of safety.

Additionally, shared rides were even canceled to comply with social distancing guidelines. These measures aimed to prioritize drivers' and passengers' health and safety, but they undoubtedly posed financial and emotional challenges for ride-share drivers. The need to adapt to new protocols while still providing an essential service added an extra layer of difficulty to an already uncertain and trying time.

In the face of countless challenges that defined 2020, I persisted as a beacon of resilience amidst an unforgiving storm. The trials I encountered were just a fraction of the immense difficulties that unfolded during that time. However, my unwavering determination allowed me to navigate the uncharted waters and became a testament to the indomitable human spirit. As the world slowly began its healing process, I gained a newfound appreciation for the fragility of life. Amidst the chaos, a sense of gratitude blossomed within me. I realized the importance of cherishing each moment and valuing what truly matters.

In addition to these personal reflections, I am a member of the Independent Driver Guild of Chicago (IDG). During the pandemic, I was deeply saddened to learn about the lives lost among drivers and non-drivers due to COVID-19. The situation brought about numerous uncertainties, as even those who took the vaccine were still susceptible to the virus. In the face of the tensions and concerns that permeated every aspect of life during the pandemic, I found myself standing at a crossroads, faced with a difficult choice. The weight of responsibility bore down, urging me to consider the best course of action for my safety and well-being.

After much contemplation, I took a break, temporarily stepping away from my role as a ride-share driver. It was a roadblock, an interruption in the flow of my everyday life. But within that pause, a newfound opportunity emerged—a chance to gather wisdom and insight from the world unfolding before me. During those few months of respite, I immersed myself in observing and analyzing the situation. I delved into the vast sea of information, seeking knowledge that would empower me to make informed decisions and navigate the challenges posed by the pandemic. I witnessed the ebb and flow of the world around me from a distance. I saw the resilience of communities coming together, supporting one another in the face of adversity. I witnessed the tireless efforts of healthcare workers, essential workers, and countless unsung heroes who fought tirelessly to keep society afloat.

In this period of reflection, I gained a deeper understanding of the magnitude of the situation. I grasped the importance of putting safety and well-being at the forefront of every decision. I recognized that sometimes, taking a step back is the best way to move forward, allowing oneself to gather strength, knowledge, and perspective. Armed with this newfound wisdom, I eventually returned to my role as a ride-share driver. But this time, I approached it with a renewed sense of purpose and vigilance. I understood the importance of adhering to safety protocols and being cautious and considerate in every interaction.

Though initially perceived as a roadblock, the break I took ultimately became a catalyst for growth and resilience. It taught me the value of self-care, of taking a moment to reassess and recalibrate amidst the chaos. It taught me that gathering information and understanding the bigger picture can be a powerful tool for navigating uncharted territory in times of uncertainty. As I ventured back into the world, I carried the lessons learned during my challenging hiatus. I embraced the challenges with a newfound resilience, armed with the knowledge and wisdom forged through the crucible of the pandemic. With determination and caution, I continued my journey on the frontline, adapting to the ever-changing landscape with an unwavering commitment to safety and well-being. The road ahead may still be filled with challenges, but I face them confidently, knowing that my choices are guided by the wisdom gained during my pause—a pause that transformed into a pivotal moment of growth and understanding. Though filled with uncertainty and hardship, the pandemic held unexpected treasures. With newfound free time and strict adherence to CDC guidelines, I journeyed to different countries, seeking solace and adventure.

It was during one of these remarkable encounters, amidst my travels to various countries, that fate intervened in the most enchanting way, leading me to the love of my life, Natalia, from

Colombia. From the first moment our eyes locked, time seemed to stand still, as if the universe had conspired to bring us together. In her presence, I was instantly captivated by her radiant beauty, which emanated from the depths of her soul and shone through her eyes. It wasn't just her physical appearance that drew me in; it was the warmth of her spirit, the kindness in her words, and the genuine love she exuded.

Every conversation with Natalia felt like a symphony of laughter and shared dreams. We would lose track of time as we delved into the depths of our souls, exploring our passions, fears, and aspirations. With every word exchanged, a fire within me that had long been dormant was reignited, filling me with a renewed sense of purpose and joy. In Natalia, I found a partner and a soulmate who understood me in ways I never thought possible. As our relationship blossomed, we embarked on countless adventures fueled by love and the desire to create beautiful memories together. I have traveled to Colombia at least nine times in the past two years, each visit filled with romance, exploration, and a deepening connection. We would wander through picturesque streets hand in hand, savoring the magic of cobblestone alleys and vibrant plazas. We would indulge in intimate candlelit dinners, savoring the flavors of Colombian cuisine while sharing stories of our past and dreams for the future. And in those precious moments, surrounded by the beauty of our surroundings and the love in our hearts, time seemed to stand still, fully immersing ourselves in the bliss of our togetherness.

It wasn't just grand gestures and exotic locations that defined our relationship. We found joy in the simplicity of everyday moments, cooking special dinners for each other and exchanging heartfelt gifts that spoke volumes about our love and understanding. Whether it was a handwritten letter filled with adoration or a small trinket that held sentimental value, each gesture served as a reminder of the depth of our connection and our commitment to nurturing our love. So, dear reader, as Chapter 4 draws close, I stand in awe of the extraordinary love that has graced my life. Natalia has redefined my understanding of true love and has become my partner, confidant, and most significant source of support. Together, we continue to embark on new adventures, explore the depths of our souls, and build a future filled with endless possibilities.

As I gaze into Natalia's eyes, I am reminded of the extraordinary power of love to transcend boundaries, heal wounds, and inspire us to become the best versions of ourselves. With each passing day, I am eternally grateful for the serendipitous encounter that led me to the love of my life, a love that has forever transformed the landscape of my heart. The red light loomed before me again; its presence seemed almost poetic, symbolizing the countless mishaps, roadblocks, and challenges that had defined Chapter 4 of my life's journey. However, within the chaos and uncertainty, I discovered a truth that would forever alter the course of my story. In embracing the imperfect, the unexpected, and the wondrous, I unearthed the true magic of existence.

Throughout this chapter, I encountered a myriad of experiences. I formed deep connections with neighborhood acquaintances who transformed into lifelong friends; their unwavering support reminded me of the power of human relationships and the beauty within our shared humanity.

Not every bond is meant to withstand the test of time. I had to let go of a dear friend, once my closest confidant, for self-respect and personal growth. This challenging decision paved the way for new beginnings and discovering my worth.

Amid life's unpredictability, a sudden car accident caused by an intoxicated party bus driver shook me to my core. It shattered the illusion of invincibility and served as a poignant reminder of the fragility of existence. Yet, from the wreckage, I emerged with a renewed appreciation for the precious gift of life and a heightened sense of resilience.

And then, the world was gripped by the COVID-19 pandemic, thrusting me into a period of unemployment that lasted for months. While the challenges were immense, this unforeseen pause in my journey allowed me to embark on a different kind of adventure—one that transcended physical borders. During this time, I crossed paths with Natalia, the love of my life from Colombia.

Natalia's presence in my life was nothing short of extraordinary. Her beauty, inside and out, left me breathless from when our eyes first met. In a world turned upside down, we found solace and strength in each other's arms, forging a connection that defied distance and circumstance.

So, dear reader, as Chapter 4 draws close, I stand at the intersection of reflection and anticipation. I have celebrated the beauty of friendship, navigated the complexities of letting go but learning from negative experiences, and triumphed over adversity. Through it all, I have discovered that even in the darkest times, unexpected blessings can emerge with hard work and dedication.

As the red light finally fades into a bright green, I drive forward with a heart brimming with gratitude, ready to embrace the next chapter of my journey. As we navigate through life, it is the twists, the turns, and the unexpected trials and challenges that make every encounter worthwhile. So, I invite you to join me as we unravel the mysteries, embrace the challenges, and uncover the breathtaking magic in the chapters yet to come.

CHAPTER 5 - Happiness is a Choice

Embracing Personal Freedom

Ah, it was 2019 in January, one of the coldest times in the history of Chicago. The day after the Polar Vortex in Chicago, the city was still reeling from the freezing temperatures of minus twenty-three degrees Fahrenheit. As I picked up my passenger, Nathan, little did I know that this ride would turn into an adventure filled with laughter and insights.

Nathan, a construction worker by profession, hopped into my car, and we embarked on a pothole-filled journey close by from South Canal St. and West Roosevelt Road in South Loop towards Fullerton Ave. and Clark Street in Lincoln Park. Let me tell you, Chicago's streets had seen better days. Potholes were everywhere, and it was as if the city had become a giant obstacle course!

With his construction expertise, Nathan became my impromptu professor, educating me on the perils of the Polar Vortex. The extreme cold caused the sewer pipes to freeze, leading to bursts that wreaked havoc on the city's cement infrastructure. He even had to attend to a few buildings in Downtown Chicago areas that flooded in the basement. And let's not forget the constant salt treatment by the shovel trucks, which acted as the perfect sidekick to corrode the streets even further!

But what amazed me the most was how past potholes were hastily patched up. Instead of adequately fixing them, the city opted for quick and cheap solutions. It was like they were playing a game of hide-and-seek with the potholes, but the potholes always won. Those patch jobs were flimsy at best, and it felt like I was driving through a level of Nintendo's Mario Kart, desperately trying to dodge the treacherous obstacles. You could also tell there were past potholes in that area because you could see the repatched opened up after the water that froze in that area melted. Not just old ones, but new potholes, too, were formed. Some looked like tiny meteors that may have landed, creating those mini craters.

"Hey, Nathan, have you ever played Mario Kart?" I ask as I wipe the sweat of dangerous pothole collisions off my face.

"Oh yeah, Marshall, I'm a pro! Why do you ask?"

"Well, buckle up, my friend, because driving through these potholes feels like we're in a real-life Mario Kart game!"

"Haha, you're not kidding! It's like the city thinks they can outsmart the potholes by covering them up with those flimsy patches. But guess what? The potholes always win!"

"Exactly! It's like they're playing hide-and-seek, but these potholes have mastered the art of camouflage. They're the ultimate champions!"

Driving down Ogden Avenue, my car went over a giant block of ice that couldn't be avoided. Then afterward, I rear my vehicle to the right, avoiding a massive pothole that stretches from the right to the left side of the lane!

"O my God! Nice job, Marshall, on dodging that pothole the size of Texas! I can almost picture the city workers saying, 'Okay, guys, let's cover up this pothole with a sprinkle of asphalt and a dash of hope. Good luck, drivers!"

"The size of Texas? I didn't know Texas was that big! And then we're left here, maneuvering our way through the streets like Mario Kart racers dodging banana peels and turtle shells. It's a race against the pressure of freezing temperatures and potholes!"

"I can almost hear the sound effects as we swerve and bounce around. Watch out for that blue shell, Marshall!"

"Oh no, Nathan, a blue shell would be the final blow! It'd be like hitting a giant pothole that sends us flying into the air. Who needs a rainbow road when we have Chicago's streets?"

"You're right! We're experiencing the pothole version of Rainbow Road, complete with unexpected twists, turns, and heart-stopping moments."

"Well, at least we're getting a unique driving experience, right? We can tell our friends, 'Forget roller coasters; come to Chicago and ride the Pothole Express!'"

"Haha, that's one way to look at it, Marshall. Remember, if we survive this pothole madness, we'll be invincible on any other road!"

"Absolutely! We'll be like Mario and Luigi, the fearless pothole conquerors. No obstacle can stand in our way!"

"To victory and beyond, Marshall! Let's show these potholes who's boss!"

"You bet, Nathan! We'll navigate through this Mario Kart-inspired cityscape and emerge as the champions of the asphalt!"

Together: "Game on, potholes! We're coming for you!"

But you know what? Despite the difficult conditions, Nathan and I couldn't help but find humor. We laughed and joked, turning the bumpy ride into a hilarious adventure. It was like we were contestants on a bizarre reality show called "Pothole Warriors," battling our way through the concrete chaos with wit and laughter.

"Nathan, these potholes are like banana peels and turtle shells being aimed at us! It's like the road itself is trying to sabotage our journey!"

"Haha, you're so right, Marshall! I keep expecting a mischievous turtle popping up from the sewer, hurling shells at us. Dodge left, dodge right, just like in Mario Kart!"

"But here's the catch, Nathan. In Mario Kart, we can always rely on that green mushroom for a quick comeback if we get hit. But in real life, there's no second chance or extra life once it's game over!"

"Oh my goodness, you're right! No magical mushrooms or golden stars to save us from the perils of these treacherous potholes. It's one shot, and we better make it count!"

"It's like we're living on the edge, my friend. Every swerve, every dodge is a heart-stopping moment. We're like the daredevils of the asphalt, dancing with danger!"

"Exactly! We should get honorary licenses as professional pothole dodgers. Move over. Mario, Luigi, Marshall, and Nathan are taking the wheel!"

"I can already see the headlines: 'Dynamic Duo Masters the Art of Pothole Evasion. Chicago's Very Own Superheroes!'"
"We'll have our theme song and everything! 'Pothole Avengers, Assemble!'"

"But seriously, Nathan, let's keep our eyes peeled and our reflexes sharp. We'll conquer these potholes one dodge at a time and make it safely to our destination!"

"You're right, Marshall. We've got this! No matter how intense the road gets, we'll show these potholes who's boss. Nothing can stop us!"

"So, buckle up, my friend, and let's continue our epic adventure through the streets of Chicago. Together, we'll defy the odds and emerge victorious!"

"To victory and smooth rides, Marshall! Let's keep dodging those potholes like true Mario Kart champions!"

"Nathan, what's even scarier about these potholes? They're not just a threat to our cars but can also put us out of work!"

"Marshall! These road craters are like hidden traps waiting to sabotage our livelihoods. One wrong move, and we could be sidelined for weeks!"

"It's like a double-edged sword, Nathan. On one side, we're battling to protect our vehicles from the pothole apocalypse. Conversely, we're fighting to keep our jobs intact!"

"You're so right, Marshall. If our cars suffer severe damage, it means costly repairs and precious time away from work. We can't afford to take that risk."

"Every swerve, every dodge becomes more than just avoiding a bump in the road. It becomes a desperate plea to the car gods to protect our means of earning a living."

"I find myself praying with every pothole we narrowly avoid. 'Please, car gods, let us emerge unscathed! Our livelihoods depend on it!'"

"And in those heart-stopping moments, we hold our breath, hoping that the wheels don't get misaligned, the rotors don't break, and the engine remains intact. The possibilities are endless, and the consequences are dire!"

"A flat tire could mean days without work, a misaligned wheel could throw off our entire schedule, and internal engine damage could put us out of commission for weeks."

"It's like playing a high-stakes game, where our cars are our players, and the potholes are the formidable opponents. We can't afford to lose this battle!"

"So, let's channel our inner Mario Kart champions, Marshall! With every dodge, we're not just protecting our vehicles, but safeguarding our livelihoods."

"Nathan! We'll navigate this pothole-ridden battlefield with precision and skill. We won't let these road hazards knock us out of the game!"

"To all the hardworking drivers, may the car gods be on our side. Let's conquer these potholes and keep our wheels rolling!"

"Here's to a smooth ride and uninterrupted workdays. We've got this, Nathan! We won't let the potholes defeat us!"

Together: "Onward, fellow road warriors! Let's ensure our livelihoods stay on track!"

We had formed an unbreakable bond by reaching Lincoln Park through our shared pothole escapades. Still chuckling, Nathan stepped out of the car and thanked me for the ride filled with unexpected thrills. We said our goodbyes, holding back the urge to do a victory lap to conquer Chicago's pothole madness.

As I drove away, I couldn't help but appreciate the absurdity of it all. Who knew a simple ride through the city could turn into a wild, Mario Kart-inspired adventure? It was a day I will never forget when ride-share trips dodging potholes became an art form, and laughter became the fuel that propelled us forward.

So, if you ever find yourself driving through Chicago after a Polar Vortex, buckle up and prepare for a pothole-infested ride. Just remember to bring your sense of humor because sometimes, the craziest moments become the most unforgettable memories.

During one of my recent journeys, I had the pleasure of meeting a passenger who left a lasting impression on me. When he stepped into my vehicle, his warm and friendly demeanor made me feel at ease during South Lake Shore Drive traffic. As we embarked on our ride, we struck up a conversation about his life.

As we chatted, the topic of upcoming holidays and Thanksgiving came up. The passenger excitedly told me about his plans, where he would be spending the holidays, and the cherished traditions he held dear. Hearing his enthusiasm and the joy he found in celebrating with loved ones was heartwarming.

It wasn't just their holiday plans that captivated me; it was the wisdom he shared through a quote from Ralph Kiner, which his father had once told him. The quote perfectly encapsulates the ever-changing weather patterns that Chicago is known for.

"If you don't like the Chicago weather, wait 15 minutes."
Don't worry, the weather will be something completely
different after that. It was a lighthearted reminder of how
unpredictable life can be and to embrace the constant
fluctuations with a sense of humor.

Safety became an important topic during our conversation. He emphasized the importance of avoiding distractions while driving, particularly texting, and the grave consequences of drinking and driving. I wholeheartedly agreed with his stance, as road safety is a responsibility we all share.

As our journey ended, I couldn't help but feel grateful for the encounter. The passenger's friendly nature, insightful stories, and commitment to spreading awareness about safe driving left a lasting impact on me. It reminded me of the power of human connection and the meaningful conversations that can occur in unexpected circumstances. This comical observation perfectly captures the unpredictable nature of Chicago's climate. Mother Nature enjoys playing tricks on us, keeping us on our toes and forever guessing what meteorological surprises await us around the corner.

One moment, the sun shines brightly, casting its warm golden rays upon the city, creating a picturesque scene. In the blink of an eye, dark clouds roll in, transforming the sky into a gloomy canvas. Rain pours relentlessly as if the heavens have decided to release their reservoir upon unsuspecting pedestrians. Yet, when you reach for your umbrella, the rain abruptly ceases, and the clouds part to reveal a radiant blue sky. The sun returns in all its glory, breathing life back into the city. It's as if the weather is engaged in a whimsical dance, constantly changing its tune with every passing moment.

This phenomenon has become ingrained in the collective consciousness of Chicagoans, who have learned to embrace the unpredictability with a sense of humor. We've come to expect the unexpected, knowing that the weather can shift from extreme to extreme in the blink of an eye.

So, when someone mentions the saying, "If you don't like the Chicago weather, just wait 15 minutes," it elicits chuckles and knowing nods of agreement. It serves as a reminder always to be prepared for anything, whether carrying an umbrella, layering clothing, or simply adapting our plans to accommodate the whims of the weather gods.

Despite the comical nature of this saying, a sense of camaraderie stems from experiencing these meteorological roller coasters together. We bond over it, sharing stories of how we've been caught off guard or pleasantly surprised by the ever-changing weather patterns. In the end, this funny saying about Chicago weather reflects the resilient spirit of the city and its inhabitants. We've learned to adapt, to find humor in the face of uncertainty, and to appreciate the beauty of each fleeting weather moment. So, if you see yourself in Chicago and the weather doesn't suit your preferences, fear not. Just wait 15 minutes, and you'll witness a complete transformation, leaving you in awe and chuckling at the whimsical nature of Chicago's weather.

Since then, I've carried his words with me: the lighthearted quote about Chicago's weather and the valuable reminder to prioritize safety on the road. It's a reminder to not only adapt to life's changes with a smile but also to make responsible choices that ensure the well-being of myself and others.

As I continue my journey as a driver, I look forward to more encounters and conversations that enrich my experiences and leave me with lasting lessons. I've realized that happiness is a choice, and embracing personal freedom is the key to unlocking its true potential. As I drive through the vast expanse of the entire Chicagoland area in Illinois, I encounter individuals from all walks of life, each with their own stories and aspirations.

In this exciting chapter of my story, I immerse myself in the diversity of Chicago's neighborhoods, connecting with people from different backgrounds, cultures, and perspectives. Every passenger entering my vehicle brings a unique energy, a glimpse into their lives, and a reminder that happiness depends not on external circumstances but on our conscious decisions.

Navigating the busy streets, I witness the resilience and strength of the human spirit. I meet individuals who have faced adversity with unwavering determination and embrace personal freedom despite challenges. Their stories inspire me to cultivate a sense of gratitude for my independence, shape my destiny, and find happiness amidst the chaos of life.

Conversations with my passengers taught me that happiness is not a destination but a journey. It's about finding joy in the present moment, appreciating the small victories, and cherishing the connections we forge. It's about embracing freedom and making choices that align with our values and aspirations. I could have chosen to be bitter and angry in challenging situations, but why? Things like potholes and constant weather changes are beyond my control. I could be happy, try to make things light-hearted, and save myself from stress and increased blood pressure. It is much more healing to be satisfied and be wondered than to be angry and depressed. To me, it became a choice. To you, with conscious decisions, it can be too!

As the miles pass, I realize that my role as a driver goes beyond simply ferrying passengers from point A to point B. I can create a positive atmosphere within my vehicle, fostering an environment where conversations flourish, dreams are shared, and laughter echoes through the car's cabin.

I embrace the profound truth that happiness is a choice. As I continue to weave through the intricate streets of Chicago and the surrounding areas, I am reminded to savor the journey, appreciate the diversity surrounding me, and empower others to embrace their freedom.

In these moments, as I witness the resilience and determination of those I encounter, I am reminded that happiness is not a fleeting destination but a lifelong pursuit, a choice to be made every day on every mile of this incredible journey.

Some trips have been brief, lasting only half a mile, while others have extended for an astonishing 300 miles. On occasion, I've embarked on long-haul journeys that spanned up to 10 hours, accounting for the five-hour drive to the destination, five hours for the return trip, and the necessary stops for fuel and restroom breaks. The passengers, too, have been troopers, enduring these extensive journeys with patience and grace. My trips have taken me far and wide, from the streets of Milwaukee, Green Bay, and Racine in Wisconsin to the historic cities of Springfield, Decatur, Peoria, Rockford, and Galena in Illinois. I've even embarked on ventures reaching as far as South Bend and Valparaiso in Indiana. Occasionally, I've been fortunate enough to transport passengers to the vibrant city of Cincinnati, Ohio.

Throughout these countless miles, as the wheels of my vehicle have carried me through bustling streets and serene neighborhoods, I've had the privilege of engaging in numerous conversations with people of varied job positions and perspectives. These diverse excursions have become windows into the lives and stories of individuals from all walks of life. From the backseat of my car, I have witnessed the unfolding narratives of humanity, each passenger offering a snippet of their journey.

In the realm of my backseat confessions, I have immersed myself in the world of business executives, their voices resonating with ambition and determination as they discuss their latest endeavors and strategies for success. Their stories have painted a vivid picture of the challenges and triumphs that accompany the pursuit of professional greatness.

Conversely, I have been privileged to listen to students' dreams and aspirations, their youthful enthusiasm fueling conversations that teem with hope and possibility. From aspiring doctors and lawyers to aspiring artists and writers, their passions have breathed life into my car, transforming it into a haven of dreams and aspirations.

But it doesn't stop there. The kaleidoscope of human experience continues to unfold as I encounter artists who pour their souls onto canvases, scientists who unravel the mysteries of the universe, athletes who push the boundaries of physical achievement, and adventurers who seek thrills and exploration. Like a carefully woven thread, each interaction adds to the rich tapestry of human existence.

These encounters have expanded my understanding of the world, broadening my horizons beyond the confines of my own experiences. They have taught me that beauty and wisdom can be found in the stories of others, regardless of their background or occupation. Each conversation has been an opportunity for growth, a chance to learn from the remarkable individuals who have graced my car with their presence.

As I continue this journey as a ride-share driver, I eagerly anticipate the next passenger and story waiting to be shared. In each interaction, I am reminded of humanity's profound interconnectedness and the power of dialogue to bridge the gaps that separate us from the highways of the Chicagoland area; I look forward to countless adventures. Every turn of the wheel promises new encounters and captivating stories, ensuring that no day behind the wheel is ever mundane.

In my exhilarating journeys through the vast expanse of the Chicagoland area, I've had the extraordinary privilege of encountering everyday individuals and notable figures from various fields. Along the way, I've had the pleasure of meeting famous newscasters who have graced our television screens with their commanding presence and eloquent delivery. Their insights into the world of journalism and their firsthand experiences have left an indelible mark on me.

Additionally, I've had the honor of meeting renowned weather forecasters whose voices have become synonymous with accurate forecasts and the ever-changing moods of the sky. Their passion for understanding atmospheric phenomena and their ability to convey complex weather patterns to the public have fascinated and educated me.

Interacting with renowned weather forecasters and experiencing their expertise in accurately predicting weather patterns can be a remarkable and enlightening experience. These individuals possess a deep passion for understanding the intricacies of atmospheric phenomena and are skilled at communicating complex weather information to the general public. Weathermen play a vital role in our lives, helping us prepare for and navigate through the ever-changing moods of the sky. They study meteorology, analyzing data from various sources such as satellites, radars, and weather models to develop forecasts that can guide our daily activities and long-term planning. Their knowledge extends beyond simply predicting whether it will rain or shine. They delve into the science of weather systems, including high and low-pressure systems, atmospheric conditions, wind patterns, and precipitation. By interpreting these factors, they can provide accurate and detailed forecasts, enabling individuals, communities, and organizations to make informed decisions and take necessary precautions.

Weather forecasters can effectively convey these complex weather patterns to the public, which is an actual skill. They use various communication channels, such as television, radio, websites, and mobile apps, to disseminate weather information that is accessible and understandable to a broad audience. Clear explanations, visuals, and engaging storytelling help us comprehend the weather dynamics, its potential impacts, and how to stay safe and prepared.

Their dedication to their craft and commitment to keeping the public informed and safe is admirable. Their work goes beyond just providing forecasts; they often play a significant role during severe weather events, providing real-time updates, warnings, and guidance to ensure public safety. Interacting with renowned weather forecasters can be inspiring as their passion, knowledge, and educational ability have a profound impact. Their expertise enhances our understanding of weather and fosters a sense of curiosity and appreciation for the natural world around us.

In summary, encountering renowned weather forecasters who possess a deep passion for understanding atmospheric phenomena and can convey complex weather patterns to the public can be a fascinating and educational experience. Their accurate forecasts and dedication to keeping the public informed contribute to our understanding of weather and help us make informed decisions. Their work serves as a reminder of the intricate and ever-changing nature of our environment, inspiring us to appreciate and respect the forces of nature.

It's genuinely serendipitous when life presents us with unexpected encounters that leave a lasting impact. The opportunity to transport Ashton, the drummer from the Five Seconds of Summer, was an extraordinary experience, especially when their rhythmic talents have captivated audiences worldwide. Drummers often hold a unique position within a band, as their beats and rhythms provide the backbone of the music, setting the pace and energy for the entire performance. Hearing about his experiences on the road and the stories he had to share was incredibly inspiring, offering insights into the world of music and the creative process.

The ability to communicate with Ashton during stressful rush hour traffic demonstrated that even though he was a celebrity, it's always great to be humble and maintain a down-to-earth nature. Despite fame and success, he remained approachable and open to connecting with others, even in mundane situations. This encounter showcases the power of genuine human connection and its impact on our sense of freedom and happiness. With the chaotic rush hour traffic, the drummer's willingness to converse and share their stories becomes a source of hope. It reminds us that even amid external pressures and challenges, there is the potential for authentic connection and meaningful interactions. It serves as a reminder that happiness and freedom can be found in the simplest of moments when we allow ourselves to be open to the experiences and stories of others.

This encounter inspired a sense of liberation, reminding me of the importance of embracing freedom and finding happiness in the present moment. It highlights the transformative power of human connection, as the drummer's ability to share their experiences and engage with you during that traffic-filled journey left a profound impact. The unexpected encounter with a renowned drummer from a famous band offers a unique perspective on the power of human connection and the potential for inspiration in everyday moments. Their rhythmic talents, experiences on the road, and willingness to share their stories demonstrate the transformative impact of music and authentic communication. This encounter serves as a reminder to find freedom and happiness by embracing the present moment and being open to the experiences and stories of others.

Furthermore, I was extremely fortunate to have a conversation with a NASA astronaut recently. What made it even more special was that their brother was also a part of NASA and had just returned from a thrilling space expedition. As I spoke with this astronaut, I couldn't help but feel a sense of awe and admiration for these brave men and women who venture beyond our atmosphere to explore the vast unknown. Listening to his firsthand accounts of space missions and the wonders he had witnessed from afar was genuinely captivating. It was as if I was transported to another world, hearing stories that seemed straight out of a science fiction novel. The sheer magnitude of his experiences and the breathtaking sights they encountered left me in awe.

As the astronaut passenger described the feeling of weightlessness, the beauty of Earth from space, and the challenges he faced during the missions, I couldn't help but feel a renewed appreciation for human exploration's boundless possibilities. These astronauts are pioneers, pushing the boundaries of what we thought was possible and expanding our understanding of the universe.

Interacting with someone who has been to space and witnessed the wonders of the cosmos firsthand made me realize how privileged we are to live in a time where such incredible feats are achievable. It reminded me of the indomitable spirit of exploration that has driven humanity throughout history. The conversation left me with a deep sense of gratitude for the dedication and courage of these astronauts. They willingly embark on perilous journeys into the unknown, facing countless challenges and risks, all in the pursuit of advancing our knowledge and understanding of the universe. Their stories have ignited a spark, fueling my curiosity about space and its possibilities. They have inspired me to continue exploring and learning, to embrace the unknown with courage and wonder.

Ultimately, my conversation with the NASA astronaut and hearing about his brother's space expedition were unforgettable experiences. They reinforced my belief in the power of human exploration and left me with a profound admiration for those who dare to venture beyond our atmosphere into the vastness of space.

On certain occasions, I've been honored with the opportunity to transport military personnel who have served in high-tech weapons divisions. Interacting with these remarkable individuals has been nothing short of awe-inspiring. Their unwavering dedication to protecting our nation and their profound expertise in cutting-edge technologies have left a lasting impression on me.

To witness firsthand the commitment and bravery of these men and women is truly humbling. They carry the weight of immense responsibility on their shoulders, knowing that their expertise and skills play a crucial role in ensuring the safety and security of our country. Their unwavering devotion to duty is evident in every conversation and interaction.

What strikes me the most is their deep knowledge and understanding of advanced technologies. These military personnel possess a truly remarkable level of expertise. They have honed their skills to operate and maintain intricate systems and weaponry to defend our nation against evolving threats.

My conversations with them have opened my eyes to modern warfare's complex and ever-evolving nature. They have shared stories of training in state-of-the-art facilities, mastering sophisticated equipment, and adapting to the rapidly changing warfare landscape. Their ability to stay ahead of the curve in an era of technological advancements is impressive and inspiring.

Moreover, their level of professionalism and discipline is unparalleled. These military personnel exemplify the values of honor, integrity, and selflessness. Their unwavering commitment to duty and willingness to risk their lives for the greater good are commendable.

Transporting these individuals has given me a deeper appreciation for the sacrifices they make and the challenges they face. Their unwavering dedication and expertise remind us of our armed forces' immense capabilities and resilience. It has instilled in me a profound gratitude for those who serve and protect our nation. Because of them, we get to do whatever we want in this beautiful country, like writing a book and having freedom of speech.

In conclusion, the privilege of interacting with military personnel from high-tech weapons divisions has left an indelible mark on me. Their commitment to safeguarding our nation, mastery of cutting-edge technologies, and unwavering bravery have deepened my admiration for their service. It is an honor to be in the presence of such remarkable individuals who embody the very essence of dedication and sacrifice.

Indeed, I've also had the pleasure of encountering ambitious students who aspire to become our nation's future. Interacting with these driven and enthusiastic young minds has been incredibly inspiring. They embody the hope and potential that lies within the next generation.

In conversations with these students, I have witnessed their unwavering determination and hunger for knowledge and growth. They possess a remarkable thirst for learning and constantly seek opportunities to expand their horizons and excel in their chosen fields.

What impresses me the most is their vision for the future and eagerness to make a positive impact. They are not content with merely following in the footsteps of those who came before them; instead, they aspire to be trailblazers and shape the trajectory of our society. Their ambition knows no bounds as they dream of creating innovative solutions, advancing technology, fostering social change, and contributing to the betterment of our nation.

These students are unafraid to challenge the status quo and think outside the box. They are willing to take risks, embrace failure as an opportunity to learn, and persist in adversity. Their remarkable resilience and determination are testaments to their unwavering belief in their abilities and the power of their dreams.

Moreover, their passion and enthusiasm are contagious. Interacting with them ignites a sense of optimism and reminds me of each individual's incredible potential. They remind me that our nation's future is in capable hands and that as they grow and develop, they will contribute to the progress and prosperity of our society. They always remind my friends Manolo and Clyde to never give up and to do their best in anything.

Witnessing their journey as they navigate their education, pursue internships, research, and participate in various extracurricular activities is genuinely inspiring. Their commitment to personal growth and dedication to making a difference in their respective fields is commendable.

Encountering these ambitious students reaffirms my belief in the power of education and its transformative impact on individuals and society. They represent the hope and promise of a brighter future filled with innovation, progress, and positive change.

The encounters I've had with ambitious students aspiring to become the future leaders of our nation have been incredibly uplifting. Their determination, passion, and vision for the future instill a sense of optimism and excitement. They are a constant reminder of the potential that lies within each individual and the transformative power of education and ambition. It is a privilege to witness their journey and to be a part of their growth as they shape the future of our nation.

They have made my journeys even more extraordinary. Each interaction has expanded my horizons, offering unique insights into their respective fields and reaffirming the limitless potential within each individual. The prospect of meeting more inspiring figures and hearing their captivating stories constantly reminds us of our world's incredible diversity and boundless opportunities.

Amidst my eventful journeys, I've had the privilege of transporting incredibly talented architectural designers who have played a pivotal role in shaping the magnificent cityscape of Chicago. It was a unique experience to be entrusted with their precious blueprints, carefully rolled up in tubes and safely stored in the trunk of my car. As we navigated the bustling city streets, these visionary designers would enthusiastically share intricate details about the buildings they had meticulously crafted, leaving an indelible mark on the urban landscape.

Listening to these architects passionately discuss their creations was like embarking on a captivating journey through the city's architectural history. With every turn of the wheel, they pointed out their masterpieces, eagerly sharing stories behind their inspiration, design principles, and challenges. Their deep knowledge and understanding of their craft brought a new dimension to my appreciation of the Chicago skyline.

Each building had its own unique story. They would describe the fusion of art and engineering, the innovative use of materials, and the careful consideration of functionality and aesthetics that went into their designs. From soaring skyscrapers to elegant bridges, every architectural marvel seemed to have a tale to tell.

What struck me most was the passion that radiated from these designers. Their love for their craft was evident in every word they spoke, and their eyes would light up as they shared their vision for the city's future. Their dedication to creating spaces harmonizing with the surrounding environment and enhancing the human experience was truly inspiring.

As I drove through the city, accompanied by these architectural visionaries, I saw familiar buildings in a new light. The details and nuances I had previously overlooked now came to life, as I could appreciate the thoughtfulness and creativity that went into their construction.

Transporting these talented designers not only deepened my admiration for their work but also instilled in me a renewed appreciation for the power of architecture to shape our experiences and define the character of a city. Their creations stood as testaments to the transformative impact that visionary design can have on a community.

In conclusion, the journeys I've had the pleasure of undertaking with talented architectural designers in Chicago have been truly memorable. Their passion, knowledge, and dedication have left an indelible mark on the city's skyline. Transporting their precious blueprints and hearing their stories has enriched my understanding of the architectural wonders that grace the city. It is a testament to the power of design to shape our surroundings and inspire us to see the world in new and extraordinary ways.

In addition to transporting talented architectural designers, I've had the delightful opportunity to pick up tour guides with an incredible wealth of knowledge about the city's history and landmarks. These passionate individuals can transform each ride into an immersive cultural experience as they weave captivating tales of bygone eras and unveil hidden gems in the city's streets.

Their enthusiasm for the city's history was palpable when they entered my car. They would greet me with a warm smile and begin painting vivid pictures of the past, transporting me back in time to witness the events and experiences that shaped the very fabric of the city. As we traversed the streets, these tour guides would point out significant landmarks, sharing captivating stories behind each one. They would recount the historical significance, architectural details, and the people who played critical roles in shaping these iconic sites. Their wealth of knowledge extended beyond the well-known landmarks, as they would also introduce me to hidden gems that only the most astute locals could uncover. These lesser-known places held countless stories, allowing me to see the city through a new lens and appreciate its rich tapestry of history and culture.

What truly stood out was their passion for their craft. It was evident in their animated storytelling, attention to detail, and genuine excitement as they uncovered the layers of the city's past. Their dedication to preserving and sharing the city's history was inspiring. These tour guides taught me about the city through their expertise and instilled a profound connection and belonging. They made me realize that a city is more than just concrete and steel—it is a living, breathing entity with a vibrant history and vast knowledge cemented in its very existence.

The conversations with these tour guides have left a lasting impression on me, fostering a deep appreciation for the cities I traverse. They have taught me that behind every building, every street, and every neighborhood, there is a story waiting to be discovered. They have encouraged me to explore, delve into the hidden corners of cities, and uncover the narratives that bring them to life.

Picking up tour guides who share fascinating stories about the city's history and landmarks has been an enriching experience. Their expertise, passion, and dedication to their craft have transformed each ride into a cultural journey filled with captivating tales and hidden treasures. They have deepened my appreciation for the cities I encounter, revealing the layers of history and culture that make them truly remarkable.

Among the diverse range of passengers I've had the pleasure of transporting, I've encountered hotel workers, servers, and chefs who have all played a crucial role in shaping the vibrant hospitality scene of Chicago. These individuals, with their unique perspectives and experiences, have provided fascinating insights into the city's hotels and restaurants' inner workings and unwavering commitment to delivering exceptional experiences to visitors and locals alike.

Their passion for their work was evident when they stepped into my car. Whether they worked at renowned hotels or bustling restaurants, their enthusiasm for the hospitality industry shone through in every conversation. They would eagerly share stories of their daily routines, their challenges, and the joy they derived from creating memorable moments for guests.

Hotel workers, in particular, would describe the behind-the-scenes operations that often go unnoticed by visitors. They would discuss the meticulous planning and coordination required to ensure a seamless guest experience, from check-in to check-out. They would also share anecdotes about going the extra mile to accommodate special requests, guaranteeing each guest felt valued and cared for.

Servers and chefs, on the other hand, would delight in discussing the artistry and creativity that goes into crafting a memorable dining experience. They would describe the careful selection of ingredients, the precision in preparing each dish, and the joy of seeing the delight on diners' faces. Their passion for their craft was infectious, making me appreciate the Chicago dining scene on a new level.

What struck me the most about these individuals was their dedication to excellence. They took immense pride in their work and were continuously striving to exceed expectations. Their commitment to providing exceptional experiences was unwavering, even amid long hours and demanding customers. They embodied the spirit of hospitality, ensuring every interaction was imbued with warmth, attentiveness, and genuine care.

The hospitality workers I encountered were often the city's unsung heroes. They worked tirelessly behind the scenes, making the city come alive through their efforts. Their commitment to creating memorable experiences for visitors and residents played a vital role in shaping Chicago's reputation as a top-notch hospitality destination.

My encounters with industry workers have added a delightful flavor to my experiences as a transportation provider. Their insights into the inner workings of the Chicago hospitality industry and their unwavering dedication to providing exceptional experiences have enriched our conversations. They are the driving force behind the vibrant hospitality scene, and their passion and commitment are commendable.

Furthermore, I've had the privilege of transporting hardworking construction workers who have played a vital role in shaping the city's ever-evolving landscape. These dedicated individuals have shared their stories of teamwork, craftsmanship, and unwavering commitment to their craft, leaving me in awe of the intricate process behind bringing architectural dreams to life.

As these construction workers stepped into my car, their worn-out boots and tools were a testament to their tireless efforts. Their hands, calloused from years of labor, spoke volumes about the hard work and dedication they put into their craft. They took immense pride in their role as builders, shaping the city with their hands and expertise.

During our rides, they would passionately recount the projects they had worked on, sharing the challenges they encountered and the triumphs they celebrated. From towering skyscrapers to intricate bridges, they describe the careful planning, precise execution, and collaborative effort that went into each construction endeavor.

Their stories illuminated the behind-the-scenes construction world, revealing the intricacies and complexities of turning architectural designs into physical realities. They explained the meticulous attention to detail required to ensure structural integrity, the coordination among various trades, and the constant adaptation to changing conditions on the job site.

What struck me the most was their unwavering dedication to their craft. They spoke of long hours, physically demanding work, and the need to continuously learn and adapt to new techniques and technologies. Despite these challenges, their passion for construction remained unwavering. They took immense pride in their ability to contribute to the city's growth and development, knowing that their hard work would leave a lasting impact on the urban landscape.

Moreover, their stories highlighted the power of teamwork and collaboration. They emphasized the importance of effective communication, trust, and mutual respect among the professionals involved in a construction project. From architects and engineers to electricians and plumbers, they spoke of the collective effort required to bring a vision to life.

Encountering these hardworking construction workers has deepened my appreciation for their transformational impact on our cities. Their dedication, craftsmanship, and unwavering commitment to their craft are awe-inspiring. They are the unsung heroes behind every architectural marvel, shaping the city's skyline and creating spaces that enrich our lives.

In conclusion, the privilege of transporting hardworking construction workers has shed light on the remarkable process behind shaping the city's landscape. Their stories of teamwork, craftsmanship, and dedication to their craft have left me in awe of their contributions. They embody the spirit of hard work, resilience, and passion, reminding us of the immense effort required to turn architectural dreams into tangible realities. Their unwavering commitment to their craft is commendable, and their impact on our cities is immeasurable.

Engaging in conversations with these diverse individuals has been a source of great joy for me. While some passengers preferred to remain silent, I always deeply respected their choices. I understood that there are times when people want to enjoy a quiet journey or reflect on their thoughts. Respecting their boundaries and understanding their need for solitude was essential to my role as a driver.

Each interaction with these remarkable individuals has taught me valuable lessons about the power of human connection and the rich tapestry of experiences within a lively city like Chicago. As I continue my driving adventures, I respect every passenger's preferences, knowing that each journey holds the potential for meaningful connections and the discovery of new perspectives.

In addition to celebrating the remarkable individuals I've encountered, it is essential to recognize that happiness is a choice that encompasses embracing personal freedom. Amidst the diverse array of passengers I've had the pleasure of driving, I've witnessed firsthand the profound impact that individual liberty and the power of choice can have on one's happiness.

Throughout my journeys, I've encountered individuals from all walks of life who have exemplified the transformative effects of choosing personal freedom. Some passengers radiated joy and contentment, embracing their passions and making conscious decisions to live on their terms. Whether pursuing a creative endeavor, embarking on an adventurous journey, or cultivating meaningful relationships, they demonstrated the liberating power of choosing a path that aligns with their true selves.]

Conversely, I've encountered numerous individuals who appeared burdened by circumstances or trapped within societal expectations. However, even within these challenging situations, I witnessed the resilience of the human spirit. Some passengers expressed a desire for change, a longing to break free from the shackles that held them back. In these moments, I realized the importance of personal freedom and its profound impact on one's overall well-being.

While external factors may impose limitations, the power of choice lies within each individual. By embracing personal freedom, we can make conscious decisions that align with our values, passions, and desires. In these choices, we find the path to happiness and fulfillment. I'm reminded of the significance of personal freedom and its transformative effect on our lives. I encourage each passenger I encounter to embrace their choices, pursue their dreams, and find joy in their journey. May we all seize the moment to exercise personal freedom, making choices that bring us closer to a life filled with happiness, purpose, and personal fulfillment.

One day, as I navigated the city streets, I welcomed a new passenger named Mina into my car. It was one of the hottest days of the year during the summertime. The atmosphere was tinged with an unspoken unease, and I couldn't help but notice the distress that lingered in the air. It was as if the weight of the world rested upon her shoulders. Intrigued by her energy, I turned my attention to her, ready to embark on a journey that would transcend the physical miles we would cover.

Mina said, "It's getting hot in here. Can I turn up the air conditioner?"

"Of course. It's only full blast now at the lowest temperature possible", I replied.

As we embarked on our shared adventure, she found solace in her mom's and friend's familiar voices, pouring her heart out over her cell phone. The turmoil in her voice revealed a relationship teetering on the edge, a precarious balance between holding on and letting go. It was a crossroads that demanded her attention, a fork in the road where diverging paths beckoned her to choose her destiny.

All of a sudden, Mina made contact with the rear mirror. *She asked, "Tell me what you think from what you just heard."*

Moved by her vulnerability, Mina turned to me, seeking wisdom and perspective. With genuine care in my voice, I offered her a safe space to explore her thoughts and emotions. She shared the intricacies of her situation, and I listened intently, absorbing the layers of her story.

I replied, "I'm not sure. You mean to tell me what I think?"

She replied, "Yes, I'm asking for advice. We have an over-an-hour trip together to talk on the way to Rockford. We might as well get more comfortable in our conversation. Don't worry, you won't get in trouble."

"Haha, thanks. I appreciate it. I may have a lot of experience in life and relationships, and I have been a driver for ten years, dealing with many personalities of all differences and countless experiences. I'd be happy to share my knowledge with you in any way I can."

As the car's wheels spun onward, our conversation became a dance of introspection and exploration. I gently prodded her to examine the depths of her heart, to question her desires and motivations. We delved into the complexities of relationships, peeling back the layers to reveal the nuanced dynamics at play.

Together, we navigated the labyrinth of emotions on the interstate highway, pondering the delicate balance between her personal happiness and her partner's well-being. I encouraged her to consider the power of open communication, the strength of understanding each other's needs, and the significance of finding common ground. We explored the art of compromise, recognizing the sacrifices required to create a harmonious union.

As our journey unfolded, she absorbed the insights and perspectives that danced between us. I saw the flicker of clarity ignite within her eyes, a flame of understanding and self-awareness. While the decision before her remained daunting, she now possessed a more profound sense of her values and aspirations.

With a concerned look on Mina's face, "I'm struggling with something lately. It's about my partner's friends. They've been gossiping about me behind my back, making me uncomfortable. I don't know how to handle this situation. What should I do?"

I lower the air conditioner's setting and say, "Oh, I'm sorry to hear that, Mina. Gossip can be hurtful and create unnecessary tension. It's essential to address it and find a resolution. Have you talked to your partner about this?"

"Yes, I did, but he hesitates to confront his friends. He doesn't want to cause any conflicts or strain their

relationship. But it's bothering me, and I feel he should stand up for me," she said as she fixed her makeup.

"I completely understand where you're coming from, Mina. In such a situation, your partner must prioritize your feelings and relationship over his friends. He needs to clarify that he won't tolerate gossip about you. He is in a relationship with you, not with his friends. He needs to prioritize you over them."

"That's exactly what I've been thinking. But how do I make him understand that it's important?"

"Communication is key here. Have an open and honest conversation with your partner. Express your concerns and how the gossip is affecting you. Let him know that he needs to find courage and that you need his support. He should firmly respond to his friends when they bring up these negative discussions."

"I see. So, I should tell him how I want him to reply and that he should prioritize me over them?"

"Exactly, Mina. Let him know that you expect him to defend you and your relationship. He needs to show that your well-being and happiness come first. Trust and loyalty are vital in any relationship, and he should tell his friends that he won't tolerate negative talk about you."

"Thank you so much for your advice. I needed someone to talk this through with. I'll talk with my partner and tell him how much it means to me."

"You're welcome, Mina. I'm glad I could provide some guidance. Remember, you deserve to be respected and supported. Don't hesitate to communicate your needs and expectations. I hope everything works out well for you and your partner."

"Thanks again, Marshall. I appreciate your perspective."

Mina then said, "You know something? You are such an inspirational person. I'll be looking forward to reading your book one day."

Laughing in shock, I replied, "How did you know I planned
to write a book? I was thinking of it, but once twenty-thirty
people say you should write a book, I guess it tells me maybe I
should write one, shouldn't I?"

Mina gave me a smirk as we both laughed. While driving on the I-90 W highway from the Hyde Park neighborhood in Chicago, a memory from the distant past re-entered my mind with a conversation I had with my first Culinary Instructor. I learned something significant in Culinary school from my first culinary instructor at CHIC (The Cooking and Hospitality Insititute of Chicago) LeCordon Bleu Chicago. He was an extraordinary Corporate Chef at the Chicago Tribune. He was always very hard on me while mentoring me, but I am very grateful for every lesson. He even offered me a position out of school.

"Chef Romaine, one of the most valuable lessons I learned at
CHIC was from you. You were my first culinary instructor,
and your mentorship profoundly impacted me. I'm incredibly
grateful for every lesson and experience."

Chef Romaine gave me a stern look. "Ah, it's wonderful to
hear that, Marshall. I remember those days well. You were

terrible. I should have failed you so you could retake Culinary 101."

I laughed because I knew receiving harsh lessons in the culinary world from one's superior meant it was a place coming from the heart. "One thing you said has always stayed with me, Chef. You asked me, 'Are you happy?"

I felt confused at the time. "Yes," I answered as I thought to myself. I guess I am happy. "Yes, I am happy", I replied.

"OK, good Marshall. As long as you are happy, that is the only thing that matters. You emphasized that happiness is the only thing that truly matters, which has stuck with me ever since."

"Indeed, happiness is the key, my young chef. In this demanding industry, it's easy to get caught up in the hustle and lose sight of what truly matters. As long as you find joy and contentment in your actions, everything else falls into place."

"Those words have guided me through my career, Chef. Whenever I face challenges or doubts, I remember your advice. It reminds me to prioritize my happiness and well-being."

Chef Romaine: "I'm glad to hear that, Marshall. It warms my heart to know that my teachings have made a positive difference in your journey. Remember, success may come in many forms, but genuine happiness is the ultimate measure of fulfillment."

"Thank you, Chef Romaine, for pushing me to be my best and instilling in me the importance of happiness. I'm forever grateful for the opportunity you offered me after culinary school. Your mentorship has truly shaped my path."

"It was my pleasure, Marshall. You showed great potential, and I knew you had a bright future. I'm proud of the chef you've become. Keep pursuing your passion and always prioritize your happiness. That is what truly matters in life."

"I will, Chef. Your words will continue to guide me as I navigate this world. Thank you for everything."

"You're most welcome, Marshall. Remember, a happy chef creates the most delicious dishes. Keep that fire alive, and I have no doubt you will continue to find success. Bon appétit!"

Those words stayed with me sincerely to this very day, and I was more than happy to share them with my passenger, who needed this advice during this delicate situation that she was dealing with.

As we drove through the long highway through the corn fields, the present came back into my mind as I asked Mina, "Are you happy? That is all that matters in life. As long as you are happy, that is the only thing that matters. To be happy in any relationship, it is important to compromise. Always ask if it is worth it. Is it worth compromising from each side to make things work, or is what's sacrificed, such as self-worth, not worth it to compromise?"

She then realized that I was right. She needed to find a way to communicate to her boyfriend that he needed to respect her and choose his girlfriend's respect over his friends' negative gossiping. I was so happy that I could have helped someone I didn't know in such a short time. As we reached her destination, a contagious positive energy filled the air. I sensed the weight of her contemplation, the gravity of the choices that awaited her. With a heart of gratitude, she stepped out of the car, ready to face her path with newfound strength and resolve.

"Have a good one," I said as she exited the car.

As Mina smiled, she said, "You have a good one, too, and I look forward to reading your book in the future."

It was funny, as if she could read my mind and knew what I was thinking. It was a reminder that the road to happiness is often paved with uncertainty, but armed with self-reflection and the wisdom gained through shared experiences, she would find the courage to make the choice that resonated with her most authentic self. As I watched her disappear into the memory of life, I knew our encounter had left an indelible mark on both of us. The roads we travel are adorned with crossroads and unknown destinations, but in these moments of self-discovery and contemplation, we find the strength to navigate the twists and turns ahead.

In this captivating exploration of personal happiness, we delve into the stories of individuals who have chosen different paths in life. From a contented friend who embraces the advantages of living alone to a passenger seeking advice from a troubled relationship, we discover the power of personal choice in shaping our happiness. By examining the importance of relationships, the pursuit of individual goals, and the willingness to compromise, we highlight the profound impact of these choices on our well-being.

Once upon a time, there was a military veteran named Todd who had endured a lifetime of challenges, including failed relationships, a difficult upbringing, and an injury sustained during their service. Despite the well-intentioned advice and support offered by those around them, this individual remained steadfast in his bitterness and negativity. He seemed trapped in a cycle of pessimism, always anticipating the worst outcomes and refusing to embrace the potential for happiness.

I tried to offer some perspective to Todd, saying, "It's about being happy in life. Are you happy?"

As I consulted with Todd, who shared an intriguing perspective on relationships, he replied, "It's not about being happy. It's about being practical and knowing how to protect yourself from situations." Curiosity piqued, I urged him to elaborate further.

I emphasized the importance of practicality, stating, "In relationships, it's crucial to make rational decisions based on practical considerations rather than being driven solely by emotions." I stressed the need to consider compatibility, financial stability, and long-term goals to ensure a solid foundation.

"Todd, I appreciate your insight on emotional vulnerability. Opening oneself up to love indeed comes with risks. Heartbreak, disappointment, and conflicts can arise from our emotional investment in a partnership."

"Absolutely. I've experienced the consequences of emotional vulnerability firsthand. I had a Colombian girlfriend whom I dated while in Colombia, but then I had to move to China. Unfortunately, I didn't give her as much attention as I should have, and she ended up dating someone else and leaving me. She even moved to Pittsburgh with the guy."

"It sounds like a tricky situation, Todd. Moving to China and not maintaining strong communication could have significantly influenced the outcome. Things might have

turned out differently if you had taken her with you or found a way to involve her in your business ventures in China. It would be best if you considered making more effort to prioritize your relationship and keep the lines of communication open. It was a missed opportunity, and you should learn from that experience.

"Looking back, I did not even think about that. I was more focused on business in China at the time. I even asked her to stop communicating as much so I could focus more on my business."

"Yes, Todd, but you brought up this relationship with your ex-girlfriend several times already. You still have feelings for her. You can't stop thinking about her and talking about her. Communication and connection are crucial, especially in long-distance relationships. It's important to make your partner feel valued and included, even when circumstances change. It's a lesson I've taken to heart as well."

"Yeah, I know what your relationship is as well. Don't worry; you'll figure it out. "

"Don't worry about my relationship, Todd. I fully know what kind of relationship I am in, and we are both happy. I'm glad I could offer some insights, Todd. Relationships require effort, understanding, and consistent communication. By learning from our experiences, we can create healthier and more fulfilling connections in the future."

Todd replied, "Do you know what you're getting yourself into? I don't think you do."

"Todd, I understand you strongly believe in adverse constructive outcomes and may not believe in happiness. It's important to respect your perspective and experiences. However, it's worth considering that life can offer a range of positive and negative experiences. While there may be challenges and disappointments, there can also be moments of joy and fulfillment."

"I appreciate your understanding, but I've seen too much evidence of the adverse outcomes in relationships and life. It's difficult for me to believe in the possibility of lasting happiness. I'm a miserable person, and misery loves company."

301

"Understandably, your experiences have shaped your beliefs, Todd. It can be challenging to see beyond the negative when that's what we've encountered. However, it's important to remain open to the possibility of positive outcomes and to keep an open mind. Life can surprise us with unexpected moments of happiness and fulfillment."

"I hear what you're saying but find it hard to let go of my skepticism. It feels safer to expect the worst rather than risk disappointment. The way you think is not how the world works. Here are all the crimes that happen in Colombia. All these tourists are getting drugged and murdered."

"It's natural to want to protect oneself from potential disappointment, Todd. However, it's important to remember that shutting ourselves off completely can prevent us from experiencing life's joys and growth. It's a delicate balance and, ultimately, a personal choice. All those tourists being targeted are such a tiny percentage. More crime happens in cities like Chicago, where we live, and other cities. Come on, Todd, stop trying to have such a negative outlook on life!"

"I understand where you're coming from, but I prefer to focus on what I know and can control. Being realistic tends to be a more predictable path for me."

"That's a valid choice, Todd. Each person has a way of navigating life and finding fulfillment. It's important to prioritize what feels right for you and to make choices that align with your values and beliefs."

"I don't think you know what you're getting yourself into in this relationship."

" I appreciate your concern, but I am very confident and know exactly what I'm getting into. I have a different approach and outlook on life. Don't worry about it. I am building a relationship based on trust, respect, and foundation. It's important to have a strong foundation, especially built on trust, to build an amazing relationship. Let's respect and support each other's choices as we continue our journeys. Wishing you all the best in finding what brings you peace and fulfillment."

As our conversation deepened, he delved into the negatives of being in a relationship. "One of the drawbacks is the potential loss of personal freedom," he explained.

I added, "Being committed to a partner often requires compromising on personal decisions, adjusting schedules, and sharing responsibilities."

He continued, shedding light on another aspect, saying, "Emotional vulnerability is a significant risk. Opening yourself up to love means exposing yourself to the possibility of heartbreak, disappointment, and conflicts that arise from the inherent emotional investment in a partnership."

I touched upon the topic of sacrifices and compromises, remarking, "Relationships often demand sacrifice and compromise. You need to be willing to adapt, compromise on personal preferences, and make concessions to meet your partner's needs and desires."

He acknowledged the challenges when discussing communication, stating, "Effective communication is vital, but it can be difficult. Misunderstandings, differing communication styles, and struggles expressing needs and concerns can strain relationships."

Lastly, he addressed trust and betrayal, cautioning, "Trust is the foundation of any relationship, but it's not immune to potential breaches. Infidelity, dishonesty, and betrayal can lead to emotional pain and severe strain on the relationship." This was what he was dealing with the most.

"Todd, I apologize for the confusion. The situation was quite challenging for you. Betrayal and dishonesty can be incredibly painful and damaging to a relationship."

"Yes, that's right. In this case, I thought a mutual acquaintance was my friend who lied about me to my girlfriend. He intentionally misled her, causing her to break up with me and prioritize him over our relationship."

"I can only imagine how difficult and hurtful that must have been for you, Todd. Deception and betrayal can shatter trust and leave deep emotional scars. It's essential to surround yourself with supportive friends and loved ones during challenging times."

"Absolutely. It was devastating to see her believe his lies and choose him over me. Trust and honesty are crucial, and this experience has made me even more cautious about who I let into my life."

"I understand why you would feel that way, Todd. Experiences like these can make us more guarded and hesitant to trust others. It's important to take the time to heal and rebuild trust within yourself before opening up to new relationships."

"You're right. Healing will take time, and I need to focus on rebuilding my sense of trust and self-worth. It's a painful process, but I'm determined to emerge stronger."

"I admire your resilience and determination, Todd. It takes strength to confront the pain caused by betrayal and work towards healing. Remember to be patient with yourself and seek support from those who genuinely care about your well-being."

"Thank you for your understanding and support. It means a lot to me. I'll do my best to navigate this difficult journey and develop a stronger sense of trust and resilience."

"You're welcome, Todd. I believe in your ability to overcome this challenging experience, find happiness, and trust again. Take the time you need to heal, and always remember that you deserve to be in a relationship built on honesty and mutual respect. I wish you all the best on your journey towards healing and finding the fulfilling and trustworthy relationships you deserve. Stay strong and take care."

Ultimately, my conversation with him painted a nuanced picture of relationships, intertwining practicality, self-protection, and the negatives one might encounter. It became evident that his perspective valued caution, self-preservation, and a realistic understanding of the challenges of a relationship.

Todd, a business consultant, shared his past relationships and reluctance to seek compromise in today's generation. Accustomed to analyzing negative and critical situations, he preferred being single rather than navigating the complexities of compromise. Operating from a place driven by fear of loss, he believed remaining unattached was more practical and self-protective. He was also a Military Veteran who was injured in the war. He ran over some dangerous stones in the sand during the Gulf War, which considerably ended up putting him in injury and life-long extreme pain. He had a very negative outlook on life, making numerous mistakes and loosely ignoring many people's advice, which led to his bitterness and pessimistic outlook.

Despite my numerous attempts to encourage positive energy and change in his perspective, the veteran remained ironclad and stationary in his decision to have a bitter life. It became evident that he had chosen to hold onto his grievances and past traumas, allowing him to overshadow any possibility of finding joy in life. He also did not believe in happiness or thought it was an option.

As observers, we can only do so much to influence another person's mindset and choices. While it can be disheartening to witness someone we care about continuously reject happiness, respecting their intention and understanding that they have reasons for choosing their path is essential.

In this case, despite my best intentions and efforts to offer guidance and support, the veteran remained steadfast in refusing to embrace the thought of happiness. To him, it was not about being happy. It was about protecting yourself and earning trust. This situation serves as a reminder that each individual has the freedom to choose their path and determine their level of happiness.

When consciously or subconsciously choosing not to be happy, it's essential to recognize that people have complex inner worlds and varying experiences that shape their perspectives. While some may appear to resist happiness, it's crucial to approach this topic with empathy and understanding.

There can be several reasons why someone might struggle to embrace happiness. Deep-seated beliefs, past traumas, or unresolved emotional issues could influence their mindset. Additionally, societal or cultural factors, personal circumstances, or a lack of self-awareness may affect their decision-making process.

However, it's essential to remember that we cannot control others' choices. Our primary focus should be on our journey towards happiness. By cultivating self-acceptance, practicing self-care, and engaging in activities that bring us joy, we create a foundation for our well-being.

While it is natural to want to help others find happiness, we should recognize our limitations. We can offer support, compassion, and understanding, but ultimately, individuals must take responsibility for their own happiness. Setting healthy boundaries and avoiding becoming emotionally drained or overly invested in others' choices is crucial.

By prioritizing our happiness and personal growth, we can positively influence the lives of those around us. Our genuine contentment can inspire others to reflect on their choices and make positive changes. Leading by example creates an environment that encourages others to explore their paths to happiness.

In summary, while it may be challenging to understand why some individuals subconsciously choose not to be happy, focusing on our journey toward happiness is essential. We can offer support and understanding, but ultimately, each person must decide on their pursuit of happiness. By prioritizing our well-being and leading by example, we can inspire others to find their path to happiness.

As readers engage with this chapter, I hope you will be inspired to assess your decisions and thoroughly consider the impact on your happiness while also considering the perspectives of those around you.

Finding the strength to fight for what truly matters and embracing the compromises necessary for lasting joy and fulfillment is a powerful journey. It requires introspection and a deep understanding of our values, goals, and aspirations.

To align our choices with our goals and aspirations, we must identify what brings us genuine happiness and fulfillment. This involves reflecting on our passions, values, and what gives our lives meaning. Understanding our priorities allows us to make intentional choices that align with our authentic selves.

Personal freedom is an integral part of this process. It means having the autonomy to make choices that align with our values and aspirations, free from external pressures or societal expectations. Embracing personal freedom allows us to live authentically, fostering a sense of authenticity and contentment.

However, personal freedom does not mean pursuing happiness at the expense of others or disregarding the consequences of our actions. It involves recognizing the importance of empathy, compassion, and ethical considerations. Sometimes, compromises are necessary to maintain harmonious relationships and contribute to the greater good. Embracing solitude, pursuing meaningful relationships, and fighting for what we believe in are different paths that can lead to joy and fulfillment. Solitude provides an opportunity for self-reflection, introspection, and personal growth. Meaningful relationships, built on trust, respect, and mutual support, can bring immense joy and a sense of belonging. Fighting for what we believe in, whether advocating for social justice or protecting the environment, can give our lives purpose and create greater fulfillment.

Understanding the nuances of personal freedom and the value of self-reflection empowers us to make choices that align with our deepest values and aspirations. Through this alignment, we can create a fulfilling life that brings us joy, contentment, and a profound sense of purpose. Personal freedom goes beyond the absence of external constraints; it encompasses the liberation of our inner selves and the ability to make conscious decisions that reflect who we are. By taking the time for self-reflection, we gain clarity about our desires, interests, and core beliefs. We explore our passions and uncover what truly matters to us.

Through this process, we become aware of the various factors that shape our lives, such as societal expectations, cultural influences, and personal conditioning. We question whether external pressures drive our choices or if they genuinely resonate with our authentic selves. This introspection allows us to break free from societal norms and embrace our power to shape our path.

We embark on self-discovery and personal fulfillment when we make choices that align with our deepest values and aspirations. These choices may involve taking risks, stepping out of our comfort zones, or pursuing unconventional paths. They may require us to let go of societal expectations and embrace the uncertainty that accompanies following our hearts. While each person's journey is unique, the underlying principle remains the same: embracing our power and living authentically allows us to create a meaningful life. We find joy, contentment, and a profound sense of purpose in this alignment space.

A life lived in alignment with our true selves is not without challenges. There may be obstacles to overcome, sacrifices, and difficult decisions. However, the rewards are immense. We cultivate a deep sense of fulfillment and inner peace by choosing authenticity. We experience a greater connection with ourselves and others as our choices and actions reflect our genuine selves. It is important to remember that the journey towards personal freedom and a fulfilling life is ongoing. As we grow and evolve, our values and aspirations may shift. Self-reflection becomes a lifelong practice, allowing us to reassess our choices and adjust as needed.

Ultimately, by embracing our power, making choices that resonate with our authentic selves, and continually reflecting on our journey, we can create a life characterized by joy, contentment, and a profound sense of purpose. It is a journey well worth embarking upon—leading us towards our own life.

CHAPTER 6 - So is Forgiveness
Free yourself to Self-Liberation and Self-Acceptance

As I reflect upon my tumultuous childhood, I recall a time when even the slightest words could ignite a raging fire within me, engulfing my soul in a storm of anger and stress. Between the ages of 12 and 15, my life was a constant battle, with each situation becoming a brick in the wall of resentment and bitterness that I had erected around myself. The weight of unresolved conflicts and unaddressed wounds consumed my thoughts and tainted my interactions with others. Amidst the chaos, I began to realize that holding onto grudges and harboring anger only served to imprison me further. It became clear that forgiveness was not a gift bestowed upon others but a liberating act of self-love and acceptance.

Fasten your seat belt as we embark on a journey filled with introspection and growth, seeking to untangle the knots that had entwined my heart. I delve into the depths of my pain and confront the wounds that have festered for far too long. It is no easy task, as forgiveness requires confronting the past and embracing vulnerability.

Yet, as I gradually let go of the weight I had carried for years, I started to experience a newfound sense of freedom. Forgiveness became my key to self-liberation, unlocking the doors that had kept me trapped in a cycle of bitterness. With each act of forgiveness, I release the shackles that bound me, allowing myself to heal and grow. Through forgiveness, I learned the power of empathy and compassion, not only towards others but also towards myself. As I extended my forgiveness to those who have caused me pain, I also permitted myself to make mistakes to learn and grow. It is an act of self-acceptance, acknowledging that I am human and deserving of love and understanding.

In this thrilling chapter, forgiveness becomes my guiding light, illuminating the path toward self-liberation and self-acceptance. As I embrace the transformative power of forgiveness, the heavy burden of anger and resentment lifts from my shoulders, making space for peace, healing, and the possibility of a brighter future. So, join me on this exhilarating journey as I navigate the intricate terrain of forgiveness, breaking free from the chains of the past and embracing the boundless potential of self-liberation and self-acceptance.

From my early days in grade school, I faced the formidable challenges of not fitting into society. I was made fun of and bullied for my weight and appearance, carrying on the burden of societal judgment. To my surprise, this journey of anger and resentment was about to take an unexpected last-second turn that would change my life forever. Having been a victim of past bullying in grade school, I felt as though my life at the time was shrouded in darkness and confusion. Plagued by ridicule and a sense of un-acceptance, feelings of rage and despair consumed my days.

High school marked a turning point in my earlier life as my peers and classmates unexpectedly began to recognize the beauty in my uniqueness. I was guided by compassionate guidance counselors with social therapy who showed me the path like a GPS I sought out for a profound transformation in life. Inspired by my different views and perspectives on the world, my peers graciously sought my company for admiration and advice. At that point, I never felt so self-liberated. I was free from the chains of difference and un-acceptance. Never once have I felt so free and accepted. I never thought I would meet people who would look up to me in such an esteemed way. That is when I realized I had been angry for so long and for the wrong reasons.

Flattered and taken aback, the college also marked another turning point. With much graciousness and my unique ability to navigate challenging situations, my peers invited me to many social gatherings. Engaging me in exciting conversations, I eventually became grateful and appreciative of the difference in my ethnic origin, cherishing my uniqueness.

As I entered my early 20s, I embarked on a career as a chef, eagerly pursuing opportunities in various prestigious hotels and restaurants. However, during this time, I carried a deep-seated anger within me, allowing it to poison my interactions and decisions. Unbeknownst to me, this negative pattern would repeat itself, leading to job losses and missed opportunities.

Amidst this tumultuous period, I was confronted with a string of personal losses that compounded my already challenging circumstances. It felt as though the universe had conspired against me as my beloved dog tragically met its end in a devastating accident. Shortly after, I received news of my grandmother's passing, leaving me feeling a profound sense of grief and loss. To add to the emotional turmoil, my girlfriend at the time decided to end our relationship, leaving me feeling abandoned and alone. As if these weren't enough, I also experienced the crushing blow of being fired, adding to the mounting sense of failure and despair.

During these trials, it felt as though the streets of a rough neighborhood were crumbling before me, and I had hit a dead end, with a "do not enter" sign blocking any potential way forward. The weight of these losses and setbacks seemed impossible, and I questioned the purpose and meaning of it all.

However, during these darkest moments, hope began to emerge. As I navigated the wreckage of my personal and professional life, I realized I had a choice. I could become consumed by anger, self-pity, and resentment, or I could use these experiences as catalysts for growth and transformation.\

This realization marked a turning point in my journey. I decided to confront my anger head-on, seeking therapy and engaging in self-reflection to understand its roots and impact on my life. Through this process, I began to unravel the layers of pain and disappointment that had accumulated over the years, learning to let go of the anger that had been holding me back.

As I gradually released the toxic emotions that had plagued me, I discovered a newfound sense of clarity and purpose. I realized I had the power to shape my destiny, regardless of the circumstances that had befallen me. I started to channel my energy into positive pursuits, seeking opportunities for personal and professional growth.

With each setback, I reminded myself I had the strength to overcome any obstacle. I embraced a mindset of resilience and perseverance, understanding that failure and loss were not endpoints but stepping stones to success.

This transformation took time and effort. It required a deep commitment to self-improvement and a willingness to confront my shortcomings. But as I continued to work on myself, I began to see the fruits of my labor. I secured new job opportunities, built healthier relationships, and developed a newfound inner peace.

Looking back, I now see that the crumbling streets and dead-end signs were not symbols of defeat but invitations to reinvent myself and forge a new path. They were reminders that there is always potential for growth and transformation, even in adversity. This journey of self-discovery and resilience has shaped me into the person I am today. It has taught me the power of introspection, forgiveness, and overcoming life's challenges. As I share my story, I inspire others who may find themselves at a similar crossroads, reminding them that even in the darkest times, there is always light at the end of the tunnel.

In the depths of my despair, I realized that something within me needed to change. I couldn't continue living a life fueled by anger and resentment. At this pivotal moment, I embarked on a journey of self-discovery and forgiveness. Learning to forgive didn't come easy; it took time, introspection, and a willingness to let go of the past. I recognized that holding onto grudges and dwelling on negative experiences only served to weigh me down. I needed to find a way to release the burden weighing on my shoulders for far too long.

Amidst the blooming dawn of my transformative adventure, I discovered a profound source of strength—a power that could reshape my entire existence. It was the power of forgiveness, a force that held the key to unlocking true liberation and manifesting a compassionate outlook. As I immersed myself in the world of the workout gym, hot yoga, and captivating social groups, I realized that forgiveness was not only a personal journey but also an essential component of my growth. It became clear that I had to broaden my horizons and embrace the connections I sought. Indeed, I needed to release the burdens of resentment and grudges that weighed me down.

Amid weightlifting sessions, my muscles straining and heart pounding, I pondered the weight of emotional baggage I had carried for far too long. In those moments of exertion and self-reflection, I discovered the immense power of forgiving others and, perhaps more importantly, forgiving myself. I let go of bitterness and resentment with each rep, allowing compassion and understanding to flourish.

Within the heated confines of the hot yoga studio, as beads of sweat dripped from my brow, I realized that forgiveness was not a sign of weakness but an act of courage. It required vulnerability and a willingness to relinquish control, allowing healing to permeate the depths of my soul. I discovered self-acceptance and inner peace by forgiving myself for past mistakes and embracing my imperfections. I encountered individuals with unique stories and perspectives in the vibrant City of Chicago of social groups. It was within these diverse encounters that forgiveness took on a communal essence. As we shared our experiences and vulnerabilities, I witnessed the transformative power of extending forgiveness to others. It became a bridge that connected us, fostering empathy and deepening our connections. In the act of forgiveness, we found solace and the freedom to grow together, united by our shared humanity.

And then, in the serenity of the Vipassana meditation retreat, forgiveness bloomed like a lotus in the still waters of my mind. As I delved into the depths of introspection, I recognized the interconnectedness of forgiveness and compassion. The act of forgiving, whether directed towards others or myself, allowed me to release the chains of resentment and embrace a more expansive heart. I found the strength to embody the compassionate outlook I yearned for through forgiveness.

With each step of my journey, forgiveness became a guiding light, illuminating the path to personal growth and transformation. It taught me that in forgiving others, I freed myself from the shackles of the past. It showed me that I opened the door to self-love and acceptance in forgiving myself. Ultimately, forgiveness allowed me to view the world through a lens of empathy, understanding, and boundless compassion.

In this extraordinary tale, forgiveness remained etched within the fabric of my being—a constant reminder of the power to heal, embrace connections, and manifest a life filled with love and understanding. With renewed purpose and a heart brimming with forgiveness, I eagerly turned the page, ready to embrace the new journey toward enlightenment and self-discovery. Amid my personal growth, the clouds of confusion and un-acceptance cleared as I realized I was not alone in my struggles. Many others face their hardships, and these experiences turn into threads that weave the fabric of collective humanity with empathy and understanding, becoming the pillars of newfound strength.

In the face of an incredibly challenging situation, insults were hurled at me within the confines of my vehicle while I was providing service, and I found myself tested to the core. One afternoon filled with traffic and construction, I picked up a passenger who seemed visibly upset as the city lights reflected in the slick streets. His furrowed brows and clenched fists hinted at a troubled mind. As we embarked on our journey, tensions filled the air, and the silence grew heavy.

Suddenly, the passenger turned to me and unleashed a barrage of insults. His words stung like a swarm of angry hornets, but I resisted the urge to retaliate. Instead, I reminded myself of the importance of my professionalism training and empathy.

Joe, with a disgruntled look, said, "Are you stupid? Can't you even read a map? You're a complete idiot!"

Taking a deep breath, "I understand that you may be frustrated, but I kindly ask you to refrain from using derogatory language. Let's focus on reaching your destination safely and smoothly."

You're a moron! I can't believe I got stuck with you as my driver. You're useless!"

Behind the wheel, my mind raced with possibilities. Perhaps he had received bad news, lost a job, or experienced heartache. Regardless of the reason, I understood that his outburst did not reflect who I was. My role was to provide a safe and comfortable experience, even when faced with adversity.

Yet, amidst the storm of negativity, a powerful voice within me whispered, "Just relax." I reminded myself that the passenger's behavior may result from their struggles—a bad day at work, a strained personal relationship, or the weight of a family illness. With this realization, I tapped into the reservoir of my hospitality management training and experience working in hotels.

"I apologize for giving you the wrong impression. I assure you, I am here to provide the best service possible."

"You don't know how to drive! It's like you're blind behind the wheel. Are you even qualified to be a driver?"

"I am following the directions on the GPS. Waze/Google Maps works with traffic reports and algorithms in the city to find the best and fastest route. I am doing my best to navigate the city. Everyone has challenges, and I appreciate your understanding in this difficult situation."

"You're a complete waste of space! I can't believe you're getting paid for this. I should have taken a different ride."

"I want to create a positive and respectful environment in my vehicle. We kindly treat each other with kindness and respect. Together, we can make this journey a more pleasant one."

Joe then pauses in silence as he considers his actions. "Thank you for your cooperation. Let's work together to ensure a safe and enjoyable ride for both of us."

I took a deep breath and responded kindly, offering him a reassuring smile. I engaged him in conversation, hoping to divert his attention away from the negative emotions that had consumed him. Slowly but surely, the tension dissipated, and a flicker of gratitude replaced his initial hostility.

After reflecting on his behavior, Joe said, "I'm sorry for how I treated you earlier. It was uncalled for, and I apologize. I've had a terrible day with my wife and a rough time at work."

I smile genuinely and say, "Thank you for acknowledging that. We all have bad days, and I understand how it can affect our behavior. I appreciate your apology."

I shared stories of resilience and personal triumphs as we continued our journey. I focused on the positive aspects of life, highlighting the power of forgiveness and how it had transformed my own experiences. I spoke of my joy in connecting with others and the satisfaction of brightening someone's day.

To my surprise, the passenger's demeanor gradually shifted. His stern expression softened, and a glimmer of appreciation shone through. As we arrived at his destination, he turned to me and apologized for his earlier behavior. He confessed that he had been dealing with personal issues that had clouded his judgment.

Joe starts to hand over a twenty-dollar tip to my hand and says, "You know what? Despite my bad mood, this has been the best trip I've had in a while. Your professionalism and kindness made a difference. I'm sorry again, and thank you for being so understanding."

Gracefully accepting the tip, I say, "I genuinely appreciate your kind words and the gesture. It means a lot to me. I'm glad I could make a positive impact on your day. Let's hope the rest of your day gets better."

At that moment, I realized the impact I had made by choosing forgiveness over anger. Not only had I diffused a potentially volatile situation, but I had also offered a moment of solace to someone in distress.

As the passenger exited my vehicle, he reached into his pocket and gave me a generous tip. It was a tangible symbol of gratitude for the understanding and compassion I had shown him during our journey together. With a heartfelt smile, he disappeared into the night, and I continued on my path, inspired by the power of forgiveness. The passenger and I part ways, with the passenger reflecting on the transformation their encounter had brought about. I, too, feel a sense of fulfillment, knowing that my commitment to professionalism and forgiveness had not only diffused a tense situation but also left a lasting impression on the passenger. We both carry the lessons learned from this encounter, recognizing the power of empathy and the potential for positive change, even amid challenging circumstances.

Guided by the principles of professionalism and a commitment to exceptional service, I vowed to conduct myself with unwavering grace and composure. In the face of adversity, I understood that my role was to transport passengers from one point to another and be a beacon of positivity and upliftment. In those trying moments, I tapped into the secret power of forgiveness—a force that had repeatedly proven to work wonders in my life. I chose to release any anger or resentment that arose, recognizing that it served no purpose other than to dampen my spirit. Instead, I directed my energy towards empathy, understanding that the passenger's behavior might reflect their inner turmoil.

By embracing forgiveness, I could rise above the insults and maintain a professional demeanor. I responded to their negativity with kindness, refusing to let their words tarnish my character. Little did I know that this secret power of forgiveness would shield me from their negativity and bring unexpected rewards.

Incredibly, my commitment to maintaining a positive influence in the face of adversity began to yield surprising results. Passengers who witnessed my calm and composed response to insults were moved by the power of forgiveness radiating from within me. Some recognized the strength it took to remain optimistic amid such challenging circumstances. These encounters turned into transformative moments, where I became more than just a driver for them—I became a source of inspiration and hope.

The ripple effects of forgiveness were tangible, transcending the confines of that vehicle. Passengers started expressing their gratitude through generous cash tips, recognizing the profound impact a positive influence can have on their lives. It was a testament to the transformative power of forgiveness— the ability to heal wounds, create meaningful connections, and leave a lasting impact.

I realized forgiveness was a personal tool for navigating difficult situations and a catalyst for positive change in the world around me. By embracing forgiveness, I became a conduit for compassion and understanding, touching the lives of those I encountered on the platform. Reflecting on those challenging moments, I am grateful for the secret power of forgiveness that guided me through. It has taught me I can choose love, understanding, and forgiveness even in adversity. It has shown me that by embodying these qualities, I can transcend difficult circumstances and make a profound difference in the lives of others. With each encounter, I am reminded of the incredible power we hold within ourselves—the power to forgive, heal, and create a more compassionate world.

In the following days, I reflected on this experience and the countless others I encountered as a service provider. Each interaction presented an opportunity to make a positive impact, to be a beacon of light in someone's darkness. The secret power of forgiveness had not only helped me navigate difficult situations but had also brought unexpected rewards. Through understanding and compassion, I transformed moments of conflict into opportunities for growth and connection.

So, as I embarked on my next ride, I carried this lesson with me, ready to face whatever challenges lay ahead. With an open heart and a commitment to kindness, I knew I could continue to make a difference, one passenger at a time.

During a ride-share pick-up, I picked up a passenger named Andrew, who was Filipino-American like myself. As we conversed, we discovered shared experiences and childhoods shaped by the guilt and shame society often ingrained in us. Growing up Asian, I had been taught to internalize these feelings, but I realized that it was essential to break free from these limiting beliefs.

As we exited Jackson from du Sable Lake Shore Drive, we discussed, "To overcome the guilt and shame, I channeled my energy into becoming more assertive. I recognized that assertiveness was a healthy and balanced way to express myself rather than becoming passive or exhibiting aggression. It required self-reflection and self-empowerment to find my voice and assert my needs and boundaries." The passenger and I bonded as we agreed that fogginess is an ancient and essential aspect of life that must be practiced more.

By practicing assertiveness, I could release the weight of societal expectations and embrace a more authentic version of myself. It was a gradual process, but each step forward brought me closer to a life founded on self-acceptance and forgiveness.

"Hey, Andrew, I wanted to share something with you. After all these years, I finally forgave my youngest brother for his wrongdoings. It feels like a weight has been lifted off my shoulders."

"That's great to hear! Forgiveness can be a powerful way to heal and move forward. Let me share my experience with forgiveness. My father and older brother recently apologized for not accepting me for who I truly am."

"Oh, I see. How did that come about?"

"Well, my older brother admitted that he was always jealous of me because he felt I was better than him in many ways. He finally realized his mistake and sincerely apologized for his behavior. It was a heartfelt moment for both of us."

"Admitting his jealousy and apologizing must have taken a lot of courage. It's truly a sign of growth and maturity."

"Absolutely. And it didn't stop there. On my father's deathbed, he, too, apologized to me. He was a Colonel in the Philippines, and many people struggled with acceptance in that society. But in his final moments, he expressed his deep regret for not fully understanding and accepting me. He wanted nothing but the best for his son."

"I can only imagine the mixed emotions you must have felt during that conversation. It's heartwarming to see that your father found peace and understanding before he passed away."

"It was indeed a bittersweet moment. I'm glad we were able to reconcile and have those conversations. It taught me the importance of forgiveness and understanding, even in the face of past pain."

"Absolutely. Forgiveness can be a transformative experience for both parties involved. It allows us to let go of resentment and create room for healing and growth."

"I couldn't agree more. Forgiveness is a powerful journey, and it takes strength to do so. But in the end, it brings inner peace and harmony."

Thank you for sharing your story, Andrew. It is truly inspiring to see how forgiveness has significantly impacted your life. It reminds me of the profound impact it can have on our relationships and overall well-being."

"You're welcome. Forgiveness is a gift we give ourselves as much as others. It's a step towards emotional freedom and a brighter future."

"Well said, Andrew. Let's continue to embrace forgiveness and create a more compassionate world."

These experiences of connecting with others and challenging societal norms became integral to my journey of forgiveness and personal growth. They reinforced the importance of embracing our identities and acknowledging the cultural influences shaping our perspectives.

These experiences of connecting with others and challenging societal norms became integral to my journey of forgiveness and personal growth. They reinforced the importance of embracing our identities and acknowledging the cultural influences shaping our perspectives.

"Wow, that was a powerful discussion on forgiveness. It resonates with me. Growing up, I faced my fair share of challenges, including being made fun of and feeling like I didn't fit in. It's amazing how forgiveness can be crucial in overcoming those experiences and finding self-acceptance."

"Absolutely! Forgiveness can be a transformative practice, especially regarding the emotional scars we carry from our past. Unfortunately, many of us have experienced being made fun of or feeling like we don't belong. But by embracing

forgiveness, we can break free from resentment and open ourselves up to new possibilities."

"Yes, exactly! It's easy to hold onto anger and bitterness, but I've learned it only weighs me down. Forgiving those who may have hurt us is not always easy, but it allows us to reclaim our power and move forward with a sense of freedom."

"You're right. Forgiveness is not about condoning the actions of others but rather about freeing ourselves from the burden of negativity. Letting go takes strength and courage, but the rewards can be liberating. By forgiving, we create space for personal growth, healing, and ultimately, a more fulfilling life."

"I couldn't agree more. Forgiveness benefits us in many ways. It allows us to break the cycle of negativity and promote empathy and understanding. It's a way to dismantle the barriers that divide us and foster a more compassionate and inclusive society."

"Absolutely! Forgiveness can heal not only our wounds but also the wounds within our communities. We contribute to a culture of empathy, understanding, and unity by extending forgiveness. It's a powerful tool for creating positive change and fostering stronger connections with others."

"It's incredible to think about how forgiveness can have a far-reaching impact. It's not just a personal journey but a collective one. I'm inspired to practice forgiveness more consciously and encourage others to do the same."

"That's wonderful to hear! Remember, forgiveness is a process, and it may take time. But by cultivating forgiveness in our lives and sharing its importance with others, we can create a ripple effect of healing and transformation. Together, we can foster a more inclusive and compassionate world."

"Thank you for this enlightening conversation. It's given me a lot to reflect on and reinforces the power of forgiveness in my own life."

However, a profound realization shatters my chains: forgiveness is the key to my liberation. By releasing the shackles of anger and resentment, forgiveness frees my spirit, allowing me to embrace self-acceptance wholeheartedly. Whispering to myself, I feel the resonating truth within those words, understanding that forgiveness is the ultimate act of self-liberation. It liberates me from the burdens of past pain and empowers me to move forward with grace and compassion.

This exciting chapter of my journey embarks upon a path of forgiveness, harnessing its transformative power to reshape my life. With each release of grudges and extension of forgiveness, I experience a liberating wave washing over me. Bitterness and resentment recede, making way for a newfound serenity and self-acceptance. Through these acts of forgiveness, I discovered the strength to relinquish the past and embrace a brighter future. No longer bound by the chains of anger, I embark upon life with renewed vigor and a sense of purpose.

I also recognize the far-reaching implications of forgiveness within the realm of career and business. Letting go of past grievances opens doors to new job opportunities and fosters success in the business world. By releasing resentment, we create space for collaboration, understanding, and growth, ultimately leading to the best outcomes for all parties involved. Forgiveness catalyzes personal and professional liberation, enhancing working relationships and creating an environment conducive to success. Through forgiveness, we approach challenges with clarity and empathy, navigating the complexities of the business world with grace and integrity.

As forgiveness becomes part of our professional approach, job opportunities present themselves more readily. Closed doors open, offering fresh avenues for growth, networking, and advancement. The act of forgiveness not only enhances our well-being but also contributes to the collective success of the business community.

In this exciting chapter of my journey, I find the wisdom of forgiveness. I know that forgiveness brings personal liberation and shapes a thriving business landscape. With forgiveness as my guiding principle, I confidently navigate the professional world, embracing opportunities and fostering a culture of success, unity, and prosperity.

The wisdom of forgiveness accompanies me on this journey, reminding me that I possess the key to my liberation. It is a precious gift I bestow upon myself, a pathway to personal growth and inner peace. As I forge ahead, I carry the transformative power of forgiveness, knowing that through this act of grace, I can genuinely set myself free.

While becoming upgraded with this new wisdom, I consciously decided to shape my destiny by learning to choose behaviors that eventually resonate with what I desire to become. By embracing my uniqueness and striving to rise to the occasion,

I gained personal satisfaction by becoming a beacon of a GPS point of hope for others. As my story unfolds, this journey of acceptance, resilience, and self-discovery aims to serve as a testament to the human spirit's indomitable nature for happiness. With every mile driven, I hope this story may one day inspire others to embrace their own story to unveil a path toward a brighter and more savory future built on self-liberation and self-acceptance.

Today, as I reflect upon my past, I am grateful for the transformative power of forgiveness and the strength I gained through assertiveness. This has taught me the significance of breaking free from the rough paths of societal guilt and shame, embracing my true self with self-acceptance, and using assertiveness as my gasoline and electricity for personal empowerment, leading to a crystal clear path of self-liberation.

Free from the traffic of hatred and the construction of resentment, my car races at the speed limit towards the newly paved path of self-liberation and self-acceptance. As I embark on my journey, leaving behind the heavy burden of hatred and resentment, it symbolizes my commitment to a new path of self-liberation and self-acceptance. Within this story, I invite readers to explore forgiveness as a catalyst for personal growth. Forgiveness allows us to release the weight of past grievances, freeing ourselves from negative emotions and opening up space for personal transformation. By embracing forgiveness, we can heal wounds, nurture inner peace, and propel ourselves on self-discovery.

I've encountered my fair share of challenging passengers in the unpredictable ride-sharing world. Some have been rude, others consistently late, yet I've learned the power of forgiveness in these situations.

During these moments, I ask myself, "Do they know their issues? Or perhaps, are they unaware of their behavior?"

Deciding whether it's best to address the situation, prioritize safety, and move on becomes a delicate dance. But what I've discovered is that forgiveness, more often than not, works in my favor. One Thursday morning, I had a scheduled ride at 10:30 am to pick up a passenger named Denelly. On the way to her location, I was pleasantly surprised to find a Shell station with a decent gas price of $3.30 per gallon. It was a stroke of luck, especially considering that gas prices in Cook County were usually closer to $4.00 per gallon. I felt grateful for the opportunity to save a little on fuel costs.

Upon arriving at the apartment complex, I exited the parking spot and patiently waited for Denelly. However, as the five-minute mark passed, I wondered where she was. I texted her, introducing myself as her driver, Marshall. When I didn't receive a response, I sent another text asking about her whereabouts. Growing concerned, I attempted to call her but was met with an automated message stating that her phone didn't have voicemail set up yet.

Frustration started to creep in as I thought, "Oh no, not again!" I had received a prior message from the company stating that there would be no changes or additions to this ride, which made me wonder if something urgent had come up.

Just as I started worrying, a lady approached from a distance. Seeing her, I felt relief and hope that she was Denelly. *As she came, she asked, "Hi, is this Marshall?" I replied with a smile, "Yes, it is! Are you Denelly?"*

Confirming her identity, she apologized for not receiving my text messages. I reassured her, explaining that the company was supposed to send them. She mentioned that the signal in the area sometimes went down due to her carrier's issues and said she would call them to address the problem. She then expressed frustration, questioning what was wrong with the ride-share company for not sending her the necessary information. Believing it was due to her carrier's signal loss, I nodded in agreement.

To my surprise, the passenger suddenly remarked, "You know, I can tell from the moment I entered your vehicle that you exuded an amazing light about you and provided exceptional customer service."

I thanked her, feeling grateful for the recognition. I shared that I had recently received an award from Lyft, recognizing me as one of their Drivers of the Year, specifically for my outstanding customer service. We laughed, both finding it surreal and surprising. I explained that the award was based on high reviews and the tips I had received, as I was among the highest-earning drivers in the city. The recognition still astonishes me, and I remain immensely grateful.

As the journey continued, the passenger opened up about her past experiences with ridesharing. She recounted numerous bad rides, particularly those scheduled through the company for hospital trips. I suggested she review the driver's profile beforehand to see their ratings and experience level. She shared a particularly distressing incident where a driver insisted on taking her cell phone to change the destination, even though it was the company's request, not hers. When she couldn't comply, the driver kicked her out of the car. She was understandably upset, but the next driver who picked her up couldn't speak English.

However, he showed empathy and assured her that he would safely take her to the hospital, which comforted her.

At that moment, the lady expressed her appreciation for my role as her driver and gratitude for the compassion and empathy I demonstrated towards her circumstances. This heartfelt acknowledgment made me feel valued and affirmed in my efforts to provide a positive experience for her. Above all, I genuinely wished for her well-being and hoped that her visit to the hospital would unfold without any obstacles.

At that moment, as the lady expressed her gratitude, it reminded her of the power of forgiveness. I created a space for understanding and healing by showing compassion and empathy. Her appreciation and acknowledgment freed me from lingering doubts or insecurities, enabling self-liberation and self-acceptance. This experience reinforced the idea that forgiveness can benefit the person receiving it and the one giving it, as it allows for personal growth and emotional liberation. Ultimately, I recognized that by sincerely wishing for her well-being and a smooth hospital visit, I was embodying the spirit of forgiveness and fostering a positive connection with another human being.

In that moment of gratitude and appreciation for the lady, I forgave her for various things. Firstly, I forgave her for being 10 minutes late, understanding that it's not uncommon for passengers to have occasional delays. I recognized that most passengers usually wait at the pick-up location when I arrive, and this instance was an exception.

Furthermore, I forgave her for not responding to my texts or calls, as she claimed that the service wasn't working. While it initially seemed frustrating, I let go of any resentment and accepted her explanation, realizing that technical issues can occur.

Lastly, I forgave her for providing inconsistent explanations that needed to be added up. She attributed the issues to the company, the ride-share platform, and her phone carrier, leaving uncertainty about the actual cause. Instead of dwelling on the inconsistencies, I accepted that multiple factors could have contributed to the situation, and it was not worth dwelling on.

Through forgiveness, I released any negative emotions and embraced understanding and empathy. This allowed me to maintain a positive attitude and focus on providing passengers with a smooth and pleasant ride, fostering a harmonious and respectful interaction.

As I revved up the engine, the weight of the impending journey settled heavily on my shoulders. The atmosphere inside the car was already tense, and I could sense the mounting stress ahead. The restless and impatient teenagers radiate a vibrant mix of excitement and anxiety.

With each passing mile, the adrenaline coursed through my veins, matching the pulsating rhythm of the city streets. The distance to the Homan Neighborhood felt like an eternity, an endless stretch of road that refused to yield. The mere thought of reaching our destination sooner gripped my mind, urging me to push the boundaries of speed.

Fate had other plans with traffic and its relentless grip on time, refused to relent. The minutes they dragged, elongating into excruciating stretches of waiting. The car became a crucible of discomfort, the air thick with anticipation and impatience. The teenagers' demands, growing louder, bombarded me with requests for warmth, phone chargers, and seating arrangements.

The third passenger squeezed into the front seat beside me and exuded an odor that seemed to defy hygiene laws. The stench became tangible, invading my senses and mingling with the mounting tension. Each breath I took threatened to overwhelm me, but I persevered, determined to navigate this treacherous journey.

As the cityscape blurred past, I found myself navigating a labyrinth of obstacles. Dodging reckless drivers, maneuvering through labyrinthine streets, and battling against time itself, I fought tooth and nail to conquer the relentless distance. The car became a vessel hurtling through chaos, defying the constraints of mortality. Death lurked around every turn, its shadowy presence heightening the stakes of our harrowing expedition.

As the wheels of my car rolled along Cicero Ave., the minutes stretched into an eternity, each passing second taunting my patience.

As we drove down Cicero Ave., I thought, "O man, how much longer will this trip take? Ok, I need to act calm, cool, and collected. I am older than them and can be a good example for these young men."

The weight of the elongated journey pressed upon me, fueling my desperate desire for its abrupt end. With a deep breath, I resolved to maintain an outward facade of calm, cool, and collected composure. After all, I was the older one amongst these young men, and I must set a positive example.

Just as I willed myself to exude an air of tranquility, a sudden movement from the front seat jolted my senses. The passenger seated next to me, his jeans precariously hanging halfway down his boxer underwear, reached for his belt. In that split second, a wave of unease washed over me, and I wondered about the intentions behind this unexpected action. Was he attempting to intimidate me? I refused to buckle under the weight of his potential intimidation, silently vowing to maintain my resolve.

Suddenly, the passenger in the front seat beside me pulls out his belt, his jeans halfway down his boxer underwear.

I thought to myself, "Great! Is this passenger trying to intimidate me? It's not going to work on me." He started to fickle with the removed belt as if he were going to try to use it to strangle me.

I drove with a straight face, as I have done on many of my past trips. That has to be one of the most challenging things to do sometimes, especially given the environment and circumstances in which both the driver and passengers are in their lives.

Then the passenger asked, "Do you smoke weed? We have some to sell to you if you want." I quickly looked at the belt to see if one of the passengers asked, "Do you smoke marijuana? The other Uber allowed us to smoke marijuana in their car." I politely responded, "I apologize, as any type of substance such as marijuana would be considered a charge of a felony because they charge it like a DUI (driving under the influence)."

With a steady grip on the steering wheel, I continued driving, my eyes fixed firmly on the road ahead. Inside, a whirlwind of emotions churned, but my expression remained stoic. I refused to give in to the rising tension, determined to control the situation.

As the car weaved through the dangerous streets, I could sense the passenger's gaze fixed on me, searching for a reaction. But I remained resolute, refusing to show any signs of vulnerability. Deep down, I knew that my composed demeanor would be the shield that protected me from the moment's uncertainty.

Despite the internal turmoil, I focused on the road, navigating the labyrinthine streets with unwavering precision. Each turn and intersection became a testament to my resolve and the strength I possessed within. The passing buildings and flashing lights mirrored the intensity of my thoughts, flickering by in a blur as I pushed forward.

As the miles ticked away, the tension inside the car seemed to subside. The passenger, perhaps recognizing the futility of his attempted intimidation, eventually relinquished his grip on the belt. A fleeting sense of relief washed over me, but I remained vigilant, knowing the journey was incomplete.

In that fleeting moment, I realized that my unwavering composure had triumphed over the stressful and death-defying circumstances surrounding us. I had shown strength in the face of adversity, proving to myself and these young men that fear and intimidation would not deter me.

With a steely determination, I continued driving, the straight face I wore concealing the whirlwind of emotions raging within. The journey was far from over, but I knew that at that moment, I had emerged as a beacon of resilience and unwavering resolve. As the car pressed on, inching closer to our destination, I embraced the extraordinary nature of our shared experience, knowing that I had overcome not only the external challenges but also the internal battle of staying composed in the face of uncertainty.

As the wind rushed through the open car window, carrying a sense of reckless abandon, the passenger behind me waved and called out to random female pedestrians crossing our path. Their attention was his sole pursuit, and the audacity of his actions sent a shiver down my spine. This unexpected turn of events heightened my senses and set my heart racing in a city like Chicago, known for its vibrant energy and contrasting shades.

With every passing moment, my mind raced to prepare for the worst. I knew I had to be vigilant and ready to defend myself if the situation spiraled out of control. In this city of boundless beauty and ceaseless vitality, one must always be on guard, embracing the adrenaline-fueled dance that comes with the territory.

As the car hurtled through the urban landscape, the passenger's focus shifted from physical gestures to the digital realm. His phone emerged as a conduit for his audacious behavior, capturing videos and calling attention to his social media persona. It was in these moments that a flicker of unease danced within me. Would he catch me in an unwitting cameo of his audacious exploits? The uncertainty gnawed at me, heightening the exhilaration and danger of our shared journey.

My thoughts raced as the passenger's self-documented escapades took a sinister turn. While filming himself in the car, he brazenly threw up gang signs, accompanied by the mention of a notorious gang's name. The gravity of the situation became palpable as the line between audacity and danger blurred. In the depths of my mind, I grappled with the realization that I had unknowingly become a witness to a potential crime, a participant in a high-stakes narrative that unfolded within the confines of my car.

With a heavy weight upon my shoulders, I listened as the passenger casually discussed his plans with his friends. Their intentions were clear—to jump an unsuspecting individual, seizing their marijuana and ill-gotten wealth. The gravity of his words hung in the air, mingling with the exhilaration and fear that coursed through my veins. I was thrust into a twisted plot where right and wrong intertwined and blurred the boundaries of law and morality.

Amid this death-defying spectacle, I found myself torn between instinct and reason. Should I intervene? Should I distance myself from this dangerous entanglement? The streets of Chicago, pulsating with life and a spectrum of experiences, offered no easy answers. But within me, a fire burned a determination to navigate this treacherous path with my integrity intact.

As the journey continued, each passing moment became a testament to my resilience and my unwavering commitment to the values that define me. The thrill and terror of the situation melded into a symphony of emotions, fueling my resolve to emerge unscathed from this high-stakes adventure.

In the heart of Chicago, where the line between exhilaration and danger is razor-thin, I remained steadfast, believing that even in the face of chaos, a glimmer of hope can illuminate the way forward. As the car's wheels spun on, propelling us closer to our destination, I vowed to hold fast to my principles, navigating the treacherous currents of this death-defying passage with unwavering courage.

With nerves of steel and unwavering composure, I maintained a calm and collected attitude, my hands gripping the steering wheel with steadfast determination. The passengers in the car exchanged glances, astonished by my seemingly effortless control over the intense situation. It was as if I had become the embodiment of fearlessness.

As we neared our destination, the passengers, seemingly unfazed by the adrenaline coursing through their veins, made an unexpected request. They asked me to drop them off at the end of a dimly lit alley, a place that exuded an air of uncertainty and danger. A moment of hesitation flickered within me, but I swiftly dismissed it. I couldn't show them fear; I had to prove that I was unyielding in the face of potential threats. Thus, with unwavering resolve, I decided to navigate the car down the narrow alley, ready to confront any challenges that may come our way.

Just as I was about to execute the daring maneuver, a colossal truck thundered behind us, its presence overwhelming. It swerved dangerously close in an audacious attempt to overtake me, threatening to sideswipe our vehicle. But I was no stranger to such perilous encounters. Dodging near collisions had become an integral part of my daily routine, an art I had mastered through sheer experience and quick reflexes.

In that exhilarating moment, time seemed to slow down. I deftly steered the car, skillfully avoiding the truck's reckless advance. Every twist and turn was executed with calculated precision as if I were dancing on the edge of disaster. The passengers, their eyes wide with astonishment and admiration, could only watch in awe as I navigated the treacherous path unscathed.

Though the thrill of the near-miss surged through my veins, I remained focused, my senses heightened, ready to face any challenge that awaited us down the alley. Deep within, a determination to protect myself and those entrusted to my care simmered. I was prepared to unleash my inner warrior, to fight tooth and nail if these teenagers harbored ill intentions.

The shadows whispered secrets of danger and uncertainty as the car glided through the dimly lit alley. Yet, I pressed on, undeterred by the ominous atmosphere. I remained a beacon of strength and resilience, a symbol of unwavering bravery.

It was as if the outside world blurred into a whirlwind of motion. I realized that this exhilarating journey mirrored life. Adversity lurked around every corner, but I refused to succumb to its intimidating presence. Instead, I embraced the challenges, transforming them into opportunities to showcase my indomitable spirit.

With each passing second, I continued my death-defying drive down the alley, my heart pounding with anticipation. Once apprehensive, the passengers now witnessed the unwavering determination coursing through my veins. In their eyes, I saw a newfound respect, an acknowledgment of my unyielding courage. With resolve, I embodied fearlessness, a testament to the indomitable human spirit that refuses to be shaken by the perils of life.

As I looked back at the difficult path we had traversed, I couldn't help but feel exhilaration. The stress, the trials, and the brushes with danger had forged an unforgettable experience. I had defied the odds, pushed beyond the limits of my endurance, and emerged victorious.

As we reached the end of the narrow alley, my heart pounded in my chest, anticipation coursing through my veins. With a sudden turn to the left, we arrived at the drop-off address, and to my surprise, a fourth friend emerged from the house, joining the others already in the car. A flicker of unease passed through my mind as I contemplated the possibility of facing off against four formidable opponents.

As the passengers bid farewells, a rush of emotion surged through me. The exhilaration of the journey still lingered, but beneath the surface, a twinge of disappointment tugged at my heart. Their gratitude seemed hollow, for deep within my thoughts, I knew something wasn't right.

While the last passenger disconnected their phone from the charging wire I had thoughtfully provided, their voice echoed with assurances of a glowing five-star rating. But in the depths of my being, a fire ignited—a burning determination to take a stand, to protect myself and others from potential harm.

In that moment, a surge of courage propelled me forward. I resolved to report this incident to illuminate the shadows that threatened our safety. It wasn't an easy decision, for I understood its weight. But I knew, with every fiber of my being, that it was necessary.

Unbeknownst to them, I had sensed the dark undercurrents beneath their seemingly innocent words. A plan had been woven within their whispers, a sinister plot to rob an unsuspecting person of their marijuana and hard-earned money. I couldn't stand idly by, allowing such a crime to unfold within the confines of my car.

With my heart pounding and adrenaline coursing through my veins, I mustered the strength to assign a three-star rating. A symbol of defiance, a testament to my unwavering commitment to justice. It wasn't about personal gain or revenge; it was about safeguarding the sanctity of our journeys and protecting the innocent from the clutches of malevolence.

As the notification confirmed the submission of my report, a sense of relief washed over me. I had done what was necessary, what was right. The road ahead might be paved with uncertainty, but I knew deep down that my actions would help prevent such situations from repeating.

So, to my fellow drivers and passengers, I implore you to trust your instincts and be vigilant. We hold the power to shape the safety of our shared experiences. Let us not shy away from taking a stand, for it is in these moments of courage that we can forge a path towards a brighter, more secure future.

Together, let us ride with unwavering determination, ensuring that each journey is exhilarating and free from the shadows that seek to darken our paths.

Fortune smiled upon me that night, for no harm befell me during this dangerous encounter. I navigated this challenging situation unscathed through the accumulation of knowledge and expertise gained from over 25,000 trips and a decade of experience in the hospitality industry. The skills honed through countless encounters with unpredictable circumstances allowed me to maintain composure in the face of uncertainty.

However, I couldn't help but acknowledge that a less-seasoned driver or someone lacking the depth of experience I possessed might not have fared as well. This death-defying episode was a stark reminder of the importance of expertise, wisdom, and know-how to navigate the uncharted territory of challenging and unpredictable scenarios.

As I reflected on the journey's conclusion, relief and exhilaration surged. It was a testament to the countless hours spent perfecting my craft and the numerous stories etched into my memory, each contributing to the tapestry of my expertise.

With gratitude, I continued, ready to face the next thrilling, death-defying adventure that awaited me on the open road.

I bid farewell to the teenagers, and a profound realization washed over me, intertwining with the exhilaration of our death-defying passage. It was a realization of the transformative power of forgiveness. In that moment, I understood that we can embark on a journey of self-liberation and self-acceptance by forgiving others and ourselves.

The courage displayed by those young souls and their unwavering determination to overcome their fears mirrored the resilience of the human spirit. It reminded me that forgiveness is an act of compassion towards others and a means to free ourselves from resentment and bitterness. In facing the uncertainties and perils of our shared adventure, we discovered forgiveness's profound strength.

As I drove away, the echoes of that life-altering journey reverberated within me as a powerful reminder of the extraordinary lengths we can reach when pushed to the edge. It was a testament to the indomitable human spirit and our capacity to rise above our circumstances and embrace the power of forgiveness.

In embracing forgiveness, we liberate ourselves from the burdens of the past, allowing us to fully embrace the present and chart a brighter future. Through forgiveness, we find the strength to persevere, even in fear and uncertainty. Through forgiveness, we unlock the door to self-acceptance, embracing our flaws and imperfections with compassion and grace.

The memory of that death-defying passage etched itself into my memory. I recognized that forgiveness had played a vital role in our shared experience. It fostered a sense of unity and understanding, paving the way for personal growth and transformation.

So, let us remember the power of forgiveness as we navigate the twists and turns of our journeys. Let us free ourselves from the weight of grudges and resentments, allowing forgiveness to guide us toward self-liberation and self-acceptance. And in doing so, may we discover the exhilarating heights we can reach, embracing our humanity's fullness and our spirit's resilience.

As a ride-share driver, my main focus is the safety and satisfaction of my passengers. While it can be tempting to confront rude or inconsiderate individuals, sometimes it's best to let it slide to maintain a peaceful and secure environment. By forgiving these passengers, I prevent potential conflicts and ensure a smooth journey for everyone involved.

What's fascinating is that choosing forgiveness often results in a beautiful transformation. Those passengers who I initially thought disliked me or were unappreciative of my services surprised me with their gratitude. They were some of the most generous, showering me with cash tips and expressing their appreciation through online tipping. It was as if my forgiveness broke down barriers and allowed their true nature to shine through.

By extending understanding and empathy, I created a space for them to reflect on their behavior and recognize its impact on others. In forgiving them, I inadvertently created an opportunity for growth and connection. It's a testament to the power of forgiveness and the potential for positive change that lies within us all.

Moreover, forgiving these passengers freed me from resentment and negativity. Instead of harboring grudges or dwelling on negative experiences, I focused on the positive interactions and joy of providing a safe and enjoyable ride. This shift in perspective improved my overall well-being and allowed me to approach each new passenger with renewed enthusiasm and an open heart.

So, while forgiveness may not always be the easiest path, it leads to unexpected rewards. By forgiving, I create a harmonious environment for my passengers and open doors to kindness, generosity, and appreciation. It's a reminder that in ride-sharing, as in life, forgiveness can transform and elevate our experiences.

Moreover, this story emphasizes the power of embracing assertiveness to overcome societal expectations. It encourages readers to challenge cultural norms that may confine or limit their true identities. By assertively asserting their beliefs, values, and aspirations, individuals can break free from societal constraints and pave the way for a more authentic existence.

In this narrative, I aim to inspire readers to connect with others who have shared similar experiences. We can find strength and support in our collective journey of self-discovery and growth by finding solace and understanding in those who have walked similar paths. Through these connections, we can challenge societal norms, celebrate our unique identities, and empower others to embrace our authentic voices.

Ultimately, this story serves as a potent reminder for readers to embrace forgiveness as a pathway to self-liberation and personal growth. It highlights the transformative power of letting go of grudges and embracing compassion towards ourselves and others.

By forgiving, we release the burden of anger and revenge, allowing us to focus on what truly matters in life. It encourages us to shift our perspective and invest our energy in cultivating happiness, fostering meaningful connections, and pursuing our passions. Instead of dwelling on past hurts, forgiveness opens the door to healing and creates space for new possibilities and positive experiences.

Moreover, this story emphasizes the brevity and preciousness of life. It reminds us that our time on this Earth is limited and should not be wasted on holding onto resentment. By choosing forgiveness over anger, we free ourselves from negativity and create a pathway to happiness and fulfillment.

Living a life grounded in forgiveness and focusing on what truly matters enables us to cultivate authenticity, resilience, and compassion. It allows us to build stronger relationships, nurture our well-being, and contribute positively to the world.

This narrative serves as an inspiring call to action, inviting readers to embark on their transformative journeys of forgiveness. It encourages them to let go of past grievances, embrace self-acceptance, and forge a path toward a more fulfilling life characterized by forgiveness, happiness, and a deep appreciation for what truly matters: happiness.

CHAPTER 7 - Happiness is Everything

Create a World with Love, Happiness, and Joy

Ah, buckle up and prepare for a laughter-filled journey down memory lane! Let me regale you with an exhilarating tale from the early days of my rideshare adventures back in 2013. Picture this: my trusty steed, a humble 2009 grey Toyota Corolla, ready to conquer the roads and transport passengers to their destinations. Little did I know what hilarity awaited me!

With a touch of naivety, I welcomed passengers into my car, oblivious to the rules and regulations that would soon become my guiding light. Oh, the audacity of those early riders! They would pile in, 8-10 strong, their mischievous grins betraying the secret they were about to unleash.

"Oh yes," they would chime, "there's plenty of room in your little Corolla! Don't worry, we can all fit!"

My eyes widened, my heart racing as I tried to comprehend the physics-defying feat about to take place.

With each extra passenger, a chorus of laughter erupted, echoing through the cramped confines of my vehicle. "Wow! Really? This must be a magic trick to fit all these people in my car, similar to how they can separate the body into two parts and reconnect it like when the magician performs at the magic show!"

Their enthusiasm was infectious, and I couldn't help but join in the mirthful symphony. As we embarked on our adventure, the transformation of my Toyota Corolla into a magical clown car seemed to defy all logic and reason. The once ordinary vehicle now appeared to be stretching and contorting, accommodating an ever-increasing number of passengers. It became a whimsical spectacle that filled me with awe and amusement.

Navigating through the streets, I marveled at the ingenuity of my newfound companions. Laughter filled the air as limbs and appendages extended from unexpected places, including legs brushing against seats and arms and human heads playfully waving outside the back window. The absurdity of the situation was undeniable, and everyone couldn't help but burst into fits of laughter.

As we traversed the short distance between Lakeview and Lincoln Park along Lincoln Ave, the quirkiness of our magical

Corolla car continued to surprise and amuse us. Here are a few conversations that capture the spirit of our journey:

A passenger said, "Wait, is that an arm I feel? This car knows how to give a warm welcome!" exclaimed one passenger, their voice filled with both surprise and delight.

Another passenger chimed in, "Hold on a sec, folks! I think I just sensed a leg brushing against my seat. We're getting extra comfy on this ride!" I announced, my voice tinged with amusement.

Passenger 3 piped up, "Wait, is this someone else's leg?"

Passenger 4 joined in, "That's my leg! Is that your right arm, I feel?"

Passenger 5 exclaimed, "Oh my goodness, hold on, let me move my neck; I think I'm completely smooshed in between!"

Meanwhile, another passenger took a unique position, kneeling on the seat with their head facing the window. Another passenger plopped down on that person's calves, and the rest sat sideways on each other's laps.

It was like a real-life game of human Tetris unfolding in my
car. Trying to contain my laughter, I replied, "Don't worry,
I'm good at Tetris too!"

One of the other passengers chuckled, "Yeah! Tetris was one
of my all-time favorites on the Game Boy!"

And then, reminiscing about the good old days, another
passenger added, "Oh yeah, I remember Tetris. Hold on, I
can't breathe. Let me move a little bit. Ok, that's much
better."

Amidst the laughter and the human Tetris game in my
backseat, another passenger joined in, saying, "Yeah, this is
human Tetris for sure."

It was a hilarious and unexpected turn of events, transforming a simple car ride into a comical jumble of limbs and laughter. Who knew that my car could become a mobile comedy club where passengers became puzzle pieces in the game of life?

Amid laughter and joy, we marveled at the audacity of the experience. The fusion of laughter, conversations, and the occasional glimpse of body parts outside the windows created a carnival-like atmosphere, where rules and constraints seemed to fade into the background, replaced by a sense of wonder and limitless possibilities. Reflecting on those moments, I am grateful for the shared laughter, connections, and memories forged within the magical clown car. It was a testament to the power of spontaneity, embracing the unexpected, and finding joy in the most unlikely of circumstances.

Amidst the laughter and camaraderie, a different passenger said, "Wait, let me shift my head. I feel like a whimsical circus act surrounds me! Who needs a normal car when you can have this?"

The situation's absurdity only heightened the sense of adventure and joy within our magical Corolla. Each unexpected interaction and discovery added to the memorable experience, making our journey down Lincoln Ave. genuinely unforgettable. Amid the hilarity, I wondered: What had I gotten myself into? Yet, the infectious joy and lightheartedness of the moment washed away any doubts.

With a wide grin, I exclaimed, "Hold on tight, folks! We're about to break some rules and have the ride of our lives!"

Embracing the surreal experience, we continued our journey, defying the norms and embracing the unexpected. The magical car symbolized adventure and endless possibilities, reminding us to let go of our inhibitions and embrace the joy of the unknown.

Indeed, the magical car had a way of accommodating more passengers than its size would suggest. It wasn't uncommon to find two or three passengers squeezed into the front seat, their laughter and excitement filling the air. Despite the cozy arrangement, everyone seemed to revel in the shared camaraderie and the sheer absurdity of the situation.

Amidst the laughter and merriment, another passenger occupied a unique position, sitting right between the passenger and the driver. Nestled in the middle, this passenger became a bridge connecting the front and back of the car. It created a sense of closeness as conversations and laughter flowed effortlessly between the two sections.

This unconventional seating arrangement added to the charm and uniqueness of our journey. It fostered a sense of togetherness and shared experiences as we all marveled at the magical transformation of the humble Toyota Corolla into a vessel of adventure and delight.

As we maneuvered through the streets, passenger interactions became a dance of laughter, storytelling, and occasional exclamations of surprise. The boundaries between driver and passenger blurred as we embraced the notion of the moment. It was a reminder that the most memorable experiences are sometimes born from the unexpected and the unorthodox.

Looking back, I can't help but smile at the memories created in that little car. The shared laughter, the intertwined conversations, and the bonds formed during those rides will forever hold a special place in our hearts. They were a testament to the power of spontaneity and the joy of embracing the unconventional.

Amid the whimsical chaos in the magical clown car, more passengers added to the delightful mayhem. Some chose to kneel in the limited space, embracing the unconventional nature of our journey. Their spirits were undeterred, and they joined in the laughter and conversation, their infectious enthusiasm filling the car.

As the car ventured forward, there were moments when the laws of physics seemed to bend, and body ligaments playfully extended outside the rear windows. It was as if the car had a mischievous personality, showcasing the unexpected and pushing the boundaries of what we thought was possible. These fleeting glimpses of limbs and appendages added a layer of whimsy to our adventure, eliciting laughter and astonishment from passengers and bystanders alike.

With laughter and joy, we marveled at the audacity of the experience. The fusion of laughter, conversations, and the occasional glimpse of body parts outside the windows created a carnival-like atmosphere, where rules and constraints seemed to fade into the background, replaced by a sense of wonder and limitless possibilities. Reflecting on those moments, I am grateful for the shared laughter, connections, and memories forged within the magical clown car. It was a testament to the power of spontaneity, embracing the unexpected, and finding joy in the most unlikely of circumstances.

So let us raise our glasses once more to the laughter and camaraderie celebrating the passengers who knelt and embraced the unconventional and to those mischievous body ligaments that added an extra touch of whimsy to our journey. Here's to the laughter, the surprises, and the memories that will forever remind us of the little 2009 Toyota Corolla that defied expectations and to the memories that will forever echo in the annals of our shared stories. May they serve as a reminder that, sometimes, unexpected twists and turns make life's adventures all the more magical.

Let us not forget that times have changed, my friends. The rideshare landscape has evolved, and many regulations now ensure the safety and comfort of all involved. We may fondly remember those wild escapades, but we must also embrace the responsibility that comes with progress. So, let's raise a glass to those uproarious memories, to the passengers who pulled a fast one on me, and to the little 2009 Toyota Corolla that transformed into an iconic symbol of adventure. In the annals of our shared stories, let their quotes echo as a testament to the joy found in unexpected twists.

The magical Corolla car continued to surprise and delight us not once or twice but perhaps thrice or more. It became a cherished part of our journey, a reminder that life is meant to be embraced with open arms and a spirit of adventure. The company never stopped me from embracing the notion from the beginning, and while it took a few years to learn about the rules, I am grateful for the experiences and the knowledge I gained. As time passed and I discovered the boundaries within which our journeys could unfold, I found a new appreciation for the rules and regulations that govern our adventures. Understanding the limitations brought a sense of responsibility and safety but didn't diminish my fondness for those early uninhibited rides.

In the distant past, my friends Penelope and Haley were intrigued by the idea of driving for Uber on the side. Penelope, the Accounts Manager in the South Loop, and Haley, the newly minted Professional Therapist, were eager to learn the ropes of being ride-share drivers. What better way to make money on the side before and after work? So, I decided to take them on an Uber trip to show them the ins and outs of the app.

Penelope, always cautious, asked, "Are you sure this is okay, Marshall?"

I chuckled and replied, "Of course! It'll be like old times when I taught you both how to drive as teenagers. Wow, how time has gone by so fast!"

We eagerly waited for our first passenger as we hopped into my trusty Uber. The tension in the air was palpable, a mixture of excitement and nerves. Suddenly, the app pinged, indicating our first ride request.

Haley, biting her lip, asked, "What if we get some crazy passenger? Do we have a plan?"

With a mischievous grin, I responded, "Don't worry, ladies. I've dealt with my fair share of interesting characters. Just remember to keep your sense of humor intact!"

In the South Loop of Chicago, our first passenger, a pleasant gentleman named Edward, hopped into the car, who seemed to radiate positive energy. As we embarked on our journey, Penelope couldn't help but initiate a conversation.

"So, how's your day going today, Edward?" she asked.

"Great job, Penelope," I mentioned.

"That's exactly what you want to do at the beginning of the trip. Introduce yourself first, then confirm the passenger's name."

Edward replied, "Oh, just another day in paradise! Thanks for being my Uber fairy godmother today!"

We drove through the neighborhood of the South Loop, merging into 94 Edens and heading towards the Lake St. exit towards the River North neighborhood.

I explained to Haley and Penelope, "Do you see this is how we turn? Make sure to look to your left and right before turning to avoid pedestrians and bicyclists safely."

With a massive smile, Haley said, "O my God, I can't believe
this is happening."

We did our best to hold our faces from bursting into
laughter, but to no avail, realizing that our little adventure was
becoming a comical fairy tale. As we dropped off our first
passenger, the app again chimed, indicating a new ride request.
Excitement filled the air as we braced ourselves for the
subsequent hilarious encounter.

Unable to contain her laughter, Haley whispered to Penelope,
"Are you ready for this?"

Penelope, sparkling with amusement, replied, "Bring it on!
We're the dynamic trio of Uber!"

As we picked up our next unsuspecting passenger, we
couldn't help but notice the confusion on her face. The
passenger, Madeline, blurted out, "Oh, I didn't think I
ordered an Uber Pool!"

I quickly jumped in, wearing my best fake instructor hat, and
said with a hint of overconfidence, "Fear not, my dear

Elizabeth! This is no ordinary Uber Pool. We're trying to teach these two lovely ladies how to become the city's crème de la crème of Uber drivers! As you can see on the app, it says I'm a top driver, and this is what's best for business. What better way to teach how to drive Uber than my first experience?"

Madeline, slightly taken aback by my grandiose statement, mustered a smile and replied, "Well, thank you for being such a great instructor, Marshall. I never knew I'd stumble upon a mobile driving school in the back of an Uber!"

As the ride continued from the River North neighborhood to the Lakeview neighborhood, Penelope and Haley exchanged glances, trying to suppress their laughter. I couldn't help but join in, realizing how absurd our little adventure had become. Who knew a simple Uber ride could transform into a sidesplitting comedy sketch?

With exaggerated hand gestures and an overly dramatic tone, I continued my instruction, pretending to be the master of all things Uber. "Now, ladies, remember, it's all about the perfect balance of friendly chat and respecting personal space. And don't forget to master the art of making witty small talk while

skillfully maneuvering through traffic!"

Elizabeth, now fully embracing the comedic chaos, played

along and said, "Ah, I see! So it's like a crash course in

comedy and driving skills. Sign me up!"

We laughed, realizing just how ridiculous our impromptu driving school had become. From Uber Pool mishaps to over-the-top instructor antics, it was a perfect storm of hilarity and unexpected encounters. When we dropped off Elizabeth, the car was filled with an infectious energy of joy and laughter. She waved us goodbye, thanking us for the unique and entertaining ride. Little did she know, she had become a part of our grand comedy experiment.

As we continued our Uber escapades, Penelope, Haley, and I couldn't help but revel in the absurdity of it all. Who knew that a simple idea of teaching our friends how to drive for Uber could turn into a sidesplitting adventure filled with laughter, unexpected passengers, and comedic chaos?

With a sigh of accomplishment and relief, I said, "So, we

continued our journey, navigating the city streets with a

newfound appreciation for the comedic possibilities within the

world of Uber driving. We were determined to be the

laughter-generating, top-notch Uber drivers that Chicago had ever seen. And hey, if we could make a few people smile and chuckle along the way, then our mission was truly accomplished."

Haley, with a massive grin, said, "Absolutely! It's been an absolute blast. I never thought being an Uber driver could be this entertaining."

Penelope, unable to control her laughter any longer, said, "I couldn't agree more! Our passengers' reactions were priceless. We made their rides memorable."

"And we've learned so much along the way. Comedy truly has a way of bringing people together and brightening their day."

Haley mentioned, "That's the beauty of it. Laughter knows no boundaries. It's a universal language that connects us all."

"And it's amazing how a simple ride can become an unforgettable experience when you infuse it with humor and fun," Penelope wipes the tears of laughter from her face.

"Absolutely. We've not only made people laugh but also created memories that they'll carry with them. That's what it's all about."

Haley said, "And the best part is, we've had a blast doing it. Laughter is contagious, and spreading that contagiousness to our passengers has been a joy."

Penelope said, "So, what's next for our comedy Uber adventure? Are we ready to take our show on the road?"

"Who knows, Haley and Penelope? One day, we'll have our comedy tour. But for now, let's keep making people laugh, one Uber ride at a time."

Haley said, "I couldn't agree more. Let's continue embracing the unexpected, spreading joy, and turning each ride into a little comedy show."

"So, buckle up, my friends, because our laughter-filled journey as Uber drivers has just begun. Get ready for more hilarious adventures and unforgettable moments!"

As the sun sets and the city lights begin to twinkle, the three friends drive off into the night, ready for whatever comedic adventures await them. With their laughter-filled journey as Uber drivers, they've brought joy to others and discovered the power of humor in their lives. As they navigate the city streets, they know they're on a mission to make the world a little brighter, one ride at a time.

Penelope turned to me and said, "Marshall, this has been an absolute riot! Who knew being an Uber driver could be so much fun?"

I grinned, feeling proud and joyous. "Well, my dear friends, this is just the beginning of our comedic adventure. Buckle up because we're in for a wild ride!"

As Uber's self-proclaimed comedic instructor, I was determined to make this next passenger pickup memorable. Penelope and Haley sat eagerly in the backseat, ready to witness my comedic genius in action. Little did they know that this unsuspecting passenger was about to become the star of our impromptu comedy show.

As we arrived at the pickup location, I glanced at Penelope and Haley, mischief twinkling in my eyes.

"Alright, ladies, get ready for some top-tier comedy. Let's give this passenger a ride they'll never forget!"

With a mischievous grin, I activated the app and watched as the name of our next passenger appeared on the screen. "Ah, here comes our unsuspecting victim!" I whispered to Penelope and Haley, trying to contain my excitement.

As the passengers hopped into the car, their faces a mix of confusion and curiosity, I put on my best comedian persona.

"Welcome aboard, the laughter express! Fasten your seatbelts because we'll take comedy to new heights."

Penelope and Haley tried their best to stifle their giggles, playing along with my comedic charade. The unsuspecting passenger looked around, wondering what they had gotten into.

With a theatrical flourish, I turned to the passenger and asked, "So, are you ready to embark on this wild ride filled with laughter, hilarity, and maybe a few questionable jokes?"

The excellent sports passenger chuckled nervously and replied, "Well, I wasn't expecting a comedy show during my Uber ride, but I'm all for it!"

And with that, our laughter-filled journey began. Penelope and Haley joined in, sharing their witty banter and laughter. It was like a comedy club on wheels, with each passenger becoming an unwitting audience member. I couldn't resist throwing in classic one-liners and funny anecdotes as we drove through the city, keeping the atmosphere lighthearted and joyful. The passenger, caught up in the whirlwind of unexpected comedy, couldn't help but burst into laughter.

Between the outrageous jokes, playful banter, and unexpected comedic timing, our car became a rolling comedy show. Passersby on the streets stared in amusement as they witnessed this hilarious spectacle on wheels. The car was filled with infectious laughter, and we smiled when we reached the passengers' destination in Chicago's Uptown neighborhood. The passengers, wiping tears of laughter from their eyes, thanked us for the most entertaining Uber ride they had ever experienced.

Exiting the car, they turned to us and said, "You guys should take this show on the road! It was the Best Uber ride ever!"

We bid them farewell with a final comedic flourish, promising to bring laughter wherever we go. As we drove away, Penelope, Haley, and I couldn't help but revel in the absurdity and hilarity of it all. We may not have been the top-rated Uber drivers, but we knew how to deliver a laughter-filled experience. And so, our Uber comedy tour continued, with each passenger becoming a part of our ever-growing audience. One ride at a time, we were determined to spread joy, laughter, and comedic shenanigans throughout the city, leaving a trail of smiles in our wake.

"As time passed, I realized that attempting to train my friends while giving rides might not have been the most effective approach."

Haley said, "Yeah, it was a bit chaotic. We may have unintentionally disrupted the smooth flow of the Uber experience."

Penelope nodded, "Agreed. While our intentions were good, our attempts at comedy may have overwhelmed some passengers."

"Lesson learned. It's important to balance providing an enjoyable ride and ensuring a professional and comfortable experience for our passengers."

Haley, with a massive smile on her face, said, "Definitely. Laughter is great, but we need to respect the boundaries and preferences of our passengers, too."

Penelope said, "And perhaps, instead of trying to train while giving rides, we can find other ways to improve our comedic skills and bring joy to people's lives."

"Exactly. We can take comedy classes, perform at open mic nights, or even create online content to refine our skills and spread laughter."

In a content tone, Haley said, "That sounds like a better approach. We can still bring humor to our Uber rides but in a more controlled and considerate manner."

Penelope, with a concerned look, "Absolutely. We want to create a positive and enjoyable experience for our passengers without overwhelming them with our comedic antics."

"Let's continue our journey as Uber drivers, but with a newfound understanding and a more balanced approach to entertaining our passengers."

Haley said, "Sounds like a plan. Let's bring laughter and joy to our rides while respecting the professionalism and comfort of our passengers."

Penelope nodded, "Agreed. Here's to learning from our experiences and evolving as drivers who can bring smiles without compromising the integrity of the Uber service."

As the three friends reflect on the lessons learned, they embark on a new chapter of their Uber journey, ready to strike a balance between humor and professionalism. Their determination to bring joy and laughter remains, but now with a more thoughtful approach to ensure a positive experience for their passengers.

Looking back, I am grateful for the moments of laughter, surprise, and joy the magical clown car provided. It catalyzed unforgettable stories and forged connections with fellow passengers who shared the whimsical experience. It taught me that sometimes, the unexpected twists make the journey exciting and worth remembering. As we journey forward, let us continue to embrace the rules and regulations that guide us while cherishing the laughter-filled escapades that shaped us. And who knows, we'll look back on these current adventures with the same amusement and fondness. After all, life is a ride worth laughing about. In this captivating chapter, the theme of "Create a World with Love, Happiness, and Joy" takes center stage as the experiences and insights of my passengers shed light on the complexities and personal dilemmas we all face.

In my journey of self-discovery, I have become a living testament to the power we possess to shape our reality. I have realized that happiness is not an elusive destination but a conscious choice to break free from societal expectations and create a world that resonates with our most authentic selves.

In challenging situations, seeking inspiration and guidance from those we admire is natural. My friends Clyde, Manolo, Penelope, and Haely are the epitome of success and happiness. They have achieved their dreams, secured fulfilling careers, and enjoy a level of comfort and contentment that is truly inspiring. Whenever I find myself confronted with a daunting hurdle, I can't help but wonder: what would Clyde, Manolo, Penelope, and Haely do in this situation? Their unwavering determination, resilience, and unwavering focus have propelled them to heights, and I look up to them as beacons of inspiration.

With his brilliant mind and innovative spirit, Clyde has always been a trailblazer. He fearlessly takes on challenges, embracing them as opportunities for growth rather than obstacles. His ability to think outside the box and find creative solutions motivates me to approach the barriers with a fresh perspective, knowing there is always a way forward.

Manolo embodied charisma and confidence and could gracefully and efficiently navigate any situation. His unwavering self-belief and adaptability inspire me to cultivate my self-assurance and embrace change with an open mind. Manolo's presence reminds me that challenges are merely stepping stones to success.

With her impeccable organizational skills and unwavering work ethic, Penelope is a master of time management. She knows how to prioritize her tasks, set clear goals, and stay focused despite adversity. Penelope's discipline and dedication motivate me to structure my life, ensuring that I allocate time and energy to the things that truly matter.

Lastly, there's Haely, the embodiment of balance and harmony. She juggles her career, family, and personal well-being effortlessly, finding joy in every aspect of her life. Haely's ability to find equilibrium inspires me to strive for a harmonious existence, recognizing that success is not limited to one facet of life but is a holistic pursuit.

So, when I find myself grappling with a challenging situation, I pause and reflect on the wisdom and qualities of my dear friends. I draw from their collective strength, envisioning Clyde's confidence, Manolo's adaptability, Penelope's organization, and Haley's balance. Their triumphs and happiness remind me that I, too, have the power to overcome any obstacle that comes my way.

Ultimately, it's not about emulating their exact actions but channeling their spirit and embodying the qualities that make them successful. By seeking inspiration from those we admire, we tap into our potential and find the motivation to conquer challenges with unwavering determination. My friends have achieved their dreams so that I can forge my path to success and happiness.

As I continue to navigate this journey called life, I am driven by an unwavering belief that love, happiness, and joy are not distant dreams but tangible realities within our grasp. I understand that the key to creating a fulfilling and vibrant existence lies in being the architect of my world. With this newfound understanding, I have carefully curated a circle of loved ones who walk beside me, sharing in the mosaic of experiences and cherished memories that make life extraordinary.

In this beautiful journey, we must be discerning about the company we keep. As the saying goes, we become the average of the people we surround ourselves with. With this wisdom in mind, I have consciously chosen to align myself with individuals who embody excellence and who consistently strive to be the best versions of themselves. These people approach every situation with an unwavering commitment to excellence, transforming even the most ordinary moments into extraordinary ones.

I am constantly inspired to push beyond my limits and surpass my expectations by surrounding myself with these perfectionists. Their relentless pursuit of greatness is a beacon of motivation, reminding me there is always room for growth and improvement. Their dedication to excellence challenges me to explore new horizons and strive for greatness in every aspect of my life. It's not just about their pursuit of perfection; it's about the joy they bring to every situation. These individuals can make the most of every moment, infusing even the simplest activities with wonder and delight. Their energy is contagious, and in their presence, life becomes a vibrant tapestry of laughter, shared adventures, and unforgettable memories.

Through their influence, I have learned to embrace every experience with a zest for life. Together, we celebrate milestones, big and small, cherishing the journey as much as the destination. Whether embarking on spontaneous road trips or simply savoring a cup of coffee together, these moments become treasured gems in the tapestry of our lives.

In the grand symphony of existence, we all have the power to choose our companions, shape our reality, and create a life brimming with love, happiness, and joy. I have been blessed to find the best individuals who uplift and inspire me to live fully. Together, we embark on this incredible journey, supporting and encouraging one another every step of the way.

So, let us be selective in our choices, for the people we surround ourselves with have the power to transform our lives. Let us seek out the perfectionists, those who elevate us to new heights, who infuse every moment with a sense of wonder. Together, we will craft a breathtaking masterpiece, a life filled with love, happiness, and the magic of shared experiences. Armed with my trusty vehicle and an insatiable thirst for adventure, I delved into a world filled with captivating stories and unexpected connections.

On a late night, as I prepared to drive for the night shift, my phone buzzed with an incoming call. It was my mom seeking assistance, and my heart filled with love and determination as I answered the call.

"Hey, Mom! What's going on?" I greeted warmly, eager to lend a helping hand.

She explained that her car had encountered trouble and needed a ride to work. Without hesitation, I assured her, "Don't worry, Mom. I'll be there as soon as I finish my current trip."

With the ride-share app turned off, I embarked on a swift journey to pick up my mom. The familiar streets whizzed by as I eagerly anticipated the opportunity to follow my passion and provide much-needed support to my family.

Upon arriving at my mom's doorstep, she greeted me with a tight embrace, expressing her gratitude with heartfelt words.

"Thank you, my dear. I am so thankful for your help."

A warm smile graced my lips as I replied, "It's my pleasure, Mom. You can always count on me."

With my mom safely on her way to work, I resumed my ride-share adventures, ready to welcome new passengers into my world. Each ride brought a unique story to unfold, a chance to connect with others and make a positive impact. I listened attentively, engaging in conversations that ranged from deep and meaningful to lighthearted and joyful. The power of human connection never ceased to amaze me. As the day progressed, my phone buzzed once again. This time, it was my dad reaching out for assistance. He needed groceries from Sam's Club and knew the person to rely on—me.

Grinning excitedly, I gladly accepted the request and reassured my dad, "Consider it done, Dad. I'll take care of everything." After dropping off my current passenger, I headed towards the Sam's Club, ready to tackle the grocery mission.

Wandering through the aisles, I meticulously selected each item on my dad's grocery list, ensuring I chose the freshest produce and their family's favorite treats. I felt fulfilled as I loaded the groceries into my car, knowing I was making life a little easier for my loved ones. Returning home, my parents' faces lit up with gratitude. Their smiles spoke volumes, filled with appreciation for my unwavering support.

As the day continued, fate seemed to have another surprise for me. While I was on my ride-share adventures, my phone rang once again. This time, my aunt from Carol Stream needed a ride to the doctor's office.

With a smile, I assured her, "I'll be there, Auntie. Let me finish my current trip, and I'll head straight to your place."

Auntie replied gratefully, "Oh, thank you, dear! You're a lifesaver. I appreciate your willingness to help me out."

A sense of purpose and excitement filled the air as I dropped off my current passenger. I navigated the streets with a heightened sense of anticipation, knowing I was about to assist my aunt in her time of need. Arriving at my aunt's home, I greeted her with a warm embrace, grateful for the opportunity to be there for her.

She smiled and said, "It's so wonderful to have family we can rely on. I'm fortunate to have you in my life."

With a reassuring nod, I replied, "And I'm lucky to have you too, Auntie. We'll get through this together."

We embarked on a journey together, from Carol Stream to the doctor's office, sharing stories and laughter. The car became a sanctuary of connection and support as we reminisced about old family traditions and shared life updates. Through our conversations, I could sense Auntie's worries easing, replaced by a sense of comfort and reassurance. When we arrived at the doctor's office, Auntie turned to me with a grateful smile.

"Thank you, my dear. Not just for the ride but for being there and brightening my day. You truly have a gift for bringing joy to others."

I couldn't help but feel a swell of pride and gratitude. "It's my pleasure, Auntie. Knowing I could make a difference in your day means the world. And remember, I'm just a call away whenever you need anything."

With a heartfelt hug, we parted ways, both uplifted by the shared experience. As I continued my day as a ride-share driver, I carried that sense of fulfillment and connection, reminding myself of the profound impact we can have on each other's lives, even in the simplest of moments. The universe aligned perfectly, allowing me to assist not only my immediate family but also my extended family members. Through the flexibility and freedom of my ride-share work, I could be there for those who needed me, creating a world filled with love, support, and genuine connections.

As I dropped my aunt off at the doctor's office, she expressed her heartfelt gratitude, thanking me for being her reliable source of support. I smiled and reassured her that it was my pleasure to be there for her.

With a renewed sense of purpose, I continued my ride-share adventures, knowing each trip could positively impact someone's life. Whether driving passengers to their destinations or assisting my loved ones, I cherished the ability to create time and space for the people who mattered most in my life.

In the vibrant mosaic of my life, work, personal life, and the cherished presence of my beloved Yorkshire Terrier, Louie, have seamlessly intertwined. Despite knowing Louie only had a few more years to live, I consciously embraced each day with my furry companion. Together, we embarked on adventures, creating unforgettable memories that will forever be etched in the tapestry of my life.

Louie became integral to my journey, accompanying me on trips and sharing the joy of exploration. Whether on a road trip to a picturesque destination or a stroll through a local park, his presence added an extra layer of happiness and companionship. I delighted in witnessing his excitement as he breathed in the fresh air while the wind gently tousled his fur, his face adorned with a contented smile.

I wanted Louie to experience the best of life, including delectable human food. Chicken, beef, and bacon were some of his favorite foods. He was a true meat lover. He was very picky and never ate any vegetables. He would stare at me with that look when I offered him something other than meat. You are not planning to feed that to me, are you? Would I eat something different other than meat? Give me the good stuff, please. I lovingly fed him the delicious treats he desired, savoring the joyous moments of watching him relish every bite. His happiness became my own, and our bond grew more robust with each shared meal.

Louie's zest for life extended beyond our adventures and culinary indulgences. There were moments when he would perch on my lap, with his paws gently resting on the steering wheel, as we navigated Chicago's diverse neighborhoods and suburbs. Together, we explored the vibrant tapestry of the city, discovering hidden gems and embracing the unique experiences each locale had to offer. At the same time, his eyes watched away far and wide while his eyes looked out the front drier window.

Through Louie's presence, my life became a symphony woven with love, joy, and the unconditional companionship of a faithful friend. Every moment spent with him reminded me to cherish the present and live life fully and authentically. Louie taught me the importance of embracing simple pleasures, finding happiness in the smallest moments, and treasuring our bond. His magnetic personality and affectionate nature drew people towards him, even beyond our little bubble.

During our adventures together, whether on trips or simply going about our day-to-day routines, Louie became a source of delight not just for me but also for others. His irresistible charm and warm presence touched the hearts of those we encountered. Passengers on our journeys would often find themselves drawn to Louie, unable to resist his playful nature and the love he exuded.

People would eagerly engage with Louie, showering him affectionately, playing with him, and even giving him heartfelt hugs. The joy and love that radiated from Louie became contagious, spreading to those around us. It was heartwarming to witness the smiles on people's faces as they interacted with him, their eyes lighting up with the same love and joy he brought into my life.

Louie's ability to connect with others transcended boundaries and brought people together, even if just for a brief moment. The shared experience of enjoying his company created a sense of camaraderie, fostering connections that might not have otherwise been made. Through Louie, strangers became friends, united by their affection for this furry bundle of happiness.

Witnessing Louie's impact on others reinforced the profound lesson he taught me about the power of love and the importance of cherishing connections. His presence enriched my life and brought joy and happiness to those who crossed our paths. Louie's ability to spread love and joy amongst others became integral to our shared journey in this symphony of life.

Louie's legacy lives on in the memories we created together, both for me and those touched by his presence. He reminded us of the simple pleasure of connecting with others and sharing love and joy freely. Through him, I learned the immeasurable value of creating moments that bring happiness to ourselves and those around us.

As I reflect on the symphony of my life, Louie's paw prints are forever embedded within its notes. His ability to bring love and joy to others reminds him to continue fostering connections, embracing the simple pleasures, and sharing the unconditional love he so beautifully epitomized. In the symphony of life, Louie's impact extends far beyond our own experiences, weaving a legacy of passion and joy that will forever be cherished.

Overwhelmed with emotions, I tightly hugged Louie, my loyal furry companion. Tears welled in my eyes as I expressed gratitude for everything he had brought into my life.

"Thank you, my forever little boy," I whispered, my voice filled with love and appreciation. *"I know our time together is limited, but I want you to know that I have cherished every moment and done everything I could to give you the best life possible."*

I could feel Louie nuzzling against me as if he understood every word I said. His warm presence comforted me, reminding me of the unconditional love and joy he had brought into my world.

I continued, my voice filled with sadness and gratitude, "You've been there for me through thick and thin, through all the ups and downs. You were right by my side even during my Lyft rides, spreading your infectious happiness to me and our passengers."

With his wagging tail and bright eyes, Louie had become a beloved part of my Lyft journeys. Passengers often smiled and laughed as he eagerly accepted treats or playfully interacted with them. He brought an extra layer of joy and excitement to our rides, making them unforgettable.

"And let's not forget the indulgences," I chuckled, fondly remembering when we shared delicious burgers and sizzling bacon. "You've had the best feasts, my little foodie, and I'm glad I could spoil you with those treats."

Holding Louie close and gently kissing him on the forehead, I felt overwhelming love and gratitude. He had shown me the true meaning of unconditional love and forgiveness, even during the most challenging times in my life. His presence had brought healing and joy that I could never express appropriately in words or repay.

"Thank you, Louie," I whispered, my voice filled with emotions as he licked my face. "Thank you for showing me the power of love and forgiveness. You've touched my heart in ways I can't describe, and I will always carry your presence with me."

Louie looked up at me, his eyes filled with warmth and affection, as if he understood every sentiment that flowed from my heart. We stayed in that embrace for a while, cherishing the precious moments we had left together. In that tender moment, I knew that even though our time together would eventually end, the love and lessons Louie had taught me would endure. His paw prints will forever be imprinted on my heart, a reminder of his profound impact on my life.

With a deep sigh, I released my embrace, knowing that our journey together would be filled with beautiful memories and an everlasting bond of love. As we continued our rides, Louie by my side, we would continue spreading passion, joy, and forgiveness to everyone who stepped into our Lyft car.

As Louie's years dwindled, I was grateful for the opportunity to live a life intertwined with his. Our time together was a tapestry of love, adventure, and companionship that will forever hold a special place in my heart. And even though he is no longer physically by my side, his spirit inspires me to live life to the fullest, follow my passions, and cherish the cherished memories we created together.

In the grand tapestry of life, Louie's presence will always be a vibrant thread, a reminder of the beauty and joy of embracing every moment with those we hold dear. His unconditional love and zest for life have left an indelible mark on my journey, forever shaping the tapestry of my existence.

Each day presents new opportunities to create a world brimming with love, happiness, and joy. By prioritizing my loved ones and embracing the freedom of my chosen path, I have crafted a life that resonates with my most authentic self. Through my ride-share adventures, I not only fulfill my thirst for experience but also touch the lives of those around me in the most beautiful and meaningful ways.

In this newfound way of being, the aura of love, happiness, and joy permeates every aspect of my existence. It radiates from within me, touching the lives of those around me. They bask in the warmth of my presence, and together, we create a symphony of shared experiences and cherished memories. We can explore, live authentically, no longer bound by societal constraints, and cherish every precious moment.

With each step forward, our world expands, and the possibilities become limitless. We nurture our connections, lending a helping hand to friends and family whenever they need it. We understand that self-care and self-love are essential and prioritize activities that bring us joy and rejuvenation. In this creation of our reality, we have discovered a life beyond our wildest imagination—a life where love triumphs, happiness abounds, and joy dances in every step. Together, we embrace the freedom to live on our terms, to be present for one another, and to nurture a world filled with love, happiness, and joy.

As I navigate the city of Chicago, I encounter a diverse array of passengers, each carrying their own stories and perspectives. Through heartfelt conversations and shared moments, their tales weave together to form a tapestry of human experiences, revealing our choices' profound impact on our happiness and the world around us.

One passenger named Richard, a successful entrepreneur, shares their journey of chasing material wealth and societal recognition. Despite their accomplishments, they confess to feeling a void within, a longing for something more meaningful. Through their story, I understand the importance of prioritizing love, happiness, and joy over external accolades.

As Richard pointed at a towering building, their eyes filled with ambition, they declared, "I will live in that big building one day." However, a sense of emptiness lingered in their voice, which sparked my concern. "You've achieved so much already," I said gently, "but it seems like something is missing. Happiness is what truly matters in life."

The passenger sighed, shifting their gaze from the building to the passing scenery. "You're right," they admitted, their voice tinged with vulnerability. "I've chased material wealth and societal recognition, thinking they would fulfill me. But despite my accomplishments, there's this void inside that I can't seem to fill."

I nodded, understanding their struggle. "Sometimes, we get caught up in pursuing external markers of success," I said, my voice filled with empathy. True happiness isn't found solely in material possessions or societal recognition. It lies in the moments of joy, love, and connection we experience along the journey."

The passenger looked at me, searching for answers. "Though, how do I find that happiness?" they asked, their eyes a mix of curiosity and longing.

I smiled, knowing that the answer lay not in acquiring more but in embracing the present and finding fulfillment in life's simple pleasures.

"It starts with shifting our focus," I replied. "Instead of solely chasing external achievements, let's prioritize enjoying the journey. Take time to savor the little moments, nurture relationships, and pursue activities that bring you genuine joy."

Richard confessed, "I've neglected those aspects of my life." His voice was tinged with regret. I've been so consumed by pursuing success that I've forgotten how it truly feels like to live."

"I understand how easy it can be to get caught up in the chase," I empathized. "Remember, life is about more than just achievements. It's about the moments that take your breath away and the connections that fill your heart."

Their eyes met mine, searching for reassurance. "Do you think it's too late for me to change my life?" he asked, his voice tinged with hope.

With a reassuring smile, I replied, "It's never too late to refocus and realign your priorities. Every day is a new opportunity to make choices that bring you closer to a life that truly resonates with your heart."

They nodded slowly as if pondering the possibilities. "But where do I start? How do I even begin to rediscover what truly brings me happiness?"

I paused for a moment, carefully choosing my words. "Start by carving out time to reflect and explore your passions. Engage in activities that ignite a fire within you, and pay attention to the moments that make you feel alive. That's where your true happiness lies."

Their expressions softened, and a glimmer of excitement danced in their eyes. "I've been so focused on the destination that I forgot to appreciate the journey," he mused.

I nodded, understanding his sentiment completely. "Indeed, life's true beauty lies not only in the achievements but also in the experiences, connections, and growth we encounter. Embrace the journey, and you'll find a renewed sense of purpose."

Richard took a deep breath as if exhaling the weight of their past choices. "I'm ready to make a change," he declared, determination shining through.

With genuine encouragement, I replied, "That's the spirit!
Remember, this is your life, and you have the power to shape
it. Embrace the opportunities that come your way, and savor
the richness of each moment. You're on the path to
rediscovering what it truly means to live."

Together, we embarked on a journey of self-discovery, weaving an experience of purpose, fulfillment, and appreciation for the beauty of life. As we continued our drive, the passengers' demeanor shifted, a glimmer of hope replacing the emptiness they once expressed.

"You're right," they said, a newfound determination in his
voice. "Happiness is not found in a big building or external
validations. It's about finding joy in the present and
embracing the journey, no matter where it takes us."

I smiled, proud to have sparked a shift in perspective.
"Exactly," I replied. "Remember, life is a collection of
moments, and pursuing happiness is a lifelong journey.
Embrace the journey, and you'll find that true fulfillment lies
not in the destination but in the experiences and connections
we make along the way."

As we reached his destination, the passenger stepped out of the car, his face adorned with a genuine smile. "Thank you, Marshall," he said, gratitude filling their voice. "I needed this reminder. From now on, I'll prioritize happiness and enjoy every step of the journey."

I waved off to him, filled with satisfaction, knowing I had played a small part in their realization. As I continued to drive, I couldn't help but reflect on the profound truth that happiness is everything – a treasure worth pursuing and cherishing throughout our lives.

Another passenger, a young artist named Ana, opens up about their struggle to pursue their passion in a world that often undervalues creative pursuits. Their determination to create a world filled with love, happiness, and joy inspires me, reminding me that we can shape our reality through our choices and actions.

As the young artist settled into the backseat, I could sense excitement and apprehension in her demeanor. Curiosity got the better of me, and I asked, "What brings you to Chicago, Ana?"

She smiled, her eyes sparkling with passion. "I moved here because I believe this city appreciates and embraces the arts," she explained. "I want to attend the Art Institute of Chicago to pursue my dreams of becoming a professional artist."

Impressed by her determination, I couldn't help but feel inspired. "That's incredible," I said, my voice filled with admiration. "It takes courage to follow your passion, especially in a world that often undervalues creative pursuits. What drives you to pursue art?"

Ana's gaze turned introspective as if searching for the right words. "For me, art is a way to create a world filled with love, happiness, and joy," she expressed, her voice filled with conviction. "I believe that through my art, I can inspire others to see the beauty that exists in every moment and find happiness in their lives."

Her words resonated deeply, reminding me of the power we hold to shape our reality through our choices and actions. "You're right," I replied with a newfound determination. "Happiness is everything, and it's up to us to create a world that reflects that."

406

The artist nodded, her eyes shining with understanding.
"Exactly," she agreed. "We can infuse love, happiness, and
joy into every aspect of our lives. It starts with embracing our
passions and sharing our unique gifts with the world."

As we drove through the vibrant streets of Chicago, the
artist shared her dreams and the challenges she faced in pursuing
her artistic journey. She spoke of the moments of self-doubt and
the pressures to conform to societal norms. Yet, through it all, her
unwavering belief in the power of art to bring happiness and
inspire change fueled her determination.

Moved by her story, I couldn't help but offer
encouragement," Remember, your art has the potential to
touch hearts, ignite creativity, and bring joy to others," I
said, my voice filled with conviction. By pursuing your
passion, you are creating a path to your happiness and
spreading happiness to the world around you."

The artist smiled, and gratitude was evident in her eyes.
"Thank you," she said softly. Sometimes, it feels like an uphill
battle, but conversations like this remind me that I'm on the

right path. It's about staying true to myself and using my art to make a positive impact."

As we neared her destination, I couldn't help but feel grateful for our shared connection. The artist stepped out of the car, her spirit uplifted and determined. "Remember," she said, her voice filled with hope, "happiness is not just a destination but a state of being. Let's continue creating and inspiring one brushstroke at a time."

I waved goodbye, inspired and reminded of our incredible power to shape our reality and spread happiness through our passions. As I continued to drive, I carried her words with me, fueling my determination to create a world filled with love, happiness, and joy.

Yet another passenger, a wise elderly gentleman, imparts invaluable lessons learned through a lifetime of experiences. He emphasizes that true happiness lies not in accumulating possessions or achievements but in nurturing genuine connections, spreading kindness, and finding joy in the simplest moments.

As the wise elderly gentleman settled into the backseat, a sense of wisdom emanated. Intrigued by his presence, I couldn't help but initiate a conversation.

"What has life taught you about happiness?" I asked, my
voice filled with curiosity.

He smiled warmly, his eyes twinkling with a lifetime of
memories.

"Happiness," he said, his voice carrying a gentle depth, "is
not found in the accumulation of possessions or the pursuit of
achievements. True happiness lies in the connections we
forge, the kindness we spread, and the joy we find in the
simplest moments."

His words intrigued me, and I leaned in, eager to learn
more.

"Could you share an example from your own life?" I asked,
hoping for a glimpse into his experiences.

He nodded, a nostalgic smile gracing his lips. "Certainly, I
spent decades chasing career success, always striving for the
next promotion and accolade. But in pursuing external
validation, I neglected my relationships and the small
moments that truly matter."

Curiosity piqued, I asked, "So, what changed? How did you find true happiness?"

He chuckled softly as if reminiscing about a well-kept secret. "It was a simple realization," he said. "I discovered that the true richness of life is found in the love and connection we share with others. The laughter shared with friends, the warmth of an embrace, and the moments of pure joy fill our hearts."

I nodded, understanding the profound truth in his words. "But in a world that often prioritizes material success, how can we find that true happiness?" I asked, my voice filled with genuine curiosity.

He sat back, thoughtful for a moment. "It begins with a shift in perspective," he answered. "Instead of measuring our worth by external achievements, let's focus on nurturing our relationships, being present in the moment, and finding joy in the simplest pleasures."

I couldn't help but feel inspired, imagining a world where happiness was not tied to possessions or accomplishments but to the connections we fostered and the love we shared. "That

sounds truly fulfilling," I said, my voice filled with

admiration. "But how can we apply this wisdom in our own

lives?"

He smiled, a twinkle of wisdom in his eyes. "It starts with

small acts of kindness," he advised. "A genuine smile, a

helping hand, or a thoughtful word can go a long way in

brightening someone's day. By spreading kindness, we create

ripples of happiness that touch the lives of others."

As we continued our journey, his words resonated deeply within me. I couldn't help but reflect on cherishing genuine connections and finding joy in the simplest moments. The wise elderly gentleman had reminded me that true happiness is not elusive; it's within our grasp, waiting to be nurtured and shared.

He turned to me with a gentle smile as we reached his

destination. "Remember," he said, his voice filled with

warmth, "happiness is not a distant dream. It's woven into

the fabric of our daily lives, waiting to be discovered and

embraced."

I thanked him for his wisdom and was grateful for the reminder of what truly matters. As he stepped out of the car, I couldn't help but carry his words with me, inspired to nurture connections, spread kindness, and find joy in the simplest moments.

Through the diverse narratives shared by my passengers, I am reminded that creating a world with love, happiness, and joy begins with our choices. It is about cultivating meaningful relationships, pursuing our passions, and embracing gratitude for the present moment.

Listening to his stories inspires me to reflect on my path and the impact I can have on the world around me. I realize that by consciously choosing love, happiness, and joy in every interaction, I can become an agent of positive change, planting seeds of compassion and spreading joy throughout my journey.

In this exciting chapter, the experiences and insights of my passengers serve as a potent reminder that our choices matter. They shape not only our happiness but also the world we inhabit. So, let us embark on this adventure together, creating a world filled with love, happiness, and joy, one choice at a time.

It was a cold winter night on New Year's Eve. I eagerly assisted passengers, racing to their rescue while navigating the night of New Year's Eve celebrations. As fireworks exploded into the air off Navy Pier, excitement and festivities filled the atmosphere. Along the way to the next party, I picked up two passengers.

One of the passengers conversed with her friend Loren, urging her to break up with her boyfriend. "He is no good for you," she insisted. "He isn't your match," she added, disapproving. The friend replied hesitantly, "She doesn't know what to do."

Once her friend left, Loren approached me and asked for advice. "What should she do?" she questioned.

I took a moment to explain and then asked her, "Are you happy? That is all that matters. It doesn't matter what your friends say or anyone else says. As long as you are happy, you can make the relationship work. You are the one in a relationship with your boyfriend, not her. If your friend is truly your friend, she will respect your decision."

I could see Loren pondering my words, her eyes filled with contemplation. At that moment, the weight of choice hung in the air, waiting for her to decide her path. Her thoughts seemed to dance between doubt and determination. The neon lights and laughter from the New Year's celebrations outside mirrored the emotions swirling within her.

Finally, with a deep breath, she broke the silence.

"You're right," Loren said, her voice filled with a newfound conviction. I need to follow my heart and make my own choices, regardless of what others think. It is my relationship, not hers. It's my happiness that matters most."

Loren expressed deep gratitude, stating that it was one of the best pieces of advice she had received in a long time. A smile of relief and determination spread across her face as if a heavy burden had been lifted. At that moment, she decided to take control of her happiness and pave her path. She thanked me sincerely for the guidance, giving me an unexpected kiss on the cheek and telling me she loved me.

In that simple interaction, I realized the power we hold as individuals to shape our lives and the lives of those around us. Our choices, big or small, have ripple effects that extend far beyond ourselves. We can inspire, encourage, and support others in their journeys.

As the night progressed, I encountered passengers from various walks of life, each with unique stories and perspectives. Some were celebrating new beginnings, while others were reflecting on the year that had passed. Through their conversations, I witnessed the power of choice once again.

A young couple, holding hands tightly, shared their decision to pursue a long-distance relationship despite the challenges ahead. Their commitment to love and willingness to sacrifice for each other reminded me of the power of choosing love over fear.

I grinned with excitement and the freshness of the upcoming New Year."So, here we are on this wild New Year's Eve adventure! Buckle up, folks; it will be one unforgettable ride!"

As Sean's hand gripped his partner's hand tighter, "I can't believe we're starting the new year like this, babe. It's bittersweet, but I believe in us."

Savanna gazed affectionately into her partner's eyes, "I know, love. Distance may separate us physically, but our hearts will always be connected. This journey is just another chapter in our love story."

As I glanced at the couple through the rearview mirror, I said, "You know, folks, love like yours is a rare gem. It takes courage and determination to pursue a long-distance relationship. What's your secret?"

Sean smiled softly and said, "Communication, Marshall. We promised each other open and honest communication. We'll share our triumphs, our struggles, and everything in between. And we'll make every moment count when we're together."

Savannah gently nudged her partner and said, "And a sprinkle of spontaneity! Surprise visits, spontaneous trips, and even virtual date nights—we'll find creative ways to keep the spark alive."

I nodded approvingly, "I like your style, lovebirds! Remember, distance is just a test of how far love can travel. And I feel your love will soar higher than any plane or cross any ocean to be together."

Sean giggled, "You're right, Marshall! Our love knows no boundaries. We'll conquer the miles and make every reunion a grand celebration."

Savannah mischievously grinned, "And when midnight strikes, we'll make a wish together — a wish for a year filled with adventures, surprises, and love that grows stronger with each passing day."

I raised my hand in a mock toast To love that defies distance, to the power of commitment, and to a year ahead filled with endless possibilities. Cheers, my friends!"

Sean and Savannah both raised their hands and intertwined their fingers, "Cheers!"

As the car continued on its journey, the young couple held each other's hands, their hearts brimming with hope, knowing their love was strong enough to weather any storm. At that moment, they felt a sense of exhilaration, embarking on a new year together and ready to conquer the world, one mile at a time.

Another middle-aged passenger spoke of his choice to leave a high-paying job that had left him unfulfilled. With a sparkle in his eyes, he shared his decision to pursue his true passion, even if it meant taking a leap of faith into the unknown. His courage inspired me to embrace my passions and dreams.

In each interaction, I realized that our choices not only shape our happiness but also have the potential to create a ripple effect of positivity and fulfillment in the world. Our choices, no matter how small or insignificant they may seem, matter. They have the power to transform our lives and the lives of those around us.

So, let us embark on this adventure together, committed to making choices that align with our hearts and bring joy into our lives. Let us choose love, compassion, and kindness, knowing that these choices can ripple outwards, creating a world filled with love, happiness, and joy, one option at a time.

As the clock struck midnight and the city erupted into cheers and fireworks, I couldn't help but feel a renewed sense of purpose. Our journey as Lyft drivers had become more than just providing rides. It had become an opportunity to touch lives, inspire change, and remind ourselves of the power we hold within us.

The road stretched before me, a blank canvas filled with limitless possibilities. The air was charged with the energy of a fresh start, and as the clock struck midnight, I felt a surge of excitement coursing through my veins. This wasn't just any ordinary day; it was the dawning of a new year, a chance to leave behind the old and embrace the new.

With each passing mile, I reflected on the significance of this moment. I realized that as the driver, I held a unique role in transporting my passengers physically and creating an atmosphere of positivity, connection, and inspiration.

I turned up the radio, filling the car with joyful melodies that seemed to dance in sync with the beating of my heart. The passengers, caught up in the infectious rhythm, tapped their feet and exchanged broad smiles. It was a small gesture, but it set the tone for what lay ahead—a journey filled with optimism and shared experiences.

As we traveled through the city streets, I consciously embraced each interaction as an opportunity to make a difference. Whether it was a friendly wave to a passerby or a kind word exchanged with a fellow driver, I knew that every action had the potential to create a ripple effect of positivity.

At a stoplight, I glanced at my passengers through the rearview mirror, their eyes alive with anticipation. I spoke up, my voice filled with enthusiasm, "You know, folks, this new year isn't just about resolutions or grand plans. It's about the small choices we make every day to bring joy, kindness, and compassion into the world."

Nate nodded, their expression thoughtful. "You're right, Marshall. It's those little acts of kindness that can have a profound impact on someone's day. A smile, a helping hand,

or even a listening ear can make all the difference."

Miguel chimed in, their voice filled with conviction. "And

it's not just about making a difference for others. It's about

cultivating our well-being, too. Taking care of ourselves,

pursuing our passions, and embracing positivity can radiate

outward and inspire those around us."

I smiled, grateful for their insights. It reminded me that my role as a driver went beyond the steering wheel; it was an opportunity to foster a sense of community and uplift the spirits of those who embarked on this journey with me.

The night sky twinkled with fireworks; I made a silent promise to myself—to approach each interaction with an open heart, to spread kindness like confetti, and to be a beacon of positivity on this road of life. As I continued driving through the new day of the New Year, I knew that with every choice I made, I could create a positive impact for my passengers and myself. Together, we would navigate the twists and turns of the road, embracing the magic of possibility and the joy of shared experiences. Let's make every New Year an unforgettable chapter in each of our stories, filled with love, growth, and the power to create a brighter tomorrow.

One fateful day, as I embarked on my usual Lyft driving shift, I picked up a passenger named Tasha. Her vibrant energy and determination filled the car, instantly brightening my day. Little did I know that this ride would become a memorable journey for both of us.

Tasha, a dreamer from Englewood in Chicago, had recently moved to Lakeview to pursue her lifelong aspiration of becoming a nurse. Her enthusiasm for making a difference in people's lives. I chuckled as I recounted how I fantasized about retiring to a tropical paradise, sipping coconut water, and enjoying the warm sun.

As we chatted, the topic of retirement emerged, and I couldn't help but share a humorous anecdote about my mother's retirement plans with Tasha.

Tasha's eyes lit up, and she leaned forward, intrigued. "That sounds like a dream," she said. "But what about making a difference in retirement?"

With a mischievous grin, I responded, "Well, Tasha, picture this: after a fulfilling nursing career, you retire and decide to use your skills to volunteer in underprivileged communities. You could travel the world, providing medical care to those in

*need. Your kindness and expertise would touch countless
lives."*

*Tasha's excitement was palpable. "Wow," she exclaimed,
"that would be incredible!"*

*I nodded, feeling inspired myself. "Tasha. Retirement isn't
just about relaxing; it's an opportunity to continue making a
positive impact. It's a chance to embark on new adventures,
explore passions, and leave a lasting legacy."*

Our conversation continued, filled with laughter, quotes, and shared dreams. The Lyft ride turned into a journey of inspiration and possibility. Tasha and I formed a bond, united by our desire to chase our dreams and make a difference in the world.

*As we arrived at Tasha's destination, she turned to me with a
grateful smile. "Thank you for reminding me that retirement
is not the end but a new beginning," she said. "I will keep
pursuing my dreams and using my skills to change lives."*

With a final farewell, Tasha stepped out of the car, her determination radiating. As I continued my Lyft driving, I couldn't help but feel a sense of fulfillment. Our encounter reminded me that every interaction can uplift and inspire others, no matter how brief.

As I navigated the streets, I remembered Tasha's unwavering spirit of living life to the fullest. Our chance meeting reaffirmed my belief that I can touch lives, share stories, and ignite dreams as a Lyft driver.

I told my mom, "I am concerned for you."

"Why?" my mom replied.

"Because you are in your 70s now. You could have retired when you were 65. You can find all sorts of things to do, like going to the gym to take care of yourself, going on vacation with dad, spending more time with friends and relatives, and going to church with your friends," I continued. She has been a registered nurse at the government hospital for nearly 30 years and will retire with one of the best government-graded pensions.

My mom countered, "Many people retire, and the ones I know pass away within a few years."

At first, I didn't believe her, so I told my Auntie Lora to convince my mom to retire.

My aunt replied, "It's her choice if she wants to work. You cannot decide for her what to do."

Later, I met a passenger who worked in waste management for the city. He asked me what I thought about retirement.

She explained, "I had a few coworkers who worked until retirement. They were so happy, but a few years after retiring, many people became depressed because they lost their purpose and motivation every morning."

It's straightforward to say what you will do when it happens, but it's always a different situation when one stands at the dangerous decision bridge. When I expressed my wish for my mother's retirement, I highlighted the benefits she could enjoy after fifty years of dedicated service to her field in healthcare. The allure of restful nights and the freedom to prioritize her health, spend time with loved ones, and indulge in personal interests seemed enticing.

Throughout my journeys, I encountered numerous passengers who confidently asserted that retirement would grant them ample opportunities for leisure. Vacations, quality time with family and friends, fitness routines—these were among the activities they eagerly anticipated. Yet, I also met those who echoed my mother's sentiment, recounting stories of friends who had passed away soon after retiring.

Amid a long ride-share journey, I picked up another passenger, Daniel, who exuded an air of contentment. His silver hair and gentle smile hinted at a life well-lived, and his kind eyes seemed to hold a wealth of stories. He mentioned that he is retired at 75 years old.

Engaged in casual conversation, Daniel asked me, "How old are you, young one?"

I replied, "I'm in my 30s, sir." His eyes sparkled with memories as he leaned back in his seat. "Ah, the 30s," he mused, "such busy years, full of excitement and ambition."

Curiosity got the better of me, so I inquired about Daniel's plans for the evening. With a twinkle in his eye, he responded, "I'm going for dinner with some old friends tonight." Intrigued, I couldn't help but ask, "Are you going for Italian food tonight?"

To my surprise, Daniel burst into laughter, his cheerful voice filling the air. "How did you know?" he exclaimed, clearly amused.

I chuckled in response. "Oh, it was just a lucky guess," I said with a grin. "Most people I speak to enjoy going to Italian restaurants."

As my car drove on, we continued our conversation, sharing stories and laughter. In that fleeting moment, I realized that age was no barrier to happiness and that chance encounters with strangers could bring unexpected joy. Little did I know that this brief encounter would leave a lasting impression, reminding me to appreciate the simple pleasures and the connections we make along life's journey.

Reflecting on the contrasting viewpoints, I realized both sides held valid arguments. Ultimately, the decision to retire or continue working is profoundly personal and varies from individual to individual. The allure of retirement's promises must be weighed against the potential consequences of an idle existence. As our conversation deepened, the older man confided in me about his struggle to fill his days with meaningful activities. He admitted it was becoming a problem as the hours seemed to stretch endlessly. His voice carried a tinge of sadness, hinting at the void he felt in his daily routine. Listening to Daniel's words, I couldn't help but recall my mother's sentiments about retirement. She had always maintained a strong desire to keep working, fearing that a lack of purpose would lead to a similar sense of restlessness and dissatisfaction.

Daniel sighs, "You know, Marshall, as I've grown older, I've faced a new challenge. The struggle to fill my days with meaningful activities has become overwhelming."

Listening attentively, I reply, "I can understand how that could affect you. It's important to find purpose and fulfillment in our daily lives. What seems to be causing this void, if I may ask?"

Daniel's expression, fixed on the passing scenery, says, "Well, Marshall, the truth is, the hours seem to stretch endlessly, and I often find myself longing for something more. Retired from work, my days lack structure and purpose. It's difficult to find meaningful activities that bring me joy and a sense of fulfillment."

"I can imagine how that can be challenging. But you know, the little things can sometimes make a big difference. Have you considered exploring new hobbies or reconnecting with old passions?" I said as I nodded emphatically.

Daniel pauses momentarily as his facial expression seems pondering, and then he says, "You're right, Marshall. I used to love painting, but it's been years since I picked up a brush. Perhaps it's time to revisit that passion and let the strokes of colors fill my days once again."

"Absolutely! Rediscovering a hobby can bring so much joy and purpose. You never know; your paintings might inspire others and bring beauty into their lives. Remember, it's never too late to pursue your passions", I said encouragingly as we both witnessed the beautiful art structures off Michigan Avenue.

"Thank you, Marshall. Your words give me hope. I realize now that I can shape my days and seek out meaningful activities that ignite my soul. It's time to embrace this chapter of life and fill it with purpose and fulfillment," Daniel smiles faintly.

As I rolled down the window and felt Chicago's Fall breeze

flow through my hair, I said, "That's the spirit! Life is a

journey; each day is a chance to create something

extraordinary. Don't hesitate to step outside your comfort

zone and explore new horizons. I do not doubt you'll find a

treasure trove of experiences waiting to be discovered."

As the conversation continued, Marshall and the passenger delved deeper into the possibilities ahead. The passenger's voice carried a newfound sense of hope and determination with each passing mile. It was a reminder that even in the face of uncertainty, there was always an opportunity to fill one's days with purpose, joy, and the pursuit of passions. Together, they embarked on this journey of self-discovery, eager to embrace the endless possibilities that awaited them. Daniel's predicament resonated with me, highlighting the importance of finding fulfillment beyond our careers. It made me realize that retirement should not be merely stopping work but embracing new passions, hobbies, and connections.

At that moment, I shared my mother's perspective with the retired passenger, explaining how she believed that work provided a sense of purpose and fulfillment. He nodded thoughtfully, understanding the wisdom in her mindset. He even described his concern that he is living a great retired life, but he also expressed his worries about running out of activities to do in his retirement lifestyle.

As we continued our journey to the drop-off address and our conversation continued, we exchanged ideas and suggestions for ways he could explore new interests and engage in more activities that would bring him joy. It became apparent that the key lay in discovering what sparked his curiosity and ignited his spirit.

Our encounter left me pondering the delicate balance between work and leisure and the importance of finding personal fulfillment in every stage of life. It served as a gentle reminder to cherish the present, embrace new experiences, and never stop seeking the things that make our hearts come alive. I learned from these encounters that it is easy to speculate on what one would do in another person's shoes. However, when faced with the decision in the present moment, the situation's complexity becomes more apparent. The realities and emotions will always shape our choices, which may not or defy easy predictions.

In a different story that contains more novels, a serendipitous encounter unfolded as I picked up a passenger named Elana, who happened to be a therapist. Intrigued by her remark about my positive energy, she shared something deeply personal, confiding in me in a way she rarely did with others.

Eagerly, I leaned in and said, "I'm here to listen; please go ahead."

In delicate conversations, it's crucial to approach them with care and empathy. I can establish a foundation of understanding and respect by creating a safe space and actively listening. I acknowledge that words hold immense power—they can heal wounds, bridge gaps, and ignite positive change. As I engage in this delicate conversation, I commit to being open-minded, patient, and compassionate. I understand that my words can shape the outcome of this discussion, and I strive to use them wisely, fostering understanding and connection. With a mix of vulnerability and strength, Elana revealed a poignant family history.

"My father and aunt were both Holocaust survivors," she started. "Growing up, my hair was naturally blonde, but my aunt insisted that I dye it even blonder as I got older. She carried the weight of past traumas and wanted to shield me, even though I wasn't directly part of the war."

Moved by her story, I responded with genuine empathy, expressing my admiration for her family's resilience.

"Congratulations to your family for surviving unimaginable hardships," I said softly. "I can only begin to fathom the lasting trauma they must have endured. I am truly sorry your family had to go through that."

As the conversation continued, the passenger revealed another incredible survival tale.

"My uncle, too, managed to survive three years in a concentration camp," she shared. "The Nazis singled him out because, despite his blonde hair and blue eyes, he didn't fit their stereotypical image of a Jewish person. They could tell from his ears that he was Jewish."

As the therapist shared her connection to the story of her uncle, I couldn't help but feel a surge of anger and disbelief at the cruelty inflicted upon him and so many others during that dark period of history.

"I am utterly horrified by the dehumanizing treatment your uncle endured," I expressed, my voice filled with righteous indignation. To think that the Nazis would base their judgment on something as arbitrary as the shape of his ears is

beyond comprehension. It speaks volumes about the depths of

their hatred and prejudice."

The passenger's admission that she still covers her ears as a tribute to her uncle struck a chord deep within me. It was a poignant reminder that the impact of the past could linger in our present lives, even decades later. The resilience and determination of her family to survive had left an indelible mark on her, a reminder of the profound sacrifices made by those who came before us. Moved by the passenger's dedication to honoring her uncle's experience, I couldn't help but admire her empathy and resilience. The passenger said that is why she covered her ears.

"You are indeed an extraordinary person," I shared with genuine admiration. "The fact that you carry the pain and empathy of your uncle and choose to pay tribute to him is a testament to your strength and compassion. It is a beautiful way to honor his memory and ensure his story lives on."

In that moment, a profound connection was forged between us, a shared understanding of the importance of remembering and honoring the victims of the Holocaust. We stood together, united in our commitment never to forget and to ensure that the stories of those who suffered are told and heard. In response, I acknowledged the pain she carried, understanding the deep connection she felt to her uncle's experience.

"I am so sorry," I said sincerely. "I can see you are an empath, feeling and expressing the same pain your uncle endured. Again, I am deeply sorry, but I am also grateful that your family survived."

Moved by her strength and resilience, the passenger turned to me and said, "You are such a remarkable person. You have the qualities of a therapist, just like me."

I chuckled and replied, "Haha, my friend Haley, who happens to be a therapist as well, often tells me the same thing. I always supported her during her time at the University of Chicago in Hyde Park."

To my surprise, the therapist laughed and shared that she attended the same university and held the same degree. This incredible coincidence brought us closer.

"Funny how life works, isn't it?" I remarked. "My friend Haley is an incredible person, and we would often motivate and encourage each other with a quirky phrase: 'How bad do you want it? Do you want it? I don't think you want it bad enough.' It became our way of pushing each other forward during challenging times."

In that moment, a connection was forged between strangers, bound by shared experiences, empathy, and the power of friendship. Stories intertwined, shrinking the world and reminding us of the unexpected connections we can form and the strength we can find in each other. In response to the therapist's revelations, I felt compelled to share my own experiences with Holocaust survivors.

"Throughout my life, I have had the privilege of meeting many incredible individuals who survived the Holocaust," I began. "I am filled with immense happiness and gratitude for their survival and the stories they have shared with me. Yet, I still can't fully comprehend the depths of their trauma and grief."

I recounted a remarkable encounter with a Rabbi whose resilience and determination left a lasting impact on me.

"I once had the honor of picking up a Rabbi who shared his harrowing experience as an orphan during World War II. As the city became desolate and abandoned, he and his friends had to find a way to survive without any food. They resorted to scraping tar off the streets with knives, using it as a substitute to keep their stomachs full. They lived in constant fear, knowing that the Nazis were supposed to invade England within two weeks. But miraculously, the war ended, leading to their survival."

Growing up Catholic and attending a private Catholic school, St. Lambert, from pre-kindergarten to 8th grade, gave me a unique educational experience. As part of our curriculum, we had several field trips to the Holocaust Museum in Skokie and had the opportunity to visit synagogues. Our school's efforts garnered attention, as we were featured on Channel 7 news. From a young age, we were taught the values of respect and appreciation for everyone, regardless of their background.

My exposure to the Holocaust and Jewish culture continued when I attended Notre Dame High School for Boys for two years. We also had field trips to the Holocaust Museum, further deepening my understanding of this tragic event in history. These visits impacted me, and I developed a profound appreciation for the survivors I encountered.

Moved by the stories shared by a Rabbi, I expressed my deep appreciation for the Holocaust survivors I had encountered and the profound impact they had on me. I acknowledged the importance of visiting numerous Holocaust museums, paying tribute to the memory of those who perished, and holding deep wonder and appreciation for the survivors who played a vital role in shaping my perspective on humanity.

"I have also visited numerous Holocaust museums, paying tribute to the memory of those who perished and holding deep wonder and appreciation for the survivors I have been fortunate enough to meet," I shared.

At that moment, the passenger and I shared an understanding—a recognition of the incredible strength and resilience displayed by those who endured such unspeakable horrors. This recognition reminded us of the importance of honoring their memory, listening to their stories, and learning from their experiences.

As our journey continued, the weight of these stories lingered in the air, reminding us of the indomitable human spirit that can rise above even the darkest of times. As I dropped off the passenger, we exchanged heartfelt gratitude and a shared commitment to carry these stories forward, ensuring that the lessons of the past are never forgotten. While the wheels continued to turn and the road stretched out before us, I couldn't help but marvel at the incredible stories that had unfolded within the confines of my car. Each encounter and conversation added a vivid brushstroke to the ever-evolving canvas of my journey. As I continued to navigate the roads of life, I carried with me the profound wisdom gained from these encounters—a reminder of the resilience of the human spirit. These bonds can form between strangers and the transformative power of compassion and understanding. The passenger's words resonated deep within me; their impact was immediate and profound.

"You are such a great person," she said, her voice sincere. Sometimes in life, it's essential to free ourselves."

Her words struck a chord, and I responded with a heartfelt understanding.

"Yes, I hope that during this short ride together, you could find some release from the trauma,"

I replied, my voice filled with compassion. "I understand that

healing takes time, and nothing can be released

simultaneously. But I am here to listen and support you, even

if just a little bit of that burden can be lifted, helping you find

freedom."

The passenger's gratitude and appreciation flowed from her, a testament to the power of empathy and understanding.

"You are such a great person," she expressed, her voice filled

with warmth. You deserve to have friends in which you

deserve to be yourself, to be free, who are good-hearted and as

happy as you are, not ever having to be worried of ever being

judged."

Filled with humility, I thanked the passenger, Elana, for her kind words. The exchange touched me deeply, reminding me of the importance of providing a safe and non-judgmental space for others to share their stories and heal. It reminded us that we all deserve compassion, understanding, and genuine connections.

As Elana exited the car, a sense of fulfillment and gratitude washed over me. Our encounter had been more than just a ride—an opportunity to offer support, listen, and help someone find a sense of release. And at that moment, I felt grateful for the ability to make a positive impact, no matter how small, in the lives of others.

As I continued on my journey, I carried with me the lessons learned from Elana's story—a reminder to always approach others with kindness and empathy, to create spaces where people feel safe to share their struggles, and to understand the power of freeing ourselves from the weight of our past.

As we parted ways, the image of the passenger, her hands gently covering her ears, stayed with me. It symbolized her connection to her family's history, the power of remembrance, and the importance of honoring the stories of those who suffered. It was a reminder that the past is not something to be forgotten or brushed aside but rather to be acknowledged, understood, and learned from.

As the ride ended, we exchanged heartfelt gratitude for our shared conversation, knowing it had deeply touched us. As I watched the passenger walk away, her head held high, I couldn't help but feel a renewed sense of purpose and a determination to continue spreading awareness and empathy in the world.

In the face of darkness, the light of empathy, compassion, and remembrance can bring healing and hope. Through our actions, big and small, we can contribute to a world that cherishes and protects the dignity and humanity of all people.

In the following days, I couldn't help but reflect on the passenger's journey and our conversations. It reminded me of the responsibility we all hold to carry the torch of remembrance, to ensure that the stories of the Holocaust are never silenced or erased. Each act of memory, whether covering one's ears or visiting museums, becomes a testament to the resilience of the human spirit and a commitment to a world free from hatred and prejudice.

And so, I made a vow to myself: to continue seeking out stories, to listen with empathy, and to honor the memory of those who suffered, for it is through these small acts that we can contribute to a collective consciousness, one that embraces compassion, understanding, and the unwavering belief that the atrocities of the past must never be repeated.

As I embarked on future journeys, I carried with me the weight of the passenger's story and the countless others that have left an imprint on my heart. As I navigated the roads, I hoped that by sharing these stories and refusing to forget, we could create a world where empathy and love triumph over hatred and discrimination.

Passengers' stories on retirement highlighted the intricacies of this significant life decision. As I continued my journeys, I gained a deeper understanding of individuals' dilemmas when contemplating retirement and many other topics that may be used in the same context. The ultimate lesson learned was that empathy and an open mind are essential when considering the choices we make by others, as the situation and individual experiences will always greatly influence which paths we may take in life.

It spoke of a truth that echoed through the ages: happiness is everything. We can make our own choices and actions to shape our destinies. Happiness is not something bestowed upon us by some external circumstances but rather a conscious decision we make each day. Each person has the key to their happiness, and it is up to them to unlock their door.

Indeed, dear readers, we are all characters in life's grand story, each with unique backgrounds, experiences, and ethnic origins. Our choices and actions give us the power to influence our happiness and those around us. As we navigate the intricacies of our interconnected stories, we realize the profound impact our choices can have on the lives of others.

In a world that can sometimes be filled with adversity and challenges, choosing kindness, forgiveness, and gratitude can create a ripple effect that touches the lives of others, spreading happiness far and wide. Just as the pebble's gentle touch upon the water's surface makes expanding circles, so too can our acts of love and compassion radiate outward, reaching hearts and souls in ways we may never fully comprehend.

The air was filled with a subtle warmth, caressed by a gentle breeze that carried the scent of summer. The city streets, usually bustling with activity, seemed to have settled into a serene lull. As I navigated through the charming neighborhood of Lakeview, the soft pitter-patter of raindrops added an enchanting layer to the atmosphere.

Like a delicate symphony, the light rain played a hypnotic rhythm against the asphalt. Each droplet danced upon impact, creating ephemeral patterns on windshields and glistening surfaces. The streets, adorned with a shimmering sheen, took on an ethereal quality under the glow of streetlights.

As I continued my journey, rain became my companion, a soothing backdrop that complemented the city's serenity. The occasional splash of water from passing vehicles added a playful note to the symphony, punctuating the stillness with moments of spontaneity.

Far from being inconvenient, the rain cast a gentle spell on the surroundings. The soft glow of street lamps reflected off the wet pavement, creating a captivating interplay of light and shadow. The buildings' architecture, adorned with charming awnings and flickering signs, took on a romantic allure in this subdued ambiance.

Though the rain fell lightly, its touch was refreshing, as if nature bestowed a gentle caress upon the city. It had an almost magical effect, creating tranquility over the usually bustling streets. The familiar hustle and bustle had given way to a more contemplative mood, as if the rain had whispered to the city, urging it to slow down and savor the moment.

Like delicate messengers from the heavens, the raindrops brought a sense of renewal and rebirth. They washed away the dust of everyday life, offering a momentary respite from the mundane. The city, typically in constant motion, now seemed to take a collective breath, embracing the calmness and allowing its residents to find solace within its embrace.

A sense of serenity washed over me as I maneuvered through the rain-kissed streets. The rhythmic raindrops on my car roof provided a comforting backdrop, inviting introspection and reflection. It was as if the world had slowed its pace, granting me the opportunity to appreciate the subtle beauty that often goes unnoticed in the frenetic rhythm of daily life.

That summer evening in June 2015, as my birthday drew near, I found myself captivated by the quiet charm of the rain-soaked streets of Lakeview. It was a momentary respite, a reminder to embrace the simple pleasures and find beauty even in the most tranquil moments. As I continued my journey, I felt grateful for the unexpected gift of this serene summer rain, forever etched in my memory as a testament to the beauty of nature's gentle touch.

As I approached the junction, a burst of color caught my eye, illuminating the darkened streets with a vibrant intensity. The roads were not flooded but adorned with a multitude of red, as if the magic of a mesmerizing spell had touched the city. Curiosity ignited within me, and I found myself irresistibly drawn closer to the source of this captivating display.

With my passengers by my side, we ventured into the heart of this spectacle, eager to immerse ourselves in the pulsating energy and joy that filled the rain-soaked streets. The vibrant red Chicago Blackhawks jerseys symbolized unity and devotion, worn proudly by an army of passionate fans who had spilled into the neighborhoods.

Far from dampening spirits, the rain added an exhilarating element to the festivities. It created a glistening backdrop that reflected the vibrant lights and added magic to the scene. The streets of Wrigleyville, Lincoln Park, Roscoe Village, and the surrounding neighborhoods became a playground of celebration, with bars and establishments overflowing with fans who had poured out to revel in the victory.

Laughter, cheers, and jubilant conversations filled the air as the party on the streets continued for hours. The infectious energy spread from one street to another, drawing people out of their homes and filling every corner with camaraderie. It was a collective outpouring of joy where strangers became friends, and the city became a tapestry of shared celebration.

The bars in Wrigleyville, Lincoln Park, and Roscoe Village became epicenters of the festivities, brimming with fans clad in the iconic red jerseys. The atmosphere inside these establishments was electric, as friends and strangers alike raised their glasses in unison, toasting the success of their beloved team. The sense of unity and camaraderie was palpable as the boundaries between neighborhoods blurred, and the city came together.

The party on the streets and in the bars continued deep into the night, with the festivity refusing to recede. It was a testament to the unyielding spirit of the Blackhawks fans and the power of sports to ignite passion and forge lasting connections. The rain-soaked streets only added to the atmosphere, heightening the sense of exhilaration and creating a shared experience that would forever be etched in the memories of all fortunate enough to be a part of it. As the night drew to a close, the echoes of joy and celebration lingered in the air, leaving behind a city forever changed by the power of sports and the unity of its people. The rain may have subsided, but the spirit of that unforgettable evening continued to reverberate through the streets, reminding us of the extraordinary moments that arise when a city comes together to celebrate a common cause.

As I continued my journey, picking up and dropping off more passengers, an overwhelming wave of happiness and joy flooded me. The victory of the Blackhawks in winning the Stanley Cup in 2015 resonated deeply within me. With my birthday just a week away, this triumph became an extraordinary gift, a symbol of celebration and victory that would forever be etched in my memory.

The rain-soaked streets glistened under the glow of streetlights, reflecting the vibrant energy that permeated the air. The bars and restaurants overflowed with ecstatic fans, their voices echoing through the night. Music blared, creating a symphony of celebration that reverberated through the city.

"Marshall, can you believe the energy in this city? The Blackhawks' victory has turned Chicago into a non-stop party zone!"

"Rachel! The whole city has been injected with an extra dose of excitement. I can feel it in the air!"

As I drove through the rain-soaked streets, I noticed a group of fans hilariously attempting to recreate some of the players' moves.

"Look at those fans, trying to imitate Crawford's iconic saves! They're getting into it!" Rachel adjusted her red Black Hawks Jersey on her shoulders.

"Haha, I love their enthusiasm! Who needs a goalie when you have passionate fans diving everywhere? Maybe we should join them!"

"Oh! Let's show them our best Crawford moves. Who knows, we might get scouted for the team!"

Laughter filled the car as you and Rachel playfully imitated the fans, mimicking dramatic saves and over-the-top dives.

"Marshall, do you think we'll be able to spot any Lightning fans sulking amid all this celebration?"

"Hmm, let's keep our eyes peeled! I bet we can spot them by the way they try to hide their blue and white jerseys under their coats. Poor souls!"

The two of us laugh, imagining the Lightning fans disguised among the sea of Blackhawks jerseys, desperately trying to avoid the victorious atmosphere.

"You know, driver, with all this excitement, I wouldn't be surprised if the city starts renaming streets after our beloved Blackhawks players!"

"Oh! We'll have Crawford Court, Shaw Street, and Toews Terrace! It'll be a map of Blackhawk's greatness!"

The absurdity of the idea made both of us chuckle. We imagined a city where streets were named after the beloved Blackhawks players. As I drove through the rain-soaked neighborhoods, Rachel's comedic moments added lightheartedness to the vibrant atmosphere. The energy in the air, the overflowing bars and restaurants, and the exuberant fans created a meaningful celebration that would be remembered fondly.

At that moment, I couldn't help but marvel at sports' unifying power. It was more than just a game; it was a catalyst that brought people together, bridging divides and forging connections. In the shared jubilation of that victorious night, we were united as one, bound by a shared love for our team and a collective pride for our city.

As the raindrops pitter-pattered on my windshield, I couldn't help but feel a renewed sense of purpose. The rain, far from dampening the city's spirits, only served to intensify the atmosphere of celebration. It was as if the heavens were shedding tears of joy, joining the chorus of triumph reverberating through the city streets.

The loud music added an extra layer of vitality to the night. It was the soundtrack of our collective happiness, the rhythm that pulsed through our veins. Each beat and note reminded us of the magical moments we had experienced together. The music became an anthem of celebration, a testament to the power of victory and the unbreakable bonds forged in the name of our beloved team.

As I drove through the rain-soaked streets, the faces of the passengers I picked up and dropped off mirrored the joy that filled my heart. Each interaction carried a shared sense of pleasure as we exchanged stories and relived the incredible moments of the game. The conversations flowed effortlessly as if we had known each other for years, connected by a shared love for the Blackhawks and the euphoria that coursed through our veins.

That night, as I navigated the city, I carried with me a renewed belief in the unifying power of sports. It transcended the boundaries of age, race, and background, bringing people together in a shared celebration of triumph. The rain-soaked streets and the filled bars became symbols of our collective spirit, a testament to the beauty of unity and the profound connections that can be forged amidst jubilant moments.

"Driver, can you believe the Blackhawks' winning streak? They know how to make history!"

"Oh, absolutely, Lindsey! It's like they have a secret recipe for success. Maybe they sprinkle some hockey magic in their pre-game rituals!"

"Haha, I wouldn't be surprised! I can imagine the players doing a victory dance in their locker room, summoning the hockey gods for good luck!"

"That would explain their incredible ice skills! Those moves must be the secret to their success. I should start dancing before every drive to bring us good fortune!

451

"Hey, why not? We can have our mini dance party in the car, channeling the Blackhawks' victory energy! Just make sure to keep your eyes on the road!"

"Safety first! But a little dance groove won't hurt. We'll have the happiest passengers in town, cruising to the beat of victory!"

We both laughed, imagining a car filled with dancing passengers while the Blackhawks' spirit overtook the airwaves.

"You know, Marshall, I can't help but feel a sense of unity during these victorious moments. It's like the entire city becomes one big Blackhawks family!"

"Exactly! It's incredible how sports have this amazing ability to bring people together. We may come from different backgrounds, but when celebrating a win, we're all on the same team!"

"Hey, Marshall, do you think the rain tonight is Mother Nature's way of showering the city with good luck for the Blackhawks?"

"Well, Lindsey, they say that rain brings good fortune, so it wouldn't surprise me! We may be witnessing a little extra luck falling from the sky tonight.

"I like that idea! The raindrops are little blessings, ensuring the Blackhawks' victory is celebrated with even more joy and happiness!"

"Absolutely! The rain-soaked streets and the filled bars testify to the city's unwavering support. It's as if the entire city is joining the celebration!"

As I continued navigating the rain-soaked streets, Lindsey's comedic conversation and playful banter added a layer of joy to the already jubilant atmosphere. The unifying power of sports and the Blackhawks' victories became more than just a game—they became moments of shared triumph and connection. We laughed and marveled at the team's winning streak, imagining dances and raindrops of good luck. It was a night to remember, where the city came alive with the spirit of celebration and unity.

As the night wore on and the celebrations continued, I couldn't help but feel deeply grateful for being a part of this extraordinary experience. The Blackhawks' victory brought immense joy to the city and reminded us of the resilience and power of the human spirit. It was a night of triumph, a night of celebration, and a night that would forever be etched in my memory.

Laughter, cheers, and excited chatter reverberated through the streets, creating an electrifying atmosphere that tingled with anticipation. The air crackled with an energy that seemed to transcend the mere celebration of a victory. It was a symphony of joy, a chorus of triumph that echoed through every corner of the city.

As we made our way through the bustling streets, the rhythm of drums reverberated through the air, infusing the atmosphere with an irresistible energy. Its pulsating beat synchronized our steps, guiding us toward an epicenter of celebration. The chants of fervent fans surged like a tidal wave, rising and falling in perfect harmony as if the city's heartbeat had synchronized with its people's passion.

Each step made us part of a living collage, placed together by a shared love for the Blackhawks. The boundaries that typically divided us dissolved, allowing us to transcend age, background, and perceived differences. In that moment, we were united, an unstoppable force moving as one towards a shared euphoria.\

It felt as if the entire city of Chicago had transformed into one giant festival, a celebration of unity, joy, and the indomitable spirit of sports. The streets were alive with laughter, music blaring from every corner, and the crowd's roar reverberating through the buildings. We were transported to the very heart of the United Center, the home of the Blackhawks, where the fans' energy is legendary.

The air crackled with an electric enthusiasm, charged with anticipation and excitement. The city had shed its ordinary skin and blossomed into a vibrant, pulsating playground of jubilation. Everywhere we turned, there were smiling faces, dancing bodies, and an overwhelming sense of collective exhilaration. It was a spectacle that transcended time and space as if the boundaries between reality and the realm of dreams had blurred.

The music that filled the air was not just a backdrop but a living entity, intertwining with the city's heartbeat. It was a symphony of celebration, each note resonating with the fans' joy and passion. The sound enveloped us, captivating our senses and propelling us forward as if we were being led by an unseen conductor toward a crescendo of bliss.

In this grand festival, the streets became our stage and the people our co-stars. Strangers became friends, linked by a shared purpose and a love for the Blackhawks. High-fives and hugs were exchanged with abandon as the boundaries between individuals dissolved in a sea of camaraderie. The collective roar of the crowd became a chorus of unity, a testament to the power of sports to bring people together.

As the night wore on and the celebration intensified, the boundaries between the city and the United Center seemed to blur. The energy and passion that usually resided within the hallowed walls of the arena had spilled out onto the streets, infusing every corner with the spirit of the Blackhawks. It was a surreal experience, as if the city had become an extension of the team's home, a vibrant cathedral dedicated to the love of the game.

At that moment, as we immersed ourselves in the pulsating energy of the festival, time stood still. The rain-soaked streets, the vibrant music, and the thunderous roar of the crowd created a sensory overload that etched itself into our memories. We were no longer mere spectators driving through the neighborhood but active participants, caught in the whirlwind of celebration that enveloped the city.

Like a naughty accomplice, the rain added an extra exhilaration to the proceedings. The droplets danced upon our skin, invigorating our senses and heightening the moment's intensity. We surrendered to the elements, embracing the wild abandon of the night and allowing the rain to wash away any inhibitions. It was as if the heavens had chosen this night to join us in our revelry, showering their blessings upon the city. As the passengers hopped into my car, their faces beaming with excitement, I couldn't help but join in their jubilation. The Blackhawks' victory over the Tampa Bay Lightning in a compelling 6-game series had left a lasting impression on all of us.

"Can you believe it? The Blackhawks did it again! They never fail to keep us on the edge of our seats!" Said Jack as he jumped up and down while sitting down.

"Absolutely! It was an incredible series. Crawford's saves, Shaw's tenacity, and Toews' leadership were just out of this world. They brought their A-game!"

"I couldn't agree more! Moments like these make being a Blackhawks fan so special," said Elizabeth as she rolled down her window and started yelling, "Let's go Hawks! Let's go,

Hawks! Let's go Hawks!" Her fists pumped into the air, and roars of victory covered the entire neighborhood.

"You got that right! The energy in the city tonight is unbelievable. It's like the entire population decided to celebrate at once."

"Hey, driver, do you mind if we blast some victory music? It's time to party!" Exclaimex Maggie as she dances to her heart's content to the music blasting both inside and outside of the vehicle.

"Of course not! Let's crank up the tunes and make this ride memorable!"

As we drove through the streets, the fun and entertainment around us caused hilarious encounters and playful banter between the passengers and me.

Jack said, catching his breath from all the victory and excitement, "Hey, Marshall, can we make a detour? I heard a spontaneous dance party is happening a few blocks away!"

458

"Sure thing! Let's join in on the fun. Who knows, we'll all become expert dancers by the night's end!

Laughter filled the car as we approached the impromptu dance party, and we joined the lively crowd in their enthusiastic moves.

Elizabeth, having the time of her life in the car from the excitement of the Blackhawks winning, says, "This celebration just keeps getting better and better. I wonder what crazy shenanigans we'll encounter next!"

"Who knows? The night is young, and Chicago knows how to throw a party. Anything can happen!"

We continued to drive through the city, taking in the sights and sounds of the exuberant celebration. The streets were filled with laughter, cheers, and even amusing chants.

With an excited look, Maggie said, "Hey, Marshall, do you think we could start a 'Let's Go Hawks' chant in the car?"

"Absolutely! Let's do it! One, two, three... Let's go Hawks!"

The passengers and I start to chant, "Let's go Hawks! Let's

go Hawks!"

The car erupted in laughter and cheers as we chanted, contributing our small part to the citywide celebration. Throughout the journey, the moments of comedy and lightheartedness added a layer of joy to the already incredible atmosphere. It took us longer than usual to drive a few blocks, but none of us minded. The fun and entertainment that engulfed the city were sights to behold, creating memories that would forever be etched in our minds.

As we bid farewell to the passengers and they stepped out of the car, one final quote summed up the sentiment of the night: *"Thanks for the ride, Marshall! This was the perfect way to end an amazing night. Let's go, Hawks! Let's go, Hawks! Let's go Hawks!"*

"You're welcome! It was my pleasure. Remember, the celebration doesn't end here. The spirit of victory will live on. Go Hawks!"

As they disappeared into the sea of jubilant fans, I couldn't help but smile, grateful for the comedic moments, the joyful banter, and the shared celebration that had made this ride unforgettable. I forged through the crowds of exuberant fans as I became acutely aware of the connections I was forming. Strangers became comrades, linked by a shared love for the Blackhawks and the euphoria that coursed through our veins. High-fives and embraces were exchanged with abandon as if we had known each other forever. At that moment, we were bound by a common purpose, united in our unwavering support for our team.

Time seemed to bend and stretch, elongating the night and allowing us to savor every precious second. On a familiar and typical Monday, the streets transformed into a fantastical realm where dreams came true. It was a journey of adventure and discovery, where each twist and turn revealed new surprises and unexpected delights. The rain-soaked streets, the colorful chaos, and the pulsating energy created an intoxicating ambiance that made it impossible to resist the allure of the night.

As the rain gradually subsided and the zeal began to wane, we carried the memories of that enchanted evening. They became treasures we would forever hold close to our hearts, a testament to the power of shared experiences and the strength of a community united by a common purpose. The echoes of laughter and the fading chants reminded us that, in those fleeting moments, we were part of something larger than ourselves.

As I traversed the city streets again, the memories of that extraordinary night lingered like a sweet melody in the days that followed. They reminded me that memorable moments could be found even amid the ordinary. They became a beacon of hope, a reminder that the power of sports can ignite passions, forge bonds, and create lasting memories that will illuminate our lives' tapestry.

As the night neared its end, and we reluctantly began to depart from this magical realm, the echoes of the festival followed us. The memories of that extraordinary evening became treasures that we carried within our hearts, forever reminding us of the power of shared passion, the beauty of unity, and the exhilaration that can be found in the most unexpected moments.

As I closed my eyes and allowed the memories to wash over me that night, I carried a renewed sense of wonder and appreciation. The power of sports, the beauty of unity, and the extraordinary connections that can be forged in the most unexpected of circumstances became etched into the very fabric of my being. The incredible festival that had transformed the streets of Chicago into a vibrant mosaic of celebration became a testament to the enduring spirit of the Blackhawks and the unifying power of sports. And in my heart, I knew that the energy of that unforgettable evening would forever burn bright, an eternal flame that would inspire and uplift, reminding us of the magic that can be found when a city comes together to celebrate as one.

In 2016, specifically on November 2nd, a remarkable milestone was reached for me and the City of Chicago. It was a momentous day when our beloved baseball team, the Chicago Cubs, emerged victorious and clinched the World Series title. I can't even begin to express the significance of this achievement for me.

As I reflect on that unforgettable day, I recall a flood of memories from my childhood. I remember my grandfather, a die-hard Cubs fan, taking me to watch games of both the Chicago Cubs and the Chicago White Sox. Those moments spent together at the stadiums left an indelible mark on my heart, and my love for the game was passed down through generations.

Although my grandparents were no longer with me to witness the Cubs' World Series win, I could feel their presence in my heart. I celebrated not just for myself but also in honor of my grandparents, knowing how much this victory would have meant to them. It was a way to pay tribute to the countless memories and experiences we shared around baseball.

The year 2016 was a whirlwind of emotions and exciting events. Amidst the political turbulence and media missteps, a falsehood spread about Chicago not having won a Baseball World Series in over a hundred years. But that statement couldn't have been further from the truth. The Chicago White Sox had indeed won the World Series on October 27, 2005, and it was a momentous occasion that should be acknowledged and celebrated.

Breaking the supposed curse of the Chicago Cubs was an extraordinary feat. It took unwavering dedication and effort from the team and the loyal fans who poured their hearts into supporting the Cubs. While I may not have been directly involved in the team's success, my unwavering support and love for the Cubs contributed to their victory. Of course, it's all in good humor, but it adds to that unforgettable moment's magical aura.

The Cubs' 2016 victory was an extraordinary moment that will forever be etched in my memory. I vividly recall the electric atmosphere as I gathered at my friend Penelope's place that night in the Lincoln Square neighborhood of Chicago, eagerly watching the last game unfold on the television screen. Every pitch, every swing, held immense significance. It was a heart-wrenching experience, as if the game's fate hung in the balance, teetering between the Cleveland Indians and the Chicago Cubs.

Watching the series, it was clear that both teams, representing the proud Midwest, exuded a healthy respect for each other. The tension in the air was palpable, and the stakes couldn't have been higher. The Cubs, a team that had faced a century-long championship drought, were determined to overcome all odds and emerge victorious.

As the game progressed, the rollercoaster of emotions intensified. It seemed as if the Cubs were on the verge of being swept away by their opponents during the series. Yet, what unfolded was nothing short of miraculous. With unwavering resilience and a collective will to defy expectations, the Chicago Cubs embarked on an awe-inspiring journey of redemption, returning from what almost could have been a sweet for the Cleveland Indians.

Their comeback was a testament to the indomitable spirit of perseverance. It showcased the power of hope and the ability to rise above seemingly insurmountable obstacles. The team's grit and unwavering determination resonated with dedicated Cubs fans and people from all walks of life. It united us, transcending boundaries and igniting a shared passion for the game.

And then, as destiny would have it, the final moments arrived. The tension peaked as the Cubs fought to victory on the Cleveland Indians' territory. The eruption of joy and celebration that followed was unparalleled. It was a moment of pure pleasure, a culmination of years of heartache and longing. I honestly thought I was going to have a heart attack. It was funny as I gave my friend Penelope my cub's hat. Then her boyfriend, now her husband, texted me, saying, "There are no Cubs regalia allowed here. This is a White Sox home. " I laughed as I understood the competition stretched for generations between the White Sox and the Chicago Cubs fans.

Being a part of that incredible journey was an honor and a privilege. Witnessing history unfold stirred an overwhelming sense of pride and gratitude. The Chicago Cubs' triumph in 2016 was a momentous occasion for the team and the entire City of Chicago. It was a victory that transcended the boundaries of a mere baseball game, showcasing the unbreakable bond between a team and its fans.

As the tense series between the Cleveland Indians and the Chicago Cubs stretched into the 10th inning, the atmosphere was electric. The anticipation was palpable, and every pitch, every swing of the bat, held the potential to shift the tides of destiny. It became a teeth-grinding, heart-pounding spectacle, with sweat enveloping the players and fans alike, as we all anxiously wondered who would emerge victorious.

At that moment, I turned to my friend Penelope, unable to contain my joy, and exclaimed, "I'm so happy that the Cubs made it this far. No one thought they would come back from a 1-3 deficit. But they defied the odds, and now, it's all come down to this!"

Penelope grinned mischievously and replied, "I know, right? It's like witnessing a miracle or finding a unicorn in your backyard! This is the stuff legends are made of!"

We both laughed, caught up in the electric atmosphere. *Then, Penelope whispered, "I secretly think the Cubs have a secret weapon – a rally squirrel that brings them luck. Maybe they've been hiding it in their dugout all along!"*

I chuckled, playing along, "Oh! I heard they trained that squirrel in the art of baseball. It's got a wicked curveball and can steal bases faster than Usain Bolt!"

We couldn't help but imagine the hilarious sight of a squirrel wearing a tiny baseball cap and swinging a miniature bat. Our laughter echoed through the stadium, earning us curious glances from the nearby fans.

Penelope nudged me, pointing to a Cubs fan with an enormous foam finger. "Hey, maybe we should get one of those giant foam fingers too. We'll be the envy of the crowd!"

*I nodded enthusiastically, "Yes! And we'll paint our faces
with the team colors, wear Cubs jerseys, and become the
ultimate super fans. We'll be a force to reckon with!"*

The tension mounted during the game as we continued to
joke and dream about our future as die-hard Cubs supporters.
Little did we know that this would be a night we would
remember for the rest of our lives, filled with laughter,
camaraderie, and unforgettable moments.

Initially, I had no intention of driving, content to revel in
the celebrations surrounding Wrigley Field. However, as the
reality sunk in that we were just a few miles away from the heart
of Chicago, I couldn't resist the urge to contribute to the city's
joyous atmosphere. With a renewed sense of purpose, I offered
my services. I drove through the streets, witnessing firsthand the
jubilation and unity this historic victory had brought to the City
of Chicago.

I vividly remember getting onto Addison Street from
Lincoln Square. The energy was palpable, crackling through the
air like electricity. As I inched forward, Traders Joe's on my left;
the street turned into complete bumper-to-bumper traffic. The
tension and excitement were almost tangible as if the entire city
had held its breath and was waiting for this moment.

Suddenly, the driver directly in front of me did something completely unexpected. He abruptly exited his car, not caring about the traffic jam, and walked towards my left opposite lane. My heart raced as I wondered what he was about to do. With a sense of both awe and trepidation, he pulled out a firework and lit it right there on the street.

In that split second, fear and excitement coursed through my veins. "Oh my God! Please don't explode into me!" I exclaimed, my voice a mix of worry and anticipation.

Time seemed to slow down as I watched the fireworks shoot into the night sky, its brilliant colors painting a breathtaking picture against the darkness. Relief flooded over me as the fireworks soared higher and higher, exploding into a dazzling display of lights. The crowd around us erupted into cheers and applause, their jubilant voices blending with the crackling sounds of the fireworks. It was as if the essence of victory had ignited the sky, mirroring the triumphant spirit of the Cubs and their dedicated fans.

As I maneuvered the streets, honking horns and cheering voices filled the air. The city had transformed into a tapestry of blue and red, with ecstatic fans hugging, high-fiving, and waving flags in celebration. Strangers became friends, united by a shared

469

love for their team and the realization that they had witnessed something extraordinary.

Amidst the chaos and euphoria, I couldn't help but marvel at the sheer passion and vitality surrounding me. It was a moment etched in my memory forever, an exhilarating testament to the unifying power of sports and the unwavering spirit of a city that had come together to celebrate an unprecedented victory.

The scene was reminiscent of the last Chicago Blackhawks' victory in June of 2015, with the streets just as crowded and pulsating with excitement. However, instead of a sea of red Blackhawks hockey shirts and jerseys, the roads were filled with a vibrant ocean of white and blue Chicago Cubs baseball attire. It was a sight to behold, a testament to Cubs fans' unwavering loyalty and undying support. It was as wild as St. Patrick's Day and the Pride Parade.

Amidst the bustling chaos, a line of Chicago Police officers stood tall and proud on their majestic horses, adding a sense of order and security to the jubilant crowd. Helicopters hovered above, their blades slicing through the air, capturing breathtaking views of the celebration below. The city had come alive, transformed into a sprawling playground of joy and unity.

There were smiles, laughter, and a palpable sense of relief everywhere you looked. Cubs fans, young and old, rejoiced as they reveled in the long-awaited end of the curse that had plagued their beloved team for over a century. It was a moment of pure delight, a culmination of years of hopes, dreams, and unwavering faith.

Strangers embraced their shared love for the Cubs, forging instant connections. They exchanged high-fives and fist bumps, creating a symphony of celebratory gestures. The air was filled with a contagious energy that all could feel, an electric current that ran through the city's veins.

Amidst the sea of jubilant fans, tears of joy streamed down faces, their emotions raw and overwhelming. It was a cathartic release, a collective sigh of relief that echoed through the streets. The curse had been shattered, and the city stood united, basking in the glory of this historic victory.

As I navigated through the sea of ecstatic fans, I couldn't help but feel a surge of pride and happiness. This was a moment for the history books, a chapter that Cubs fans would forever hold close to their hearts. As the celebration continued into the night, I knew that the spirit of this remarkable triumph would linger, reminding me of the unwavering dedication and unyielding spirit of the Chicago Cubs and their loyal fans.

Being a part of that unforgettable night, feeling the pulse of the city, and witnessing the unbridled happiness on the faces of the people was a privilege beyond words. It was a reminder that sports could transcend the boundaries of a mere game, bringing together communities and instilling a sense of hope and pride. The Cubs' victory in 2016 will forever be etched in the annals of history, and I am grateful to have been a part of that magical moment. As I picked up passengers during the celebration, the details of the passengers remained blurry. The festival atmosphere and the infectious energy that permeated the entire Wrigleyville neighborhood in Chicago and its surrounding areas made it difficult to focus on individual rides. The excitement was so contagious that it swept through everyone like a tidal wave, uniting strangers in an unparalleled display of camaraderie.

Navigating ride-share, picking up passengers, and transporting them through the streets became slow and arduous, with traffic coming to a standstill for what seemed like an eternity. The honking of car horns merged with the joyful chants and cheers of the crowd, creating a symphony of jubilation. But rather than being frustrated, we found ourselves caught up in the festivities, embracing the joyful chaos around us. On Clark Street, amidst the exuberant celebration, people climbed on top of the hood and roof of my car, turning it into an impromptu dance floor. Their infectious energy and uncontainable joy radiated through their every move.

As the music blared and the beats pulsated through the speakers, the crowd moved synchronously, their bodies swaying, twisting, and grooving to the rhythm. It was a sight to behold, a spontaneous dance party that transcended any boundaries or inhibitions.

The vibrations of their footsteps reverberated through the car, creating a unique rhythm that harmonized with the music. Each step and jump sent ripples of excitement and sheer exhilaration through the crowd as if the ground beneath us was pulsing with the collective heartbeat of the city.

People twirled and spun from the hood to the roof, their laughter and cheers merging with the music. It was a beautiful chaos, an explosion of movement and uninhibited expression that mirrored the overwhelming happiness that had engulfed the streets.

At that moment, my car became a symbol of unity and celebration. Strangers became dance partners, their laughter and shared enthusiasm weaving a tapestry of joy and connection. It was as if the boundaries between us had dissolved, leaving only the shared experience of triumph and the pure pleasure of the Cubs' victory.

As the crowd danced on the car, their energy fueled my own. I couldn't resist joining in, stepping out of the driver's seat and onto the hood, letting the music guide my movements. With each leap, spin, and sway, I felt an indescribable sense of liberation and a profound connection to the collective spirit surrounding me.

The car rocked gently under the weight of the dancing crowd, its metal frame echoing the rhythm of the celebration. And in that moment, I realized that this wasn't just a car anymore —it had become a vessel of shared happiness, a symbol of unity, and a testament to the unifying power of sports. As the night continued and the dancing persisted, I couldn't help but marvel at the incredible energy and spirit that filled the air. The image of people joyfully dancing in my car will forever be etched in my memory—a vivid reminder of the extraordinary celebration that unfolded on that unforgettable night on Clark Street in Wrigleyville.

I remember cranking up the music, allowing its pulsating beats to merge with the rhythm of the celebration. The car became a mobile party, its doors flung open, inviting others to join the revelry. Passengers and strangers alike danced on the streets, their inhibitions swept away by the sheer exuberance of the moment. It was as if time stood still, and the boundaries between driver and passenger, between strangers, blurred in the shared joy of the Cubs' victory.

Amidst the revelry, I couldn't help but glance at the street corners, where brave souls climbed up light posts, their spirits soaring as high as their physical elevation. With awe and concern, I watched as they leaped off, trusting in the crowd's outstretched arms to catch them. It was a testament to the unwavering trust and unity that had permeated the city on this historic night.

Everyone became a part of something bigger than themselves in that extraordinary moment. The City of Chicago came more alive, pulsating with an energy that transcended the confines of the baseball field. It celebrated resilience, never giving up, and the unyielding belief that dreams can come true.=

As I reflect on that night, I am reminded of the power of sports to bring people together, ignite a collective spirit, and create memories that last a lifetime. The image of people dancing in my car, the exhilarating cheers that filled the air, and the sight of daredevils leaping into the waiting arms of the crowd—it all remains etched in my mind as a testament to the unifying power of the Chicago Cubs and the unwavering spirit of their devoted fans.

Whenever I reflect on that historic win, I am reminded of the power of perseverance, the beauty of hope, and the euphoria of overcoming the most significant challenges. The Cubs' victory in 2016 is a testament to the human spirit's capacity to triumph in the face of adversity. It will forever be a cherished chapter in the annals of baseball history, a tale of redemption that continues to inspire and captivate hearts worldwide.

As we cultivate our happiness, we unlock the power to transform the world. Choosing happiness, not merely as a fleeting emotion but as a conscious decision, enables us to make a difference. The accurate measure of a well-lived life lies not solely in material wealth or fleeting pleasures but in the happiness we create for ourselves and others.

This book serves as a reminder that happiness is indeed a choice that can shape our future, influence the lives of those around us, and create a world filled with love, compassion, and joy. Let its pages be etched in your memory as a constant reminder that you hold the key to your happiness and that your choices can inspire others to pursue their path to fulfillment. As you journey through the chapters of your life, may you be guided by the understanding that happiness is not a destination but a lifelong pursuit. Embrace the power within you to create moments of joy, uplift others, and spread kindness wherever you go. In doing so, you contribute to a collective narrative of love and compassion, weaving a tapestry of happiness that transcends borders and unites us all.

So, dear readers, may you carry the wisdom within these pages and let it illuminate your path. Let it be a constant reminder that your choices matter and your actions can shape the world around you. May you strive to create a life filled with happiness for yourself and the countless lives you can touch. Let us author a story of love, compassion, and boundless happiness together. May this tale inspire generations, reminding them that happiness is a choice that can transform lives, nurture connections, and create a world that radiates with the warmth of love and the joy of shared experiences.

CHAPTER 8 - Conclusion
The Sunlight Path Towards the Golden Sun

As I sit in the O'Hare Airport ride-share Parking lot, the engine of my trusty Red Toyota Corolla purrs softly. It's a moment of reflection, the perfect time to weave the final threads of this captivating tale. The pages of my book are filled with trials and challenges, each a stepping stone on my journey as a happy driver.

From the very beginning, anxiety and stress gripped my heart as I embarked on my first trip with Uber. The weight of uncertainty pressed upon me, threatening to drown my aspirations. But I persevered, pushing through the relentless snowy blizzards that tested my skills and determination. With each successful ride, I grew stronger, honing my ability to navigate the treacherous roads.

Yet, the road to success had its share of setbacks. I sought to expand my horizons by applying for Lyft, only to face the bitter disappointment of not being accepted during the try-out ride. However, fate works in strange and unpredictable ways. There is a moment that shines brightly, a sweet triumph that deserves its place in the conclusion. As luck would have it, it was during an Uber ride that I picked up a passenger who turned out to be a manager from Lyft who saw the spark within me. Little did I know that this encounter would become a pivotal moment in my story. Impressed by my professionalism, dedication, and unwavering commitment to providing the best service, the Lyft manager saw in me the qualities that transcend ride-sharing.

Their belief in my potential reignited the fire within, propelling me forward. But life has a way of throwing curveballs, and I was broken down by an unfair deactivation, forever banned from Uber. It was a blow that could have shattered my spirit, but I refused to let it define me. Instead, I rebuilt myself, brick by brick, showing the world through my experiences that success is born from countless trials and errors.

Through hard work, I stood tall, proudly accepting the prestigious Lyft Driver of the Year Award for Customer Service. Only about a hundred drivers had won out of supposedly 20,000 in Chicago. There were also different categories, but I was told that my prize in a class of drivers was the best one to win.

The accolade was more than a simple recognition. It was a testament to the countless hours spent perfecting the art of navigation, problem-solving, and delivering exceptional service to the passengers who entrusted their journeys to me. From the bustling streets of Chicago, I emerged as a beacon of excellence, embodying the essence of being a driver dedicated to customer satisfaction.

As I held that award in my hands, in the smaller shape of a key to the city, its weight was not just a symbol of my achievement but a reminder of the countless passengers whose lives I had touched. It reminded me that the true essence of being a Happy Driver resided in the miles traveled and the hearts and smiles left in my wake.

In the face of mishaps, roadblocks, and challenges, I learned the true power of choosing happiness. I embraced forgiveness, liberating myself from the chains of past non-acceptance. I focused on a world filled with love, happiness, and joy. Each red light that halted my progress became an opportunity to reflect, recalibrate, and emerge more vital than ever.

And now, as I sit here in the Alpha Ride-Share Parking lot at O'Hare Airport, the final chapter of this storybook journey unfolds. The conclusion of this book is not just a testament to my triumphs but to the indomitable spirit that resides within each of us. It is a celebration of self-liberation and self-acceptance, a reminder that the road to happiness is paved with resilience and unwavering determination.

As you turn the last page of these Tales of a Happy Driver, dear reader, let my story inspire you. Remember that even in the face of adversity, you hold the power to choose your path, gracefully navigating life's twists and turns with courage. In pursuing happiness, may forgiveness and self-acceptance be your guiding lights, leading you to the ultimate destination. Success is not solely measured by external recognition but by the lives we touch. Strive for greatness, embrace challenges, and consistently deliver your best for yourself and those beside you. May you discover your triumphs as you journey through life, steadfast in dedication, fueled by love, and committed to providing exceptional service. The journey had been long and arduous, but as I drove through the night, pursuing the elusive sunrise, a profound sense of accomplishment filled my weary heart. A tear of fulfillment rolled down my cheek, bearing witness to the trials I had conquered. With a tender brush, I wiped away the tears, embracing the cold, crisp December air that enveloped me.

The journey had been long and arduous, but as I drove through the night, pursuing the elusive sunrise, a profound sense of accomplishment filled my weary heart. A tear of fulfillment rolled down my cheek, bearing witness to the trials I had conquered. With a tender brush, I wiped away the tears, embracing the cold, crisp December air that enveloped me.

Fixing my gaze upon the radiant sun, my determination remained steadfast and unwavering. In that sublime moment, I realized that time would always be found for those who held a special place in my heart. Family and friends were the pillars of my existence, and I was resolute in showing them my unwavering love and care.

On an early Sunday morning, I picked up a young man named Jason, who was in his early 20s, and headed toward the casino. From how he spoke about the schedule at the casino when it opens and closes each day, you could tell he spent a lot of time at the River Casino located in Des Plaines, IL. He admitted to me to being a professional gambler. As he settled into the backseat, concern was shown all over his facial expression; he turned to me with a hopeful expression.

"Is it okay if I may get your advice on something?" Jason asked, a touch of vulnerability in his voice.

I smiled, eager to lend an attentive ear and offer guidance within my capacity.

"Of course, I'm always willing to share inspiration and advice with others, especially those willing to learn," I replied, my voice filled with genuine warmth.

"I'll do my best to share my experiences and assist you with whatever you're going through."

With nearly 25,000 ride-share trips under my seatbelt as a driver, I was determined to provide this young man with the utmost valuable advice. His gratitude shone through as he expressed appreciation, even promising a generous tip for my assistance.

"For that, I promise to give you a huge tip," he exclaimed, his sincerity evident. In response, I reassured him, "Don't worry about it. It's all good. I'm here to help, and any extra appreciation is always welcome."

Well, I felt like I had just won the lottery of appreciation. I mean, forget about financial rewards; this guy was about to make me the king of tips! I thanked him, trying to keep my excitement in check, but let's be honest, my heart was doing the Macarena. As we discussed different scenarios, I shared stories of my parents' dedication to staying together out of love and for the family's sake. They were practically relationship superheroes if they could survive my dad's obsession with hoarding things of the past and my mom's obsession with collecting purses and shoes.

"You know what, man?" he said, his voice filled with genuine gratitude as he had just won the gratitude Olympics. I can't thank you enough for your advice and everything you've done for me. I will give you the biggest tip that I possibly can!"

At that moment, I could practically see dollar signs flying around his head like he was a human slot machine ready to shower me with a jackpot of cash. I didn't know whether to be excited or worried that he might be planning to tip me with a solid gold yacht. Either way, I braced myself for the tip of a lifetime.

A sense of camaraderie blossomed as we continued our journey together. He shared his concerns, frustrations, and aspirations while I listened attentively, drawing upon my wealth of experiences to provide the guidance he sought. The car became a sanctuary of trust and open conversation as I offered advice with empathy and understanding.

He took a deep breath before opening up about his troubles with his child's mother and a recent car accident. I listened attentively, empathizing with the challenges life had thrown his way.

"I'm sorry to hear that," I said. "Life can be unpredictable, but it's important to remember that it's also short. Have you considered talking to her about offering forgiveness to one another? Finding a way to work things out?"

He looked at me, gratitude shining like he had just discovered a treasure chest full of gratitude.

"I appreciate you, man," he said earnestly. "I'm going to give you an even bigger tip. Your advice means a lot to me, and I appreciate you for it."

Flattered, I thanked him, assuring him his gratitude was more than enough. We delved into discussions about different scenarios. I even shared stories of my friends in relationships and their dedication to staying together out of love and for the sake of their families.

"You know what, man?" he said, his voice filled with genuine gratitude. "I can't thank you enough for your advice and everything you've done for me. I will give you the biggest tip that I possibly can!"

I tightened my face, trying to hold back laughter, thinking if this was for real. He has to be joking! The passenger's face glimmered with happiness as I tried my hardest not to explode in laughter. No one had ever said they were going to increase the tip they promised to give me, much less at least four different times during the same trip. That was a first for me!

With each passing mile, our connection deepened, and I could sense the weight lifting off his shoulders. The young man's gratitude poured forth, his words filled with genuine appreciation for my support and guidance. The late night had turned into a cold December morning as we finally arrived at the casino's entrance.

The young man asked me, "Could I share three of the most important things I had learned while driving for Lyft or in life?" I answered, "Wow, that is such a loaded question, but I will do my best to answer it with all the experience I have in my life, as well as the 25,000 trips under my belt."

"The first is always to follow the Golden Rule, which is found in almost all teachings. It is to do unto others as you would have them do unto you. Good things will eventually come back to you when you do good things. The example I set is true in countless stories. It is the ultimate rule of the universe. That is tied in with number two.

"The second is always to do the right thing no matter the situation. The world is full of bad things already. Be a light in someone else's life. Be an example. Many people are waiting for others to be the first to be nice or to do the right thing, but why not be the example to show others that it's okay to be the first to be nice or to be a good person?"

"The third is something my father once imparted to me. Always follow the rules and the law of the land," my father had said. "If you do, you'll never have to run scared alone in the dark, but you will always be able to walk in the light, without the need to run or hide because everything you do in life will be the right thing and you never have to worry about something someone trying to harm you."

The young man's face lit up as he expressed even more gratitude, shaking my hand as he said, "Thank you so much for everything. I appreciate and admire you. I don't know how much I could ever thank you enough for sharing as much advice as you did during our short trip to the River Casino. I don't know if the company will allow me to tip you on the app as much as possible. This is the best Uber ride I ever had."

We exchanged fist bumps, wishing each other well. As I drove away, I received a notification later from the ride-share company—a $50 tip. I couldn't help but feel a sense of awe and appreciation for the unexpected generosity. It reminded me of the power of human connection and how, even in the briefest of encounters, we can impact each other's lives. The young man's gratitude and the generosity of his tip reminded him of the importance of offering support and guidance to others, knowing that even the smallest act of kindness can make a world of difference.

It was not the monetary gesture that touched my heart the most. It was the knowledge that I had positively impacted someone's life as I had with thousands of other passengers, providing them with the assurance and guidance they needed in a crucial moment. The satisfaction of being able to help others is its reward, and the young man's appreciation only further affirmed the importance of lending a helping hand when we can.

With a contented smile, I drove off towards the golden sun, ready to continue my journey as a driver, knowing that the impact I could have on others extends far beyond simply transporting them from one place to another.

Without hesitation, I headed towards the sunlight path to my parents' home in the North Shore Suburbs of Chicago. My aging parents, aged 75 and 74, reside there, their home burdened by snow. With a heart brimming with love, I was prepared to relieve their worries and comfort them. My parents' anticipated smiles of gratitude would be my ultimate reward, knowing that I had lightened their burden and brought them solace. Even amidst their scolding and occasional yelling, I remained deeply grateful and appreciative, cherishing the precious experience of life and the opportunity to shovel snow for them during the harsh winters of the Chicagoland area.

Thanks to my experience as a ride-share driver, I was granted the freedom to no longer miss important events like weddings, funerals, birthdays, Christmas, New Year's, and Thanksgiving. This has paved the way towards a path of sunlight, where I can work when needed and assist friends and family in their times of need, which I had neglected during my time as a chef. I found happiness by choosing kindness, forgiveness, and spreading joy throughout my journey.

Gone are the days of feeling trapped, missing out on precious moments because of inflexible work schedules. As a ride-share driver, I can take control of my life, making a schedule that aligns with my personal life and allowing me to prioritize what truly matters.

No longer bound by the constraints of a traditional job, I can now be present for those joyous celebrations and the somber remembrances. The smiles, tears, laughter, and embraces accompanying these crucial events are no longer distant memories but tangible experiences I can fully embrace.

As a ride-share driver, I am uniquely positioned to witness life's most significant moments. Weddings, with their enchanting atmosphere and promises of forever, have become a mosaic of love and unity that I am privileged to observe. The joy in the eyes of the couples embarking on their journey together fills my heart with warmth, reminding me of the beauty of human connection.

But life is not only about beginnings; it is also about goodbyes. Funerals, once somber occasions, have transformed into opportunities for me to offer solace and support. Standing alongside grieving families and friends, I provide them with a comforting presence, reminding them that they are not alone in their sorrow. Through these moments of shared grief, I have learned the power of empathy and the importance of supporting one another, even in the darkest times.

Birthdays, once a distant celebration for others, have become moments of joy I can actively participate in. I can now join in the laughter and festivities, sharing in the delight of another year of life. The smiles on the faces of those I transport on their special day remind me of the preciousness of every moment and the value of celebrating the milestones that shape our lives.

I would no longer feel personal shame when my friends Haley and Penelope invited me to their birthday celebrations, and I had to say no because I would have had to work 10-12 long hours in the kitchen managing employees.

Furthermore, the holidays beckon with an irresistible allure, inviting us into a realm of cherished togetherness and boundless excitement. Christmas, New Year's, and Thanksgiving have transcended their mere calendar dates, assuming a profound significance in my life. Through my interactions with passengers, I have been enlightened to the transformative power of these festive occasions, which serve as precious opportunities to craft enduring memories with those we hold dear. Astonishingly, I have come to comprehend that the profound connections we cultivate imbue these moments with an extraordinary essence. Whether we are partaking in delectable feasts, weaving narratives of shared experiences, or surrendering to the enchanting allure of the holiday season, we possess the capacity to orchestrate priceless moments that will forever be etched in our hearts.

Thanks to my adventurous journey as a ride-share driver, I've had the privilege of uncovering all the hidden gems and popular hotspots in the magnificent city of Chicago. From the pulsating nightclubs and eclectic bars in Fulton Market, the old meat packaging district turned hipster haven, to the iconic landmarks that draw tourists from far and wide, I've become a human GPS of all things Chicago.

I've whisked passengers away to towering heights, taking them to the top of the Sears Tower, where the cityscape stretches out like a breathtaking tapestry beneath their feet. We've marveled at the shiny, reflective wonder of The Bean, a metallic masterpiece nestled in Millennium Park, reflecting the vibrant energy of the city.

We've strolled along the vibrant Navy Pier, basking in the whimsy of Ferris wheel rides and indulging in delectable treats. I've shared stories of artistic wonders at the Art Institute of Chicago, where masterpieces come to life and speak to the soul. Together, we've delved into the fascinating history at the Field Museum, where ancient artifacts whisper tales of civilizations long gone.

I've guided my passengers to the famous Wendella Chicago Architectural Boat Tour entrance, cruising along the majestic Chicago River, where stunning skyscrapers stand as testaments to human ingenuity. We've explored the picturesque River Walk, a serene oasis amidst the urban jungle, where the calming waters offer respite from the bustling city.

And oh, the beaches! We've soaked up the sun and dipped our toes in the refreshing waters of North Ave—Beach and Oak Street Beach, where laughter and relaxation go hand in hand.

But let's remember the laughter-inducing havens of comedy clubs. I've had the pleasure of chauffeuring passengers to The Second City in Chicago's Old Town neighborhood, where laughter echoes through the air, and to the IO Theatre in Lincoln Park, where comedic brilliance takes center stage.

How could we forget the mouthwatering famous Chicago pizza that reigns supreme in deep-dish indulgence? From the iconic Giordano's, where cheesy goodness oozes from every slice, to the delectable creations at Lou Malnati's, where the crust is a work of culinary art, and Pequod's, with its unique caramelized crust that adds a delightful twist to the classic.

And when it comes to restaurants, Chicago boasts a culinary scene that is second to none. At Au Cheval, taste buds are treated to the heavenly combination of perfectly cooked burgers and delectable toppings, creating a symphony of flavors that dance on the palate. The Girl and the Goat, helmed by the talented Stephanie Izard, offers an innovative menu that celebrates bold flavors and culinary creativity. Those are just a few of the delicious restaurants in Chicago and twenty-two Michelin-star-rated restaurants the city offers.

But let's remember the hidden gems of the Prohibition era, the speakeasy bars that transport you back in time. Shrouded in mystery, these clandestine establishments glimpse a bygone era. From cozy corners where whispered conversations and the clinking of glasses create an intimate ambiance to mixologists who craft cocktails with precision and finesse, these speakeasies are a nod to the rebellious spirit of the past.

Each of these places, whether the pizza joints that make your taste buds sing or the restaurants that push culinary boundaries, holds a unique charm and contributes to Chicago's vibrant tapestry. The city's beauty lies in its iconic landmarks and attractions, incredible dining experiences, and hidden treasures.

Chicago truly is a haven for food lovers, history buffs, and those seeking unforgettable adventures.

Ah, the cultural wonders of Chicago! The city is a symphony, with each neighborhood playing its unique tune. The Chicago Symphony Orchestra, renowned worldwide for its exceptional musicianship, fills the air with enchanting melodies that transport listeners to a realm of pure musical bliss.

The Chicago Public Library is a beacon of knowledge and imagination, inviting book lovers to explore its vast literary treasures. It's a sanctuary for those seeking intellectual nourishment and literary adventures from the classics to contemporary works.

The rhythmic pulse of the L Train and its Red, Brown, Blue, Orange, Pink, and Purple Lines traverse the city with its steel arteries, connecting neighborhoods and people. It's a symphony of movement, bustling with passengers who embark on their daily journeys and witness the vibrant tapestry of Chicago's diverse communities.

Sports enthusiasts revel in the electric atmosphere of Wrigley Field with the Cubs, where the crowd's roar and the bat's crack create a palpable energy. And let's not forget the historic Comiskey Park with the White Sox, a haven for baseball lovers, where the spirit of the game intertwines with the city's rich sports heritage.

With its historic architecture and rich heritage, Soldier Field is a testament to the city's love for football. Home to the Chicago Bears, the stadium roars with the cheers of passionate fans, creating an electrifying atmosphere that can be felt throughout the city. The echoes of legendary games and unforgettable moments reverberate within its walls, adding to the storied legacy of Chicago sports.

And then there's the United Center, a colossal arena that hosts the city's beloved basketball team, the Chicago Bulls, and the thrilling action of the Chicago Blackhawks on the ice. The energy inside the United Center is palpable, with fans chanting, cheering, and celebrating as their favorite teams battle it out for victory. It's a place where dreams are realized, legends are born, and the spirit of Chicago sports shines brightly.

These arenas serve as gathering places for sports enthusiasts, bringing the community together and creating lasting memories. From the thunderous cheers to the nail-biting moments, Soldier Field and the United Center are iconic landmarks that embody the passion and dedication of Chicago sports fans.

Whether it's the roar of the crowd at Soldier Field or the sea of red and black at the United Center, these arenas are symbols of unity, pride, and Chicago's unwavering spirit. They serve as stages for unforgettable sporting events, concerts, and performances, adding to Chicago's vibrant tapestry of entertainment.

Chicago's neighborhoods are a testament to its multicultural fabric. Little Italy is enticed by the aroma of freshly made pasta and the warmth of Italian hospitality. India Town offers a sensory delight of vibrant colors, flavorful spices, and traditional Indian cuisine. Greek Town beckons with its inviting tavernas, serving mouthwatering dishes that transport diners to the Mediterranean. And China Town, with its bustling streets and authentic eateries, takes you on a culinary journey through the diverse flavors of Chinese cuisine.

Every corner of this magnificent city has a story to tell, a culture to celebrate, and a palate to delight. Chicago is a vibrant tapestry of art, music, sports, literature, and culinary delights, inviting visitors and residents alike to immerse themselves in its rich cultural offerings.

Indeed, Chicago is a city teeming with remarkable establishments, making it a haven for food, architecture, and cultural enthusiasts. While it's impossible to cover every single one in detail, I could only provide a glimpse into some of the iconic restaurants, bars, buildings, and landmarks in the Windy City. Each one deserves their own story and book in it that I would give either of them any justice whatsoever,

As a former chef, I worked tirelessly, even during holidays and weekends, while everyone else was out enjoying their time. It often felt like I was missing out on all the fun. Sure, I was making decent money, but what was the point if I needed someone to share it with? I couldn't attend family gatherings, funerals, birthdays, or weddings because of my demanding schedule in the kitchen.

But everything changed when I decided to become a ride-share driver. Suddenly, my days took on a different rhythm. After each ride, I could end my day and be there for my loved ones. If a family member or friend needed me in an emergency, I could drop everything and rush to their side. I could partake in the joyous celebrations and create lasting memories with the people who mattered most.

This newfound flexibility became a gift I cherished deeply. I felt a sense of liberation, no longer bound by rigid schedules and demanding culinary duties. I could finally prioritize my relationships and show up for the crucial moments in life. It was a remarkable change, and I felt immensely grateful for this new experience.

Now, as a ride-share driver, I earn a living and enrich my life with meaningful connections. The smiles, the conversations, and the shared experiences during each ride remind me of the value of human relationships. This journey has taught me that true wealth lies in financial success and the bonds we forge with those we love.

Looking back, I can't help but feel grateful for the path I've chosen. No longer confined to the kitchen, ***I've discovered a newfound freedom to be present for my family and friends.*** It's a privilege I hold dear, and I treasure every opportunity to make a difference in their lives. As a ride-share driver, I've become a guide, a storyteller, and a friend, connecting people to the vibrant tapestry of experiences that Chicago offers. Each day brings new adventures, new connections, and the opportunity to share the magic of this incredible city with those who step into my car. With its rich history, diverse culture, and abundant delights, Chicago has become a playground of exploration and wonder, and I'm grateful to be a part of its ever-unfolding story.

Reflecting on my journey as a ride-share driver, I am overwhelmed with gratitude for the freedom it has granted me. This privilege allows me to balance my work responsibilities and personal life, ensuring I am there for the people who matter most. It is a gift to witness and be a part of these transformative moments, reminding me of the beauty and fragility of life and the importance of cherishing every precious moment.

As I navigate the roads, the sunlight dances through the windows of my car, casting a warm glow that symbolizes the newfound freedom and flexibility that being a ride-share driver has gifted me. With each turn of the wheel, I am reminded of the endless possibilities that lie before me. The open road becomes a metaphor for the journey I have embarked upon, not only as a driver but also as a participant in the lives of those I encounter.

I have come to cherish the true beauty of life that reveals itself in the simplest of moments. I find a profound sense of fulfillment and purpose in the selfless acts, the genuine connections, and the shared experiences. Whether offering a listening ear to a passenger in need or providing a comforting presence to someone on their way to a funeral, I realize that my role extends beyond that of a driver. I have become a facilitator of human connection, a catalyst for compassion in a world that often feels disconnected.

In these seemingly ordinary interactions, I witness the transformative power of kindness. A smile exchanged, a shared laugh, or a heartfelt conversation can brighten someone's day and create a ripple effect of positivity. In these moments, I feel a deep gratitude, knowing that I have made a difference, no matter how small it may seem. As the sun continues its ascent, casting a golden glow upon a world touched by kindness, I am filled with a profound sense of purpose. Each mile I drive and each passenger I encounter becomes an opportunity to create a meaningful impact. In this realization, I find

499

solace and joy, knowing that my journey as a ride-share driver is not just about transportation but about fostering human connection and making a positive difference in the lives of others.

So, I continue to drive onward, fueled by the desire to create space for the moments that truly matter. The road stretches before me, and with each mile, I embrace the beauty and significance of the journey. As a ride-share driver, I am not just a witness to life's moments but an active participant, weaving threads of kindness and connection into the tapestry of the lives I touch. In doing so, I realize that being a ride-share driver is not just a job—a calling, a chance to make a meaningful impact and leave a lasting legacy of compassion and love.

So, dear readers, as we close this chapter of our story, let it serve as a testament to humanity's resilience, compassion, and indomitable spirit. Within these pages, we have witnessed the power of simple acts of kindness, the beauty of forging connections, and their transformative effect on individuals and communities.

May this tale inspire you to seek out opportunities to extend a helping hand, to make time for those you hold dear, and to always choose kindness in a world that may sometimes seem devoid of it. In these small gestures, these everyday acts of goodness, we find the seeds of change, sowing the seeds of hope and creating ripples that can touch lives far beyond our own.

While you embark on your journey, remember that each act of kindness can ignite a spark of positivity, illuminating the path for others and shaping a brighter future. Whether it is a comforting word, a selfless deed, or a listening ear, never underestimate the impact of your actions. For in a world that often feels divided and disconnected, your kindness can be the bridge that brings people together, reminding us of our shared humanity.

As the pages turn and new chapters unfold, venture forth, knowing that the world eagerly awaits your acts of kindness. Embrace the stories that lie ahead, for they are waiting to be written, shaped by your compassion and guided by your unwavering spirit. Remember, you hold within you the power to make a difference, to leave an indelible mark on the lives you touch.

As we conclude this story, it is essential to reflect on the significance of embracing uniqueness, acceptance, and resilience. Throughout our journey, we have witnessed characters who have faced adversities, celebrated their differences, and found strength in their individuality. Their stories have reminded us that our experiences shape us and provide growth opportunities.

By embracing uniqueness, we acknowledge that each person is a distinct individual with their own set of talents, perspectives, and qualities. We cultivate a world rich in diversity and inclusivity by recognizing and appreciating these differences. Rather than seeking conformity, we can celebrate the beauty of our individuality and learn from one another's unique perspectives.

Acceptance plays a vital role in this narrative. It is about embracing ourselves as we are and accepting others without judgment or prejudice. When we take ourselves, flaws and all, we create a foundation of self-love and self-compassion. By extending that acceptance to others, we foster an environment of understanding and empathy where everyone feels valued and respected.

Resilience is the thread that weaves throughout our journey. The unwavering strength allows us to face challenges, overcome obstacles, and bounce back from setbacks. Resilience teaches us that setbacks are not the end of our story but opportunities for growth and transformation. It empowers us to rise above adversity, learn from our experiences, and continue moving forward with determination and courage. As we conclude, let this story be the beginning of your narrative. May you find inspiration in the tales you have read, drawing upon the lessons of embracing uniqueness, acceptance, and resilience. Carry the essence of this journey with you as you navigate the intricacies of life.

Embrace the opportunities that come your way, knowing that each experience is a chance for growth and self-discovery. Approach life with an open heart and outstretched hands, ready to create a world of love, kindness, and boundless possibility. Your story is waiting to be written, and with each step you take, you can shape it into something extraordinary.

When I speak of "always doing your best" in the context of our ride-share journey, I mean adopting a mindset of continuous improvement and putting forth your utmost effort in every aspect of life. You are first; doing your best means showing up with dedication. It implies being fully present and engaged, whether interacting with passengers, navigating through traffic, or facing other challenges. By approaching each task with a sense of commitment, you demonstrate respect for yourself and those around you.

Secondly, doing your best involves embracing challenges. The ride-share journey can be unpredictable, with unexpected twists and turns. However, by viewing these challenges as opportunities for growth, you can push beyond your comfort zone and discover new strengths and abilities within yourself.

Embracing challenges fosters resilience, adaptability, and a willingness to learn from successes and setbacks.

Lastly, doing your best means striving for excellence. It's about setting high standards for yourself and consistently working towards achieving them. Pursuing excellence helps you develop a sense of personal satisfaction and fulfillment, knowing you've given your all to each endeavor. It inspires others and creates a positive ripple effect, as your commitment and dedication can influence those around you.

By always doing your best, you will navigate the ride-share journey and the broader journey of life with intention and purpose. It's an ongoing process of growth, self-discovery, and embracing the unexpected. Remember, our stories are not defined by a definitive end but rather by the effort we put forth and the lessons we learn.

My conversations with passengers have taught me that compassion is a guiding force in our stories. Connecting with others and empathizing with their joys and sorrows brings depth and richness to our narratives. In the brief moments we share, I've witnessed the power of compassion in fostering genuine human connections.

Indeed, the power of kindness and good choices aligns beautifully with the importance of compassion in our stories. As I've talked with passengers during our ride-share journeys, I've witnessed firsthand how compassion serves as a guiding force, enriching our narratives and fostering genuine human connections.

Compassion allows us to connect with others more profoundly, transcending the boundaries that separate us. It is the ability to listen and empathize with their joys and sorrows, to understand their unique experiences and perspectives. By extending kindness and empathy, we create a space where individuals feel seen, heard, and valued.

Through these brief moments we share, I've come to appreciate how compassion can transform lives. It uplifts spirits, offers solace during difficult times, and creates a sense of belonging. By choosing kindness and making good choices in our interactions, we contribute to a positive ripple effect that extends far beyond the confines of our ride-share journey.

Furthermore, compassion reminds us that we all have stories and struggles. It encourages us to approach each encounter with an open heart and a willingness to offer support, even in the simplest ways. These small acts of compassion have the potential to significantly impact someone's life, reminding them that they are not alone on their journey.

So, as we navigate life's roads and complexities, let us remember the power of compassion. By choosing kindness, empathy, and good choices, we can create meaningful connections, inspire others, and contribute to a narrative filled with compassion and understanding.

Resilience, too, plays a significant role in our stories. Life presents us with challenges and obstacles that test our strength and determination. Yet, through adversity, we find our inner reservoirs of resilience, pushing forward when the path seems arduous. The passengers I've encountered have shared stories of triumph over hardship, inspiring me to persevere despite my challenges and setbacks.

Absolutely! The experience of encountering red lights, mishaps, roadblocks, and challenges during our ride-share journeys mirrors our life's ups and downs. During these difficult moments, the importance of resilience becomes evident. Resilience is the ability to bounce back, adapt, and persevere when faced with adversity. Just like navigating through unexpected red lights or encountering mishaps on the road, life presents us with obstacles that test our strength and determination. However, through these challenges, we discover our inner reservoirs of resilience and find the courage to keep moving forward.

The stories shared by passengers during our journeys have served as powerful reminders of the triumphs they've achieved in the face of adversity. Their tales of resilience have inspired me to confront challenges and setbacks with renewed determination and a positive mindset. Witnessing their ability to push through difficulties has shown me that setbacks are not the end of the road but opportunities for growth and transformation.

In the ride-share journey and life, resilience empowers us to navigate roadblocks, learn from our mistakes, and emerge stronger on the other side. It encourages us to embrace challenges as stepping stones to success rather than insurmountable barriers. By cultivating resilience, we develop the capacity to face adversity with unwavering resolve, knowing that setbacks are temporary detours on our journey toward our goals.

So, when confronted with the red lights, mishaps, and challenges that inevitably arise, let us remember the power of resilience. Let us draw strength from the stories of triumph we've encountered and embrace the opportunity to grow and evolve through adversity. With resilience as our companion, we can overcome obstacles, transform setbacks into stepping stones, and continue writing a narrative of courage and perseverance.

Above all, the human spirit shines brightly in these encounters. It is a spirit that transcends boundaries across diverse backgrounds and experiences. The triumph of the human soul lies in our ability to rise above hardships, to seek joy amidst chaos, and to find common ground in our shared humanity. Each passenger I've met has reminded me of the incredible resilience and strength within us all.

Certainly! Our encounters during our ride-share journeys provide us with profound insights into the incredible resilience and strength of the human spirit. In these moments, we witness firsthand how people rise above hardships, seek joy amidst chaos, and connect on a deeper level through their shared humanity. Let's dive deeper into happiness, personal freedom, forgiveness, and self-acceptance.

Happiness is a choice that resides within each of us. It is not solely dependent on external circumstances but stems from our mindset and inner state. By embracing personal freedom, we liberate ourselves from the constraints of societal expectations and external pressures. We understand that our happiness is not contingent upon achieving specific goals or material possessions but rather on cultivating a positive outlook and finding contentment in the present moment.

Part of this journey towards personal freedom is self-acceptance. It involves embracing ourselves fully, including our strengths, weaknesses, and imperfections. Through self-acceptance, we release the need for external validation and embrace a sense of inner worthiness. Accepting ourselves as we are opens the door to self-love and genuine happiness.

Forgiveness is another powerful aspect of the human journey. It is letting go of resentment, anger, and grudges toward others or ourselves. Forgiveness is not about condoning harmful actions but rather about freeing ourselves from the emotional burdens that hold us back. It allows us to heal, grow, and move forward with compassion and empathy. By practicing forgiveness, we create space for joy and love to flourish.

Cultivating personal freedom, self-acceptance, and forgiveness creates a world filled with love, happiness, and joy. Our encounters during our ride-share journeys remind us of the incredible resilience and strength that resides within every individual. Through their stories of triumph over adversity, we are inspired to tap into our inner resources and find joy even in the face of challenges.

Ultimately, the human spirit shines brightly in these encounters as we transcend boundaries and connect profoundly. We contribute to a world where love and joy prevail through embracing happiness, personal freedom, forgiveness, and self-acceptance. By nurturing these qualities within ourselves and extending them to others, we become catalysts for positive change and agents of compassion and understanding.

So, let us continue to honor the triumph of the human spirit by choosing happiness, embracing personal freedom, practicing forgiveness, and cultivating self-acceptance. Doing so creates a ripple effect that spreads love, happiness, and joy, improving our lives and the world. As you embark on the chapters of your own story, may it reflect compassion, resilience, and the indomitable spirit of the human experience.

May your journey be filled with moments of connection where you discover the profound impact you can have on others. May you find solace in knowing that your story is ever-evolving, ready to embrace new twists and turns, and ultimately, to inspire others along the way. The story never truly ends; it merely evolves, taking on new twists and turns.

As you embark on your chapters, may your story be one of compassion, resilience, and the triumph of the human spirit.

www.ingramcontent.com/pod-product-compliance
Lightning Source LLC
Chambersburg PA
CBHW030348130626
46549CB00004B/1408